IDEOLOGY AND SOCIAL CHARACTER

Jon H. Huer
University of Alabama

> FORDHAM UNIVERSITY LIBRARIES
>
> WITHDRAWN FROM COLLECTION

University Press of America™

Copyright © 1978 by

University Press of America™

division of
R.F. Publishing, Inc.
4710 Auth Place, S.E., Washington, D.C. 20023

All rights reserved

Printed in the United States of America

ISBN: 0-8191-0522-8

Library of Congress Catalog Card Number: 78-56917

To My Parents

IDEOLOGY AND SOCIAL CHARACTER:

Toward a Theory of History and Human Behavior

TABLE OF CONTENTS

CHAPTER ONE: INTRODUCTION TO HISTORY AND HUMAN BEHAVIOR	1
CHAPTER TWO: TRADITION AS IDEOLOGY AND SOCIAL CHARACTER	9
1. Introduction	9
2. Ideology and Social Character of Traditional Society	11
3. Varieties of Traditional Society	17
CHAPTER THREE: TRANSITION FROM TRADITION TO RADICAL SOCIETY	25
1. Politics of Development	25
2. Nationalism as Nation-Building Ideology	30
3. Problems of Transition	34
4. Varieties of Transition	42
5. Revolutions-by-Coup	47
CHAPTER FOUR: RADICALISM AS IDEOLOGY AND SOCIAL CHARACTER	59
1. Nationalism	59
2. The Egalitarian Spirit	69
3. Radical Secularism	80
4. Social Reform	89
5. Industrialization Effort	94
6. The Emergence of a New Epoch	97
7. The Theme of Struggle	121
8. Mass Mobilization	127
9. Oppression and Terror	135
10. Conclusion	144
CHAPTER FIVE: LIBERALISM AS IDEOLOGY AND SOCIAL CHARACTER	167
1. Liberalism as Ideology	167
2. Liberalism as Social Character	170
3. Challenge From Socialism: The Deline of Liberalism as Ideology and Social Character	174
CHAPTER SIX: POST-LIBERAL SOCIETY AND ITS IDEOLOGY AND SOCIAL CHARACTER	189
1. Utopia and Post-Liberal America	189
2. The Formation of Post-Liberal Ideology	194
3. Utopia and Mass Society	199
4. The Self and the Pursuit of Happiness in Post-Liberal Society	204
5. The Insignificant Others	209
6. On the Quality of Social Life	216
CHAPTER SEVEN: SOME FURTHER SPECULATIONS	227
APPENDIX	230
INDEX	233

CHAPTER ONE: INTRODUCTION TO HISTORY AND HUMAN BEHAVIOR

This study is an attempt to establish a broad theoretical relationship between historical events (here refered to as "ideology") and the behavior patterns of those men and women (here refered to as "social character") who experience such historical events. The relationship between social change and character formation has largely been in the domain of culture and personality. Yet few attempts have been made among social psychologists and theorists to go beyond culture (or sometimes "national character studies") to include historical events which produce massive behavioral changes. Let us first define "ideology," "social character," and "historical events" within the framework of current social science.

Broadly defined, ideology is a system of social consciousness which guides and coerces collective human action. It is the "public philosophy" of Alexis de Toqueville and Walter Lippmann, and also of the "aggregate or patterning of individual states of mind" as Richard Fagen has characterized the new Cuban ideology of Fidel Castro.[1] To the extent that ideology contributes to the molding of collective behavior, all political theories and practices may be considered ideological, which are, in C. Wright Mills's words, "intellectual and moral creations; they contain high ideals, easy slogans, dubious facts, crude propaganda, sophisticated theories. Their adherents select some facts and ignore others, urge the acceptance of ideals, the inevitability of events, argue with this theory and debunk that one."[2] All major historical events are ideological events, and as such, ideology transforms history into social character.

Broadly defined, social character refers to a set of attitudes, "tempers," and actions that are readily generalizable in a given population. This stable and "modal" pattern of behavior is guided and coerced by the collective ideology of society. In this sense, the behavioral systems of men and women in the Middle Ages, in the French Revolution or in modern industrialization may represent different social character types. Social character, as summarized by David Riesman,

> is the more or less permanent socially and historically conditioned organization of an individual's drives and satisfactions--the kind of "set" with which he approaches the world and people.

"Social character" is that part of "character" which is shared among significant social groups and which, as most contemporary social scientists define it, is the product of the experience of these groups. The notion of social character permits us to speak of the character of classes, groups, regions, and nations.[3]

Social character contrasts with "individual personality" types whose variations are often independent of the larger historical changes. It is also different from national character in that the process of character formation is seen not as the function of a particular nationality, e.g., American, Russian, Chinese, etc., but seen as products of historical events with world-wide ramifications.

Broadly defined, two major historical events have been selected as having world-wide ramifications, independent of personality and national variations: they are the "political" and the "industrial" revolutions in what historians have identified as the "modern era." The political revolution includes the English, French, Russian and Chinese Revolutions, as well as some of the more contemporary socio-political transformations, e.g., those in Cuba and Egypt. It is a historical event--whether liberal-capitalist or socialist--which transforms the basic political fabric of a society from feudal or quasi-feudal absolutism to egalitarian democracy in its varieties of practice. The industrial revolution refers to the scientific and technological breakthrough in the past three centuries--in the steam engine, electricity, steel, etc.,--which transforms the economic fabric of a society from material scarcity to affluence. These are, intertwined in the exciting repertoire of human experience, the historical events by which nations gauge their relative positions in world stratification, define the objectives of their struggle, and mold the behavioral patterns of their population. These are the historical events by which the present and future contour of international politics is to be determined. And these are the historical events by which the notion of "modern" and "pre-modern" eras in politics and economics is to be defined.

Many Western states underwent the political and industrial transformations at an early historical stage. Many others are undergoing the very process today, while still others aspire to do so in a near future. For many of the developed Western societies, political and industrial changes took place almost simultaneously as a historical process, producing a character type normally attributed to "Western man" characteristic of stable politics and affluent economics. For other developing and underdeveloped nations, political instability and economic backwardness constitute the major themes in which their collective energy finds its direction; uncertainties, hopes and conflicts in expectations, thus, are the chief ingredients of their social character systems.

Each time a society experiences one of the two events--normally the "political" and then the "industrial" for the reason given below--its social character undergoes a marked change from its previous attitudes, tempers and actions. According to this scheme of things, there emerge four distinct types of social character (shaped by the corresponding historical events and their ideologies) which form the basic outline of this study:

   Type I: societies which have experienced none of the two transformations, here refered to as Traditional Type;

   Type II: societies which have experienced only the political transformation, here refered to as Radical Type;

   Type III: societies which have experienced both the political and the industrial transformations, here refered to as Liberal Type; and

   Type IV: societies with a prolonged practice of, and exclusive commitment to, the ramifications of the two events, here refered to as Post-Liberal Type represented at present by the United States.

These four types of ideology and social character can be further elaborated:

I. TRADITIONAL TYPE: Traditional type is implicit in most historical studies as the "starting point" in the development of societies and civilizations. Neither the political transformation from absolutism to democracy, nor the economic transformation from underdevelopment to modern industrialization has taken place to alter the basic social character of this type. Socialization is based on pre-established principles so as to exclude all other alternatives, maintaining its precarious continuity of traditional saga, unwritten rules, charismatic leadership, or sheer emotive dominance over rationality in political and economic relations. This type of society and social character is similar to what David Riesman described as "tradition-directed," which is true "not only among the people of precapitalist Europe but also among such enormously different types of people as Hindus and Hopi Indians, Zulus and Chinese, North Africans and Balinese."[4] Given the universal disposition toward political and industrial modernization, it is assumed that this type will experience character changes as the process of democratization and industrialization takes place. Chapter Two discusses this type in detail.

   TRANSITION TO RADICAL SOCIETY: The transformation of a Traditional society into a Radical type is achieved by a genuine political change--be it revolution, nationhood, military coup, or reform--the criteria for which are discussed in detail in Chapter Three and Four. There has been much controversy as to at what point a society becomes "modern." Some observers have insisted on the use of political indicators for measuring modernization, while other have insisted on economic indicators.[5] However, the blanket characterizations of "underdevelopment," "developing," and "development" in traditional terms of politics and economics are often inadequate in that the transition from Tradition to Radicalism--by which a society enters the modern era --is almost always a political process. The reason for the political process taking place ahead of the industrial transformation is a logical one, although its root can be found in the notion of practicality: it is much easier to alter human ideas and attitudes and institutional arrangements (in short, political changes) than to effect the material fortunes of a society from scarcity to affluence. Political transformations can alter the system of collective behavior almost overnight, as the Russian and Chinese experiences have born out, while upgrading living standards through industrialization still remains an arduous process, taking years and decades. This process of transition is discussed in Chapter Three.

II. <u>RADICAL TYPE</u>: This type refers to the emerging new social character constellations typical of a society which has just experienced a radical political transformation from traditional absolutism to modern egalitarianism, liberal as well as socialist. The English, American, French, Russian, Chinese and Cuban Revolutions, for example, are responsible for producing this character type. Political revolutions, however, have not been the only means by which the radical social character may be forged. Acquiring an independent nationhood as in the case of Israel, political reform as in the case of Japan, or military coup d'état as in the case of Egypt can also lead to a similar character formation. A society of this type tends to display a new sense of collective direction, aggressiveness, centralized loyalty, long-term planning, secularization, and a reformist and rational outlook, among other character traits. It is in conformity with such character manifestations that the Soviet Union and its socialist bloc are identified here as Radical societies. Major components of Radical ideology and social character are discussed in detail in Chapter Four.

<u>TRANSITION TO LIBERAL SOCIETY</u>: Transition from Radical to Liberal society is determined by two indicators: political and economic. Politically, a society must maintain a relatively stable, constitutional system of human relations with all the necessary components for egalitarian democracy. Economically, a Liberal society must demonstrate--in addition to the political indicators--a relatively high standard of living through industrialization that can be objectively measured, e.g., in gross national product, income per capita, etc. Liberalism as a specific system of ideology and social character in history is thus reflective of stable politics and industrial economics prevalent in Western European nations, Australia, Canada, Japan, and the prewar United States.

III. <u>LIBERAL TYPE</u>: As a historical type, a social character unique to the now widely desired twin-goals of political and industrial development emerges, generally characterized as Liberalism. The notion of "balance" is one most telling barometer in this Liberal social character: balance between state and individual, between past and future, and between utopian aspiration and pragmatic reality. Essentially libertarian in outlook, tolerance for individual deviations from collective norms increases sharply from its level in the Radical stage. As distinct from both Radical and Post-Liberal types (see below), the sovereign state assumes a legitimate yet controlled function in the making of collective attitudes, tempers and actions. This balanced social character is facilitated in good measure by the ever-present traditional residues in collective behavior and class interests which have survived the basically equalitarian political and economic modernization. Progressive liberalism restrained by pragmatic considerations continues to be the collective behavior system of Liberal societies. Although the classic theory of politics and economics in the Liberal framework as the model of social change dominated the Western past, the "decline" of liberalism has been widely noted especially in recent decades, coinciding dramatically with the rise of socialist influence in its trail as the new ideology and social character for global changes. Chapter Five discusses this phenomenon in detail.

TRANSITION TO POST-LIBERAL SOCIETY: In the postwar era, a generation of "cultural critics" on American society has emerged whose views converged in seeing the United States as a unique ideological and characterological social type, distinct from other developed nations. These social thinkers--e.g., Riesman,[6] Potter,[7] Hacker,[8] Mills,[9] Slater,[10] among others--have emphasized certain prominent features of American civilization in its commitment to liberal egalitarianism and utilitarian technology as the collective creed and as the individual style of life. In this, what may be called a "post-liberal" pattern of behavior unique to American society has gradually crystallized.

IV. POST-LIBERAL TYPE: The Post-Liberal social character is thus a combined product of prolonged political stability and high living standards, and the historical milieu for the development of Western liberalism. It is necessarily an end-result of Liberal type discussed above, without the balancing features of tradition and class interests in its progress. Postwar United States has been the subject of many historical speculations in which its emerging social character is seen as the forerunner of Western psychology, with its far-reaching ramifications. Because of the largely speculative nature of this social character type, post-Liberal American society has been described both positively and negatively. The task of defining the American social character in the postwar era coincides intellectually with the task of defining the general perspective on Western civilization itself, the difficulty of which may be responsible for the paucity of such studies. The contemporary American social character, at any rate, may be seen as the endproduct of the classic Liberal formula which has found its full development in postwar American society because of its unique political and economic circumstances. Chapter Six discusses American society as a post-Liberal type.

In this book, there are no radically original interpretations of known historical events. By and large, traditionally accepted definitions of history have been adopted. What has been attempted, however, is a model of interaction between history and human behavior on the collective level so that a broad historical perspective on social character can be established. The basic approach is both analytic and empirical in that the standard historical phenomena are given new theoretical meaning and significance. Scaling the development and evolution of collective social characters from Traditional to post-Liberal society is an admittedly tenuous task which few prudent academicians would attempt. However, some consolation may be found in the old French saying on scholarship: "Better to make some blunders than to make the mistake of saying nothing!"

FOOTNOTES

1. Richard Fagen, *The Transformation of Political Culture in Cuba*, Stanford University Press, Stanford, California, 1969, p. 5.

2. C. Wright Mills, *The Marxists*, Dell Publishing Co., New York, 1967, p. 12.

3. David Riesman, *The Lonely Crowd*, Yale University Press, New Haven, Conn., 1971, p. 4.

4. *Ibid.* p. 12.

5. See Dunkwart Rustow, *A World of Nations*, The Brookings Institution, Washington, D. C., 1967, p. 7 for political indicators, and J. P. Nettl and Roland Robertson, *International Systems and the Modernizations of Societies*, Faber & Faber, London, 1968, p. 63 for economic indicators respectively.

6. David Riesman, *The Lonely Crowd*, op cit.

7. David Potter, *People of Plenty*, University of Chicago Press, Chicago, 1964.

8. Andrew Hacker, *The End of the American Era*, Atheneum, New York, 1973.

9. C. Wright Mills, *White Collar*, Oxford University Press, New York, 1956.

10. Philip Slater, *The Pursuit of Loneliness*, Beacon Press, Boston, 1971.

CHAPTER TWO: TRADITION AS IDEOLOGY AND SOCIAL CHARACTER

1. INTRODUCTION

When we speak of a society of the traditional type as a point of departure, we must take it to be a historical type, created and bound by epochs, stages and events in history, not by mere cultural diversities and antifacts. In this linear respect it can be defined in terms of not being modernized. In Rustow's words,

> Tribes of camel herders in the Arabian desert; the villages of Tropical Africa; and the imperial civilizations once governed by the Manchus in China and the Ottomans in Turkey-- all become similar only as they confronted in fact or contrasted in concept with modern civilization. Traditional cultures all tend to react in a number of similar ways to the uniform impact of modernity...The similarity of response in part of an early, reactive phase of modernization. Whereas modernity can be affirmatively defined, tradition remains largely a residual concept.[1]

Mannheim differentiates "traditionalism" from "conservatism." Traditionalism "simply (clings) instinctively to the old way of life." Conservatism, on the other hand, is "the intellectual, political-ideological expression of class interests and values in a dynamic historical situation."[2] "Traditionalism can only become conservatism in a society in which change occurs through the medium class conflict--in a class society. This is the sociological background of modern conservatism."[3] The distinction between Traditionalism and Conservatism rests largely on the conceptual advantage of reactions in different times and places, while the concept of Traditionalism can be used as a world-historical reference point arising from specific historical events. The specific historical events determining Traditional Society, as distinct from the "modern" state, be it Radical, Liberal or Post-Liberal, have been associated mainly with the coming of the two historic transformations: namely, the "political transformation" from feudal absolutism to modern egalitarianism, and the "technological transformation" from material scarcity to modern industry. As outlined in the preceding chapter, a Traditional Society can be simply defined as one in which its way of life reflects neither of the transformations, while the potential for doing so does exist to varying degrees. This specific definition of Traditional Society must be kept in mind, although we may borrow the more richly varying cultural studies of "traditionalism" conducted by other social scientists.

David Reisman's character typology, which "tradition-, inner-and other-directed" personality types as more or less historical varieties of social character are proposed, is one of such studies. His description of traditional society serves nicely for our introduction:

> Since the type of social order...is relatively unchanging, the conformity of the individual tends to reflect his membership in a particular age-grade, clan, or caste; he learns to understand and appreciate patterns which have endured for centuries, and are modified but slightly as the generations succeed each other. The important relationships of life may be controlled by careful and rigid etiquette, learned by the young during the years of intensive socialization that end with initiation into full adult membership. Moreover, the culture, in addition to its economic tasks, or as part of them, provides ritual, routine, and religion to occupy and to orient everyone. Little energy is directed toward finding new solutions of the age-old problems, let us say, of agricultural technique or medicine, the problems to which people are acculturated.[4]

Could there be any historical period in which all societies were all-inclusively tradition-directed, and, in our term, pre-modern Traditional types? "In Western history (writes Riesman) the Middle Ages can be considered a period in which the majority were tradition-directed. But the term tradition-directed refers to a common element, not only among the people of precapitalist Europe but also among such enormously different types of people as Hindus and Hopi Indians, Zulus and Chinese,[5] North African Arabs[6] and Balinese.[7]"

The crucial advantage of treating Traditionalism as a historically general type with empirically definable characteristics lies in the fact that many otherwise anthropologically divergent cultural artifacts and their correspondingly divergent behavioral patterns can be brought under one analytical category without mutilating the essential relevance of their presence in historical continuity. In trying to bring order into the seemingly endless diversities of human adaptations to their environment, both human and non-human, and of life styles that are almost as numerous as individual communities, it becomes necessary that we take the elements that are most significant in the long run of history. Grounded on reality and disciplined by facts, such historical inquiries must aim at achieving: (1) the desirable empirical level of generality which avoids both metaphysical and mechanistic historicism, on the other hand, and relativist-phenomenological anthropology of man in diverse cultural patterns and modes of living, on the other; hence (2) constructing a certain model of historical generality which would modestly suggest some insight into human development in historical epochs and in its contemporary meaning. It would seem in the end, however, that the most intelligently conceived and executed historical enterprise is one in which a good distinction is made between what is relevant and irrelevant, a dictum that should be borne in mind by every student of man and society in history.

2. IDEOLOGY AND SOCIAL CHARACTER IN TRADITIONAL SOCIETY

The work of Max Weber on the legitimacy of authority is perhaps unsurpassed in the sociological literature on traditionalism, although it suffers from the inevitable trend of nineteenth century historicistic idealism, or a "patronizing tendency" as H. Gerth and C. W. Mills have all characterized it.[8] His rather liberal use of "ideal" type is manifest in all of his work, which hinges upon the idealistic nature of German historicism in its most abstract and general form.[9] "For example, (concurs Reinhard Bendix) charismatic leadership is a basic relationship between ruler and ruled which is formulated in so abstract a manner that examples of it may be found in *all* historical contexts.[10]" With this due caution, however, we must rely on Weber for a sound understanding on the political structure and social relations of Traditional Society.

The matter of legitimacy in traditionalist authority, for Weber, rests on one of the two ways: (1) "Partly in terms of traditions which themselves directly determine the content of the command and the objects and extent of authority. In so far as this is true, to overstep the traditional limitations would endanger his traditional status by undermining acceptance of his legitimacy;" (2) "In part, it is a matter of the chief's free personal decision, in that tradition leaves a certain sphere open for this. This sphere of traditional prerogative rests primarily on the fact that the obligations of obedience on the basis of personal loyalty are essentially unlimited.[11]" This implies a double sphere of traditional authority in which either tradition or the "grace" of rulers becomes the sanctioned code of traditional conduct. Especially,

> In the latter sphere, the chief is free to confer "grace" on the basis of his personal pleasure or displeasure, his personal likes and dislikes, quite arbitrarily, particularly in return for gifts which often

become a source of regular income. So far as his action follows principles at all, these are principles of substantive ethical common sense, of justice, or of utilitarian expediency. They are not, however, as in the case of legal authority, formal principles. The exercise of authority is normally oriented to the questions of that the chief and his administrative staff will normally permit, in view of the traditional obedience of the subjects and what will or will not arouse their resistance.[12]

Traditionalism may be understood, then, in terms of (1) "the psychic attitude-set for the habitual workday and to the belief in the everyday routine as an inviable norm of conduct;" and (2) "the structural form of domination, or the legitimacy of authority, which is presumably rooted in tradition."[13] These two dimensions, then, reflect the function of Traditionalist ideology and social character, which determines the attitudes of the population, and, by way of the attitudes, the structural basis of institutional arrangement is maintained and strengthened. Since tradition is the reified reality of legitimacy, authority is held to be immune to public sanction through resistance. "When resistance occurs when it does, it is directed against the person of the chief or of a member of his staff. The accusation is that he had failed to observe the traditional limits of his authority. Opposition is not directed against the system as such."[14]

The seemingly precarious basis of working tradition is thus firmly enshrined in its structural permanence, although the persons temporarily occupying the status of rulers and its sanctioned authority may often be dispensed with. Limited at power change, e.a., "palace coup," in which merely the occupant has been replaced, with the structural basis of Traditionalism remaining intact, may still manifest this social type. Despite the numerous occurences of occupancy-replacement in Traditional society, we may not speak of historical transformations that affect changes in their fundamental ideology and social character. Hence as long as tradition remains intact in the main no attempt at changing society will be efficacious in producing any structural replacement. The difficulty lies essentially in the nature and mode in which the ruler exercises his authority, and the necessarily elastic sphere in which some measure of the ruler's arbitrariness may prevail is still limited by the unwritten codes of not "stepping out of bounds."

> The content of commands is bound up with, and limited by, tradition. A master who violated tradition without let or hinderance would thereby endanger the legitimacy of his own authority which is based entirely on the sanctity of that tradition. As a matter of principle it is out

of the question to create new laws which deviate from the traditional norms. However, new rights are created in fact, but only by way of "recognizing" them as having been valid "from time immemorial." Outside the norms of tradition the will of the master is limited only by considerations of equity in the individual case, and this is highly elastic limitation. Thus his domination is divided into a sphere which is strictly bound by tradition and another in which his arbitrary will prevails.[15]

As a specific form of Traditionalist domination, "Patriarchalism is by far the most important type of domination the legitimacy of which rests upon tradition. Patriarchalism means the authority of the father, the husband, the sib elder over the members of the household; the rule of the master and patron over bondsmen, serfs, free men; of the lord over the domestic servants and household officials; of the prince over house-and court-officials, nobles of office, clients, vassals; of the patrimonial lord and sovereign prince over the 'subjects'."[16] In place of "modern-rational" features of bureaucracy, i.e., "a clearly defined sphere of competence subject to impersonal rules," a rationally ordered hierarchy, a civil servant system through appointment by qualification, "technical training as a regular requirement," and "fixed salaries" properly regulated and paid in money, the following are general features of Traditional administration and the behavioral codes of that authority type, as outlined in Weber's classic study:

> (1) In place of a well-defined impersonal sphere of competence, there is a shifting series of tasks and powers commissioned and granted by a chief through his arbitrary decision of the moment. They then tend to become permanent and are often traditionally stereotyped...
>
> (2) In contrast to the rational hierarchy of authority in the bureacratic system, the question who shall decide a matter--which of his officials or the chief himself-- or who shall deal with complaints, is, in a traditional regime, treated in one of two ways: (a) Traditionally, on the basis of the authority of particular received legal norms or precedents. (b) Entirely on the basis of the arbitrary decision of the chief. Whenever he intervenes personally, all others give way to him...
>
> (3) As opposed to the bureaucratic system of free appointment, household officials and favorites are very often recruited on a purely patrimonial basis from among the slaves or serfs of the chief. If, on

the other hand, the recruitment has been extra-
patrimonial, they have tended to be holders of benefices
which he has granted as an act of grace without
being bound by any formal rules....

(4) Rational technical training as a basic
qualifications for office is scarcely to be found
at all among household officials or the favorites
of a chief. Where there is even a beginning of
technical training for appointees, regardless of
what it consists in, this fact everywhere makes
for a fundamental change in the development of
administrative practice....

(5) In place of regular salaries, household
officials and favorites are usually supported and
equipped in the household of the chief and from
the personal stores. Generally, their exclusion
from the lord's own table means the creation of
benefices in kind. It is easy for these to become
traditionally stereotyped in amount and kind. Along
with the elements supported by benefices or in place
of them, there are various agencies commissioned
by the lord outside his own household, as well as
various fees which are due him. The latter are often
collected without any regular rate or scale, being
agreed upon from case to case with those seeking
favors.[17]

A traditional form of authority, namely patriarchalism, may
reign over extended territories without changing the essential
features of traditionally defined, and arbitrarily conducted, basis
of administrative structure and the staff, thus creating a "sultan-
istic regime." Military force of various compositions and characteristics are used to rule over the regime, and now the extensive
bureaucratic necessity is staffed by those who chance to earn the
ruler's confidence and win his favor, who "in turn treat their
administrative work for the ruler as a personal service based on
their duty of obedience and respect."[18]

This traditional society emerges clearly as a type not only
when the features that are uniquely attributed to it are accentuated,
as we have done, but also when considering the structural features
and characteristics that it peculiarly lacks, that is, the structure
of "legal" (whether Radical-legal, liberal-legal, or post-liberal-
legal) society to which the former stands in clear contrast. The main
burden rests, therefore, upon how traditional authority is transformed
into "legal" authority for legitimacy, a transition from tradition to
modernity as far as the legal aspects are considered. Here, too,

Weber illuminates the path with his theoretical conceptualization of this process:

> From a theoretical point of view, the general development of law and procedure may be viewed as passing through the following stages: first, charismatic legal revelation through a "law prophets"; second, empirical creation and finding of law by legal notables....; third, imposition of law by secular or theocratic powers; fourth and finally, systematic elaboration of law and professional administration of justice by persons who have received their legal training in a learned and formally logical manner.[19]

"Charistmatic legal revelation through law prophets represents the greatest possible contrast to modern lawmaking and its adherence to enacted rules. At one time, legal prophecy was the universal practice. Its fundamental principle was that law could only be revealed." Whenever legal disputes could not be settled between feuding families or tribes by bloodshed or similarly primitive means, or when this bloodshed was desired to be avoided. "Priests and other law prophets increased their power by being called upon to dispense oracles and supervise trials by ordeal."[20] This total reliance on charasmatic legal revelation was to be modified, however, by (1) the Church's distinction between secular and sacred law, since Cannon law was strictly under the Church jurisdiction, thus facilitating "the secularization of the law;" and (2) the extended authority of secular rulers over their extended domination where the rulers wished to preserve law and order, curbing the arbitrary private exercise of law by regional cheifs and patriarchal rulers.[21] Law making by legal notables then "emerges as imperceptibly out of ancient legal practices and conventional behavior as does the imposition of laws by established authorities." The mingling of accepted tradition with new practices of law is achieved, however, through interaction among interested parties and through the work of legal notables out of which new laws are established. Legal prophecy thus gives way to public discussion even in a limited sense.

> Although it may be impossible to identify the individuals involved in this process, it is possible to see the significance of interested parties. For centuries the arrangements among them may exist on the basis of shared understandings, without any thought of explicit formulation or recourse to established authority. But whenever the belief in magic and the practice of legal revelation decline, judicial decisions become the concern of lay judges (as distinguished

from law prophets) and a subject for discussion, and the interested parties begin to estimate the probability that the judiciary will consider a given contract or association legally valid and enforceable.[22]

The gradual emergence of legal training that began to participate in the court of law and legal education in the universities made the final transformation of traditional conceptions and practices into the modern "rational" form of legal administrative structure.

The "legal order" which is a modern structural phenomenon, especially Western, for Weber, was conceived to consist of the following "ideal type" characteristics: (1) "an administrative and legal order that is subject to change by legislation; (2) an administrative apparatus that conducts official business in accordance with legislative regulation;" (3) a system of authority capable of extending itself to all persons holding citizenship and to most actions taking place within the recognized territory; (4) "the legitimation to use force within this area of coercion is either permitted or prescribed by legally constituted government. i.e. if it is in accordance with enacted statute." In sum, "Legal order, bureaucracy, compulsory jurisdiction over a territory and monopolization of the legitimate use of force are the essential characteristics of the modern state from Traditional society, of which the legal process has been mainly dealt with, is accompanied by its institutional prerequisites upon which the constitution of legal order becomes possible. These preconditions are:

> (1) Monopolization of the means of domination and administration based on: (a) the creation of centrally directed and permanent system of taxation; (b) the creation of a centrally directed and permanent military force in the hands of a central governmental authority; (2) monopolization of legal enactments and the legitimate use of force by the central authority; and (3) the organization of a rationally oriented officialdom, whose exercise of administrative functions is dependent upon the central authority. Though some of the attributes have existed elsewhere, their more or less simultaneous emergence is a distinctly Occidental phenomenon.[24]

One most significant difference in the Tradition-to-modern transition is the disappearance of the arbitrariness of the ruler and his vassals, which is characteristic of feudal absolutism. Ideally, as Bendix sums up,

> The modern nation-state presupposes that this link between governmental authority and inherited privilege in the hands of families of notables is broken. Access to important political and administrative posts in the governments of nation-states can be facilitated by wealth and high social position through their effect on social contracts and educational opportunities. But facility of access is not the same as the prerogative which aristocratic families in medieval politics claim by virtue of their "antiquity of blood," to use Machiavelle's phrase. For the decisive criterion of the Western nation-state is the substantial separation between the social structure and the exercise of judicial and administrative functions. Major functions of government such as the adjudication of legal disputes, the collection of revenue, the control of currency, military recruitment, the organization of the postal system, the construction of public facilities, and others have been removed from the political struggle in the sense that they cannot be appropriated on a hereditary basis by privileged estates and on this basis parceled out among competing jurisdictions.[25]

3. VARIETIES OF TRADITIONAL SOCIETY

In our sociological observation, what are some of the existing examples by which one may speak of Traditional social type? We already mentioned that political Radicalization (most often through revolution) is what divides a given society into Traditional or pre-modern and Radical or modern types. In reality, the Traditional type exists in diverse forms and circumstances. For the benefit of conceptual clarity, the Traditional type may be said to consist of: (1) the "aborigins-primitives" of the Pacific Islands, of Australia, and of Africa, in which structural authority and its behaviorial codes are maintained through consanguineal inheritence, traditionally defined roles or extended kinship systems without much alteration since time immemorial.

(2) The quasi-republics with some democratic appearance but with an ineffective, corruption-ridden national bureaucracy and other institutions mostly inherited from their colonial

rulers. The state machine is in such a disarray and non-rational working habit that no consciously and clearly defined collective goals or programs can be formulated, much less implemented. Lacking long term visionary objectives, compounded by internal social, economic and political instability, this type is best characterized by constant attempts of revolution and coup d'etat which fail more often than succeed. With the resulting chaos and disorder, this type is often turned into a stereotyped "Third World example."[26] One classic instance could be the Russian Duma of the pre-Bolshevik period. Following the Western parliamentary style but without the necessary functional ingredients, the state organ was an epitome of bureaucratic ineffectiveness. As W. W. Rostow observed:

> The parliamentary tradition dating, somewhat arbitrarily, from the French Revolution, had evidently grown rapidly in Russia in the pre-1914 decades. But it had struck insufficiently deep roots in the popular consciousness to dominate the chaos of 1917. Its liberal and socialist leadership was split and indecisive in the face of peasant and worker demands released by the March Revolution and the urgent requirements of either fighting the war effectively or making peace....The balance of forces represented in Constituent Assembly certainly reflected the aspirations of Russia more nearly than did the Bolsheviks. The majority simply proved incapable of making itself effective in the anarchy of 1917.[27]

This group of Traditional type represent many of the former colonies recently liberated, with a Western form of democracy which, in the course of time, becomes so ineffective and corrupt that (a) either a dictatorship (without establishing Radical ideology and corresponding social character) is created in the same manner as the former colonial rulers, (b) or countless revolutionary or coup attempts are made, some of which may have no more intention than seizing power. Except few rare cases, e.a., India, a combination of both is the main feature of these Traditional societies.

(3) Those sovereignties ruled by inherently imposed, non-constitutional monarchs, e.a., King Hussein of Jordan,[28] sheiks or tribal chieftains with a remote possibility of becoming constitutional sovereigns. In common with the group above, revolutionary potential is more evident in these nation-states than any other Traditional societies.

(4) To make this model more comprehensive and complete it must be thought of containing those isolated collective units <u>without</u> a political, geographical, social and often cultural "sovereign identity of some international recognition: Jews before the 1947 partition-decision by the U.N.; American Blacks even long after the formal Emancipation; the Gypsy nomads scattered all over Europe with more or less their own traditional protocols and modes of life; and Eskimos in some remote parts of North America and American Indians. Except in the case of Jews, it may be expected that in the long run they will be integrated into the social structure in which they now exist, sharing its political and economic fortunes as well as misfortune.

Finally, (5) it can be deductively (and even truistically) stated that those societies that can be defined as either Radical Liberal or post-Liberal types today through the two successfully and successively transformations must have been a Traditional society in some past. This observation serves no other purpose than reminding us of the essentially and imperatively sequential nature of our historical model, which is also the central theme of this inquiry into history and personality.

Sociology abounds with classic studies on this Traditional type. In fact, it seems that this type is the conceptual starting point of <u>all</u> sociological inquiries into the dichotomous models of social change: Weber's "traditional" as opposed to "rational" action and authority; Durkheim's "mechanical" as opposed to "organic" solidarity; Tonneis's "Gemainschaft" and "Gesseleschaft;" Spencer's "homogeneous" society and "heterogeneous" society; Becker's "sacred" and "secular" society; Redfield's "rural" and "urban" society, etc. It is implicitly assumed that the Traditional societies and their behavioral codes as the starting point share the essentially similar ingredients that make them resemble each other, which facilitates such analyses. Professional historians and a few anthropologists may object that grouping all these "pre-modern" communities under one heading, Traditional, may be at the expense of the intricately differentiated and dissimilar nuances of their life styles and social structures. The answer to this is rather simple: from our analytic point of view, in which larger generalizations and trend-definitions are the primary theme, disregarding petty differences, there are no intellectually conflicting differences in basic ideology and social character of the Roman Empire, the Sung Dynasty, and the Tsarist Russia. They resemble each other in all the key components of social structure, which is to say that they are dominated by traditionalism that is distinct from that of other historical epochs both empirically and theoretically, converging as a broad, yet, specific, historical type.

Finally, the following two comments must be added to the discussion of Traditional society: First, from a strictly sociological point of view, the current community of nations defined as Traditional has become, in the course of political and economic changes in the last several decades, something of an international problem. They are no longer the exotic and primitive communities which entertain tourists from the more affluent world. They are now "underdeveloped" nations, or the "Third World" nation-states with critical needs for development. In this sense, the conventional view on these less fortunate communities must be discarded, and in its place a more historically and sociologically oriented one established in tune with the revolutionary world changes. And,

Second, these revolutionary world changes have emerged as quite inevitable events for the Traditional societies. The reason for their "inevitability" may be discerned in the following two factors: (1) there is the "ideological" inevitability, i.e., given the rhetoric of either the Enlightenment-liberal (now in decline) or Marxian doctrine (now in rise), the incongruencies of Traditionalism in these nations will not go unchallenged; and (2) there is the "material" inevitability, i.e., the increased efficiency and range of modern communication by which ideas and inspirations travel fast and extensively.

In the broad historical perspective of the modern world, the future of Traditional society is essentially positive and even optimistic. Within the available varieties of future alternative for ideology and social character, that is, Radical, Liberal, and post-Liberal types, social changes in Traditional society will only improve their political and economic fortunes. But, as we shall see, the road is an ardous one indeed.

FOOTNOTES

1. Dundwart Rustow, A World of Nations, The Brookings Institution, Washington, D.C., 1967, p. 12.

2. Irving M. Zeitlin, Ideology and the Development of Sociological Theory, Prentice-Hall, Inc., Englewood Cliffs, New Jersey, 1968, p. 295.

3. Karl Mannheim, Essays on Sociology and Social Psychology, Kegan Paul, Ltd., London, 1953, p. 101 (emphasis original.)

4. David Riesman, The Lonely Crowd, op. cit., p. 11.

5. It may be understood that when Riesman wrote this in 1950, the newly succeeded Chinese Revolution did not make much impression on him; but after only two decades one wonders at the enoemous difference in Chinese character type between now and then. While the Chinese took the Marxist route to Radicalization, we might say the Taiwanese seem to have chosen the Enlightenment-liberal way.

6. Again, the Egyptian Revolution 1952 dramatically changed its traditional character into Radicalism, which is of prime importance in our character study.

7. David Riesman, The Lonely Crowd, op. cit., p. 12, cf. D. Rustow quoted above.

8. Hans Gerth and C. Wright Mills (eds.), From Max Weber: Essays in Sociology, Oxford University Press, New York, 1958, p. vi.

9. A similar style of thought and model-building in modern sociology is of course the work of Talcott Parsons who pushed the general abstraction of Weber's dangerous pure-type historical descriptions into completely non-historical concepts, categories, types, etc., which Hegel might have called a kind of "conceptual barbarism."

10. Reinhard Bendix, Max Weber: An Intellectual Portrait, Doubleday & Co., Inc., Garden City, New York, 1960, p. 330.

11. Max Weber, The Theory of Social and Economic Organization, The Free Press, New York, 1969, p. 341.

12. Ibid., p. 342.

13. Hans Gerth and C. Wright Mills, From Max Weber, op. cit., p. 296.

14. Max Weber, <u>The Theory of Social and Economic Organization</u>, op. cit., p. 342.

15. Max Weber, quoted in Reinhard Bendix, <u>Max Weber</u>, op. cit., p. 332.

16. Hans Gerth and C. Wright Mills, <u>From Max Weber</u>, op. cit., p. 296. Patriarchalism is often found within another form of authority legitimacy exclusively exercised by the "elders," or "gerontocracy."

> "The term 'gerontocracy' is applied to a situation where so far as imperative control is exercised in the group at all it is in the hands of 'elders'--which originally was understood literally as the eldest in actual years, who are the most familiar with the sacred traditions of a group. This is common in groups which are not primarily of an economic or kinship character. 'Partiarchalism' is the situation where, within a group, which is usually organized on both an economic and a kinship basis, as a household, authority is exercised by a particular individual who is designated by a definite rule of inheritance. It is not uncommon for gerontocracy and patriarchalism to be found side by side. The decisive characteristic of both is the conception which is held by those subject to the authority of either type that this authority, though its exercise is a private prerogative of the person or persons involved, is in fact pre-eminently an authority on behalf of the group as a whole. Max Weber, <u>Theory of Social and Economic Organization</u>, op. cit., p. 346.

17. Max Weber, <u>Theory of Social and Economic Organization</u>, Talcott Parsons (tr.), The Free Press, New York, 1969, pp. 343-345. "The French Revolution eliminated not only the (extended form of patriarchal) monarchy but also the system of office-purchase and hence the whole group of benefices-holders." Richard Bendix, <u>Max Weber</u>, op. cit., p. 349.

18. Richard Bendix, <u>Max Weber</u>, op. cit., pp. 341-45. In this connection, Max Weber also classified human action into four ideal-types: namely, (1) action as "strictly traditional behavior;" (2) action as "purely affectual behavior;" (3) ac-

tion as oriented "in terms of absolute value;" and (4) action as "rationally oriented to a system of discrete individual ends when the end, the means, and the secondary results are rationally taken into account and weighed." In traditional behavior, "it is often a matter of almost automatic reaction to habitual stimuli which guide behavior in a course which has been repeatedly followed. The great bulk of everyday action to which people have become habitually accustomed approaches this type." Theory of Social and Economic Organization, op. cit., pp. 115-118.

19. Max Weber, quoted by Reinhard Bendix, Max Weber, p. 388.

20. Reinhard Bendix, Max Weber, op. cit., p. 389.

21. Ibid., pp. 396-403.

22. Ibid., p. 403.

23. Ibid., p. 413.

24. Ibid., p. 380. See also Max Weber, The Theory of Social and Economic Organization, op. cit., pp. 324-341.

25. Reinhard Bendix, Nation-Building and Citizenship, op. cit. pp. 105-106.

26. An operational distinction between (failed) rebellion and (successful) revolution:

"They may succeed in these (revolutionary) aspirations without recourse to violence as in the case of England's Reform Bill of 1832, or in the face of such aspirations, the political order may prove to be inelastic, and agents of the status quo may threaten to maintain and enforce their prerogatives violently. Then a disrupture of the social structure becomes impossible, and in such crises, the middle classes may establish armed forces of their own. Against the divine right of kings, they posit the 'sovereignty of the people' or of the nation. If the king is successful in restoring his authority, disarming the insurrectionist forces, expelling, arresting, or otherwise punishing the intellectual, political and military leaders, then we speak of putsch or rebellion: the European "revolutions" of 1848. If, however, the insurrectionist forces are successful, seize power and establish a new political constitution (with or without the old king) we may speak of political revolution: The English Revolution of 1649, the American Revolution of 1776, the French Revolution of 1789." Hans Gerth and C. Wright Mills, Character and Social Structure,

Harcourt, Brace and Co., 1953, pp. 401-402n. Modern revolutions or revolutions-by-coup essentially follow the similar vein: if successful, a revolution; if not, a rebellion.

27. W. W. Rostow, <u>The Dynamics of Soviet Society</u>, The New American Library, New York, 1954, p. 129.

28. Many Jordanian intellectuals and young students regard the monarch as "destined to go" in a near future.

CHAPTER THREE: TRANSITION FROM TRADITION TO RADICAL SOCIETY

1. POLITICS OF DEVELOPMENT

Beginning roughly in the twentieth-century, a considerable portion of international politics has been centered around an aggregation of nations loosely characterized as "underdeveloped," "developing," "emerging," or the Third World." Especially in Africa, the Middle East, Asia and Latin America, these emerging nations have been undergoing an extensive experience of turmoil, political, social and economic. Angered by the memory of colonial humiliation, equipped with the ideals and rhetoric of national pride, and no less spurred by the demonstrated possibility in positive modernization, this group of emerging nation-states has occupied the stage of political theatrics and the center of revolutionary heroics. The increasing intensity and frequency in which the realistic planning and visionary programs are carried out in these nations are indicative of the world's technological changes and their subsequent ramifications on the leaders and masses of these deprived nations. The empirical proofs of technology in advanced nations "create the conditions for rebellion and revolution" in the emerging nations which "define themselves as engaged in a mortal race with the most advanced sectors of the economic world."[1]

International political trends since the end of World War II have been a move from the first phase of ideological Cold War to the second phase of economic competition, still based upon the manifest threat and implication of violence, in which "economic development (has appeared) as the primary component of real status."[2] Each nation regardless of its stage of development is accorded the formal protocol of an independent status and at the same time "the real status" is determined by its power magnitude in the competitive arena of international politics and stratification.

> All nations have the same formal status; their positions, their rights, their duties in the system of international relations are the same. The achievement of these rights and duties is not influenced by size, population, wealth, historical age, military power, or political power. In

> In opposition to the formal status of the
> nation, the real status is found. While
> the first is derived from the equalitarian
> ideology..., the second is derived from
> the position that the nation occupies
> in the system of international stratification
> in its three basic variables, economic
> stature, power and prestige. While in
> agreement with the first concept--all
> nations are equal--the structure of the
> stratified system also determines relationships
> of superordination and subordination
> among nations.[3]

The real variable on the scale of international differentiation has become the central target of social reform and political transformation of these emerging nations because of their past experience. Despite the evidence to the contrary, these emerging nations are convinced both as theory and as practice that they must narrow the gap between haves and haves-nots in a short span of time and in planned action. As the general theme of their political ideology and as the broad vision of a welfare state the emerging nation desire "to become modern and endowed with a balanced and well-developed economy; to acheive this objective within a span of time shorter than the advanced countries needed; and to enjoy the fruits of modernization (decent living standards) while still engaged in the process of development."[4]

The nations in the emerging phase of modernization conceives of national and international politics solely in terms of unilinear progress and the development, and of the techniques and resources relevant to the unilinear conception of history and scientific logic. Simplified and formalized as state ideology, this preoccupation with development function as the impetus for collective action and justifies the meaning of a revolutionary consolidation of power structure and nationalist civil organization.

> When the nationalist leaders speak
> of the "development" of the nation, they
> are speaking primarily of economic development.
> The leadership and members of nationalist
> movements are acutely aware of the
> galling contrast between the poverty,
> illiteracy, and disease of their own countries
> and the affluence of the economically
> developed areas. For them, the crucial
> division in the world is not between the
> rival political faiths of Communism and
> liberal democracy, but between the rich
> and the poor, the economically developed
> and the underdeveloped, the technically

competent and the technologically "backward" areas of the world. The key to the eradication of this difference in living standards lies in economic development, and more particularly in industrialization. With development and and industrialization, it will be possible to achieve social equality, educational opportunity, minimum standards of health and sanitation--in short, the modern welfare state. Without it, population growth and the "revolution of rising expectations" will bring about increasing suffering, political frustration, and social discontent.[5]

Social, political and economic development through technology and industrialization implies a total revolution of society. Although the ideological and circumstantial mode of modernization may vary for each society in its Traditional stage, the main thrust still retaining anti-Western ideology. The dubious East-West convergence testifies that modernity is, both ideologically and methodologically, linked to the West.[6]

Inspired and motivated by the empirical proof of technology in the advanced world, the emerging nations' aspiration is nothing less than a total transformation of society, in which new modes of consciousness, of work habit, and of structural arrangements must challenge the old order.[7] The peculiar social circumstances in these nations, however, do not seem to favor "popular war" as a method of transformation as some still argue in light of Chinese and Vietnam experience.[8] The political elites of the emerging nations are willing to adopt any methodology for the committed cause of modernization through social revolution. Steering carefully between the ideology camps of nations, they seek every source of tatics and strategies. For instance, one observer remarked on this pragmatic bent in Korea thusly: "General Park's revolution junta in South Korea has been ruthless, and indeed brutal, in eradicating corruption from official life; but the junta's first concern was to restore good relations with the United States, which had been damaged by the manner of its advent to power by overthrowing Dr. John M. Chang's American-supported civilian administration."[9]

Popular war now forced out of style by circumstances, the pragmatic bent of the Third World nations in modernization inevitably brings to the fore the role of the military in the process. "A number of studies of developing countries have pointed out that in these areas the military is the best organized institution and therefore is in the best position to give expression to the national will. This considers discipline and organization to be the key qualities necessary for the institutions to act with political effect."[10] Because of these advantages "the military is considered an instrument of change, a nation-builder, or a melting pot in which various heterogenous elements are unified as the military imposes its own sense of discipline and its own rational norms."[11] The contemporary military in the emerging nations is viewed functional in modernization primarily due to its commanding appearance as a large-scale bureaucracy,[12] to replace the faltering democratic regimes.

>The case studies show that a unified military can take power with relative ease in Asia, Africa, and Latin America. The military is thus a "heavy institution" in underdeveloped countries and can act with authority because it is first and formost an institution of force with organizational features that give it the capacity to be effective in intervening against a most modern institution in terms of its advanced technology, educated elite, absorption of rational norms, division of labor, and exposure to western influence. Although these factors do not necessarily make the military a guarantor of stability, they do facilitate decisive action in a crisis.[13]

Once the military take-over replaces the former regime, (1) the new military leaders now in power drop all pretenses of "democratic" effort; (2) they tend to consolidate the existing single mass-party (where such is the case); (3) they face the double task of "supplying national leadership" and "developing mass support" for the revolutionary programs; and (4) they develop a civilian-military alliance but under strict military rule.[14] Further,

>A new nation is confronted with the issue of whether the population at large accepts its political leaders as legitimate. New nations are countries where some form of political revolution has taken place. Those which have not had their political revolution are likely to face one. In this process of political revolution, colonial forms are eliminated. The act of national liberation--with or without force--established a pragmatic basis for a legitimate government. The military, with its symbols of authority and force, is part of the apparatus of a legitimate government.[15]

Confronted with the task of modernization, national sovereignty and independence in its post-colonial context, the new political leaders inevitably choose to mobilize and consolidate national resources under one monolithic nationalist organization, although they may allow marginal opposition parties to exist. Yet this new breed of authoritarian regimes is clearly differentiated in form and content from the totalitarian government with universalistic and expansionist doctrines. Undoubtedly,

> There are strong authoritarian tendencies in the desire of the nationalist leaders to remold their societies by government action, but thus far there is little evidence of the characteristic totalitarian attempts at thought control absolute unanimity, and the establishment of the infallibility of leaders and party. The emphasis is on persuasion, negotiation, and conciliation, while the threat or use of violence that has typically accompanied the totalitarian attempts to transform society is largely absent.[16]

It is in this context of walking a double-edged sword that the role of ideology in the emerging nations becomes crucial to the political leaders. David Apter attributes a triple-role to ideology in the modernization process of these nations. The first is the "Robin Hood" role which is prevalent during the time of political and social confusion, and the rise of self-assertion on moral rights. The second role of ideology is that of the ideologue by which a set of ideals is organized into public ideology. Hovering between reality and fantasy this role of ideology gives "exceptional opportunities to political leaders to exert their leadership in the moral sphere" after "a revolution or a new nation has obtained its independence." The scientist role of ideology, lastly, looms over the new nation as the universally recognized arbiter of rationality and certainty, in which human problems are translated into technical paradigms and rules.[17] Symbolic and moralist assertions, however, may be blended with rational and technological terms to ease out the possible conflict on the part of the population caught between tradition and modernity.

Modernization in the Third World nations, despite the optimistic rhetoric, is basically a difficult and dangerous mission for the leaders and masses alike. The leaders may face psychological mistrust and suspicion, and political intrigues. Anti-colonial ideology may breed a mentality of absolute negativism, and there must be a careful balance between economic development and political freedon and democracy.[18] At the same time, there is the lack of indigenous material source and the need for foreign capital for industrialization. The leaders of the revolutionary process, regardless of the type of state ideology, face the problem of institutionalizing the social process into a permanent feature of their national development. The basic theme of these emerging nations, then, is one of constant struggle in determination and dedication, without ignoring the force of rational control and planning. It is a process of total involvement in and dedication to change.[19]

It is this enormity and urgency of the national tasks confronted by the Third World societies that requires a historical and comparative analysis. The study of emerging nations demands insight and compassion as well as objective and empirical investigations. Most contemporary sociological analyses in this area tend to ignore the subjective and psychological element of those involved in this gigantic historical process of human development. Issues involved are national independence and industrial modernization through social revolution. Characters on the stage are visionaries and revolutionists, dreamers and fanatics, and planners and managers, with all the dramatics and heroics of a revolutionary age. The political process in the Third World nations, bound by the similar experience of colonialism, and economic backwardness, is a renewed theme of nationalism and human dignity in a world of haves and have-nots. Some succeed while others do not.

2. NATIONALISM AS NATION-BUILDING IDEOLOGY

Since the French Revolution, political ideology has been the most dominant and incessant source of human action in the slogans, visions and programs for a better life. We will briefly examine some of the political expressions of nation-building ideology in general, and the way it necessitates, and is derived from, nationalism in particular.

Political ideology has been the chief architect in a variety of political situations, e.a., revolution, nation-building, modernization, nationalism. Especially in the Third World ideology and revolution have been closely linked together with the variety of aspirations for nationhood and modernity.[20] This surge for political recognition has been facilitated, or hindered, by utilizing effective and/or ineffective ideological manifestations and implications. "The awareness of social bonds and common purpose, the identification of the individual with the group, loyalty to national, religious, or social causes and the very sense of belonging have been formed and directed by conceptual frameworks of ideologies."[21]

Nothing has played a more significant role in this political process than nationalism as ideology, unifying the unsettled population under one directional guidance, mobilizing them into state plans and movements and giving them a certain sense of identity and involvement.

> Nationalism is of fairly recent origin. It aims at the creation and maintenance of a community of life and destiny with a will and purpose expressed in the state and a unity embodied in the nation. Such unity is conscious and is maintained by a system of symbols, values, and notions which define and strengthen the awareness of a collective identity. Nationalism rises beyond the loyalties to ancient traditions or the attachment of men to their land, their homes, and the localities to which they belong. It is founded upon generalizations and a conceptual framework of orientation-- in short, upon ideology.[22]

Although "the Reformation and the victorious progress of a scientific and rationalistic world view have furthered the breakdown of traditional attitudes,"[23] most successful breaks from the Traditional past have come from the effective exploitations of nationalistic sentiments and common bonds bound together by their political and cultural identity, toward the sometimes dubious transcendent conception of nation-building.

> National-building is presumably a metaphoric rubric for the social process or processes by which <u>national consciousness appears</u> in certain groups and which, through more or less institutionalized social structure, act to attain political autonomy for their society.[24]

The modern version of true nationalism is essentially an eithteenth century product, an era of political Enlightenment and scientific rationality. First, it took up an international and humanitarian conception on manhood before it turned to a militant nationalism. "The age of reason and reasonableness which undermined theocracy ushered in a new era of national democracy. Like diesm in religion, enlightened nationalism was cultural, universal and humanitarian. (In the beginning, however,) its separatistic strain was thoroughly diluted by the solvent of international brotherhood of man. In this respect, the nationalism of the eighteenth century was as much international as it was national."[25] Nationalism as an enlightened formula for "the best way of preserving and replenishing the fountain of national genius" through national institutions, eloquently spoken of by men like Rousseau in France and Herder in Germany, had little to be desired, until patriotism emerged as an important offshot of the French Revolution. "Thus, in time, nationalism became human, tainted with the excesses of intolerant partiotism. Being human, it ceased being humanitarian or concerned with internationalism."[26] After a brief revival as a humanitarian and internationalist liberalism by the utiltarians in the nineteenth century, nationalism turned into "racial" or "fascist" system of hatred and imperialism. "This brand of nationalism was reactionary by taste, and imperialist and alienphobe by design. It was anti-Republican and Caesarian, anti-liberal, anti-humanitarian, anti-individual, as well as anti-alien and, by the same token, anti-Semitic."[27]

Nationalism, nevertheless, has sustained many wars for independence, inspired faltering forces to their revoltuionary victory, and rallied the multitude behind common themes and destiny. As a political ideology it has enjoyed unchallenged authority both in times of crises and sustained hardships, although, "nationalism, itself, does not necessarily represent a terminal point either ideologically or institutionally."[28] Our empirical observation of history suggests that this is essentially true, as attested by the decline of nationalism and with the rise of industrial liberalism, which is precisely the reverse of the early twentieth century trend in which "liberalism waned as nationalism waxed" was accorded.[29] "In Latin America, Asia and Africa, nationhood and modernity have appeared as two facets of a single transformation--a dual revolution loudly proclaimed and often ardently desired but never accomplished quickly or with ease."[30]

After the ecstasy of liberation and/or independence subsides, the indigenous new rulers naturally resort to the most effective and handy factor for social unity--nationalism. It is possible that when a sovereignty is liberated from the colonial fetters the new rulers (either through election of appointment) can initiate a Radical measure of social change, which can be similarly effective as any revolutionary Radical transformation. This is especially true in former colonies that have learned the workings of constitutional democracy, Western style, in principle but not in practice. These old colonies are simply too infatuated with Western style democracy, however, to formulate and implement drastic measures for modernization. Rather, they tend to follow the golden rule of gradualism, which is out of style in the twentieth century, in place of revolutionary changes.[31]

Nationalism, out of hatred for the former rulers from another land, serves some functions, according to Emerson. (It must be noted that the historic distinction between Traditional and Radical types is known to us but, not to these gradualist writers like D. Rustow, Emerson, etc., to whom such Radical types as Egypt or Cuba are merely more fanatical nationalists than others.) (1) nationalism can be utilized as a stepping stone to build a more orderly society; (2) "To peoples emerging imperial overlordship the major immediate contributions of nationalism are a sense of independent worth and self-respect and a new social solidarity to replace the traditional bonds....From being natives they rise to the honorable title of nationals;" (3) "For a dependent society to come to a sense of its own national existence is to make a substantial start along the road of equality with its alien rulers," to which other international privileges and recognitions are accorded; (4) the automatic status and its priviliges which the imperial rulers and lesser officials have enjoyed in the colonies, which made the colored natives only half-human, change with independence and its new nationalist ideology; "colonialism created not only the conditions which made nationalism possible, but also, as a complex of relationships subordination 'natives' to expatriate officials and employers, the conditions which made it an appropriate response for those who would regain their self-esteem;" and (5) as in the case of Egypt (after Nasser), nationalism can appeal to the emotions and appropriate responses to patriotic rhetoric.[32]

Nationalism in this process of nation-building effort is an ideology that can be used by those supporting the Traditional status quo, and also by those revolutionaries aiming at total Radicalization; to many writers, e.a., Emerson, however, the distinction between the two distinctive purposes of utilizing nationalism becomes irrelevant, for they regard the liberation or independence of a former colony as something radically different, as Emerson's optimistic view shows above. The following is one step away from this naivete:

> Nationalism in its ideological manifestation is an assertion of a people's right--however distinguished--to determine its political destiny autonomously. It is difficult to analyze this right, just as it is difficult to analyze any right. At bottom, it is merely an assertion of a value to be made good, in this case by a persuasive political dialectic. Political dialectics are not, for the most part, simply conversations. They are matters of political action by more or less organized groups of people. Political dialectics are dialogues of power. Nationalism implies democracy in the sense of public participation in politics, since its assertion of basic political right is in the form of self-determination. The sources of power supporting

the assertion of this right, if there are
any, would presumably be the organization
of the populace for political action. The
ideal type of this process might be the
levee en masse.[33]

In sum, national ideology in the political arena is
essentially an aggregate of subjective consciousness around
consciously selected goals and collective purposes. As such
nationalism has often been the basis of successful revolutionary
transition from Traditional authority and cultural patterns to a
Radical society.

3. PROBLEMS OF TRANSITION

For the most part, the transition form Traditionalism to
Radicalism is an agonizing process both for the participants and
for the spectators. The problems facing the leaders of ex-
colonies are numerous, and the fact that some of their fellow
countries have succeeded in making the Radical transition does
not help the frustrating situation. Hence, revolution becomes
the theme of their daily obsession, rather than the gradual,
popularly established democratic order taught in principle by
the West but rarely workable in reality. In Asia, Africa, Latin
America and the Middle East tension mounts and fermentation
agitates toward a new Radical order, proclaiming the Radical
ideology and envisioning the coming of a total change in social
character. Thus,

> Neither political leaders nor political
> theorists in the Middle East are concerned
> to apologize for the actual working of
> democratic institutions in their countries.
> They are concerned with why these idealized
> institutions, where they exist, have not
> worked so as to render operational the
> utopian vision of a harmonious and progressive
> society. It is they, rather more than we,
> relatively speaking, who have become
> concerned with the prerequisites of democracy
> and the methods of calling it into being.
> Above all, they have shown greater interest
> in the positive role of government in this
> transition....For Middle Eastern leaders
> and theorists, the question is "How can
> one change a culture and a society?" Their
> name for these changes is revolution.[34]

This vision of revolutionary change is as much objective
as it is subjective, for the working blueprint for democratic

institutions presupposes a measure of economic development which the Third World lacks. In most cases this revolutionary zeal is justified when the remnants of colonial mentality, traditionally backward social heirarchy, corruption and ignorance in political consciousness, among others, are presented as evidence. The contention that Radicalization through revolution, or in a manner that is similarly effective, is the sole and whole criterion that marks the entry point of a Traditional into Radicalism type is based on this historical experience that in the twentieth century time is not the same as that in previous epochs. Gradualism is both practically and morally unworkable in the Third World, although the principle is respected and often tried.

> The Middle Eastern idea of revolution is stated in terms of a social, cultural, and psychological regenration; but it also entails giving power to the many by means of what is usually referred to as an awakening. Perhaps this is a concern with the prerequisites of a democracy as we know it; creating the fundamental agreement so that smaller disagreements may be tolerated. For the time being, however, popular control of government, individual rights, and isonomy find little or no place in Middle Eastern theories of democracy. The epithets of plebiscitary democracy and totalitarian democracy come immediately to mind, but these ideas do not accord with the limited resources at the disposal of Middle Eastern governments, nor with their actual lack of strict hierarchical control. For the present, at any rate, these governments and their justifiers can rightly claim a hearing, for we have no proven alternative, only the weak suggestion that democratic institutions are firmly established by practice.[35]

Against this revolutionary necessity, many Western writers, notably D. Rustow, postulate that modernization should be achieved only gradually, and somewhat belittle the achievements brought about by revolutionary governments. "(A) critical set of alternatives that confronts modernizing societies," remarks Rustow, "relates to the timing of the three quests for authority, for identity and for participation and equality. Are all three to be undertaken at one and the same time, or are they to be pursued one by one? And if one by one, in what order are these political elements of the modern nation-state to be assembled?"[36] Further,

> If any attainment in authority, unity or equality depended on a proportionate attainment in the two others, no progress

in any of the three directions would be likely. The lack of unity and of equality would always defeat attempts at increasing authority, and the lack of authority would prevent any growth in either of the others. The result would indeed be balance, but instead of balanced growth there would be the balance of stagnation at a traditional level. Beyond such formal reasoning, several specific considerations may be adduced in favor of sequence rather than simultaneity of the three quests.[37]

There are five main factors, according to Rustow, that favor gradualism in sequence rather than to Radical revolutionary changes: (1) "Among the scarcest resources in any development process, economic or political, is the human capacity for innovation and for learning." Neither the leaders' attention nor the ability of the followers in the new order and habits is abundant enough to carry out modernization programs simultaneously; (2) promoting all three quests at once will likely lack the majority support, and likely to create oppositions among the population; (3) "There is a decisive difference in the speed appropriate to each of the three quests." Growth in modern institutions is achieved "over a period of several generations;" (4) enforcement of identity and equality, for instance, must presuppose the existence of a fairly stable authority, which means that this one must precede the others; and (5) "Authority, and in many cases identity, can grow up in a pre-modern, traditional context, whereas widespread political participation and a closer approximation to political equality are intimately bound up with other features of modernization in the intellectual, social and economic spheres."[38] Japan is given as a typical case of sequential growth in authority, identity, and equality, through the period semifeudal principalities (1338-1573), the famed Tokugawa period (1603-1868) and the Meiji Restoration (1868) in which the modernization process culminated.[39] Authority largely remained in the hands of imperial bureaucracy and of the military through of the 20's and real egalitarian participation did not occur until after the end of World War II.

The simple reality today is that the Third World cannot wait for centuries as Japan did for these modern quests to materialize. They attempt to achieve all these at once and some, like Russia, have succeeded in achieving them all simultaneously. Within a half century Russia appears to have emerged from a backward country to become a second most (or possible the most) powerful nation in the world. In one gigantic sweep of historical event, the quest for authority, identity and participation (and equality to a better degree perhaps than many Western states) has been completed, with China trailing immediately behind Russia, and Cuba and Egypt attempting to emulate the success pattern.

Weighing the empirical evidence of historic reality, which includes the desperate aspiration and determination disciplined by colonial humiliation, the sequential gradualism in modernization appears rather naive. Modernization of the Third World today must begin with a revolution and its ideology and corresponding social character, given the available sources of consciousness and the ideals of the post-feudal era that lure these desperados.

The problems of transition from Conservatism to Radicalism must be considered a little further. We must at this point emphasize the clear distinction between the Traditional -to- Radical and the Traditional-to-Modern transitions. Being "Radical" and being "modern" are in many instances not identical nor comparible. Our conception of the transition presupposes a "Radical break" from the Traditionalist ideology and its corresponding institutions and social character, which are completely replaced by a new order through Radicalization. The oft-mentioned transformation to modernity conceived generally by Western observers, on the other hand, takes the "appearance," often superficial and temporary, as the true index of modernization: Bureaucratic apparatus, elections held often enough to mold a democratic appearance, centralized authority, continuity of daily life in a predictable manner, etc., which is often the characteristic features of some of the most backward Traditionalist societies. The difficulty of obtaining some objective measure of the transformational process at the historical level, and its necessary world-historical consequences in ideology and social character is immense. Many writers especially among political scientists, have attempted to utilize or define at least some useful operational criteria, such as economic or political index, i.e., the rise and fall of gross national product street riots, peaceful exchanges of government, etc. These attempts are highly formalistic and often immaterial to reality, let alone paternalistic in the sense that Western stability is always used as the yardstick. Such textbook type conditions for, and the objective features of, modernization do not accurately reflect the reality in which both the subjective and objective aspects are intimately and dramatically interlocked as a coherent and epochal vision of world-history.

Now, the most obvious case of the elusive image of modernization as measured by the conventional Western yardstick rests with contemporary India. "That India belongs to two worlds is a familiar platitude that happens to be true. Economically it remains in the preindustrial age. It had not had an industrial revolution in either of the two capitalist vairants..., nor according to the communist one."[40] The burden of India is that the praise of the biggest working

37

democracy" and the mockery of being one of the most backward societies in the world are both correctly accorded it. On the appearance level at least, India satisfies all the conditions and structural features that characterize a modern nation. Yet historically observed, India belongs to one of the Traditional pre-modern groups discussed earlier. Barrington Moore succinctly describes the dilemma:

> There has been no bourgeois revolution, no conservative revolution from above, no peasant revolution. But as a political species it does belong to the modern world. At the time of Nehru's death in 1964 political democracy had existed for seventeen years. If imperfect, the democracy was no mere sham. There had been a working parliamentary system since Independence in 1947, and independent judiciary, and the standard liberal freedoms: free general elections in which the governing party had accepted defeat in an important part of the country, civilian control over the military, a head of state that made very limited use of formal extensive powers. There is a paradox here, but only a superficial one. Political democracy may seem strange in both an Asian setting and one without an industrial revolution until one realizes that the appalling problems facing the Indian government are due to these very facts...why the advent of the modern world has not led to political or economic upheavals in India....[41]

Plagued by the rigidity of religion, caste system, colonial mentality under British rule and other traditional obstacles, India has never had a chance for genuine Radicalization. The adherence to the non-violence rules of Gandhi's resistance that powerfully conditioned the Indian mentality in politics and actual modes of governance did not help the situation even after the Independence. Peasants, the victims of widespread poor cultivation and political docility, rebelled but their "rebellions never assumed remotely the same significance in India that they did in China."[42] The costs of maintaining features and ideals of modern liberal democracy, ironically, are both the pride and shackles of today's India. A society's entry into the modern world must be accomplished first by Radical political transformation on the world-historical level and then by developing industrial technology. The very fact that the politically pre-modern India possesses the highest capacity of industrial technology in one respect--that of producing the atomic bomb--makes our observation even more cogent.

Only one line of policy then seems to offer real hope, which implies no prediction that it will be the one adopted. In any case, <u>a strong element of coercion remains necessary if a change is to be made.</u> Barring some technical miracle that will enable every Indian peasant to grow abundant food in a glass of water or a bowl of sand, labor will have to be applied much more effectively, technical advances introduced, and means found to get food to the city dwellers in the cities. Either masked coercion of a massive scale, as in the capitalist model including even Japan, or <u>more direct coercion approaching the socialist model will remain necessary</u>. The tragic fact of the matter is that the poor bear the heaviest costs of modernization under both socialist and capitalist auspices. The only justification for imposing the costs is that they would become steadily worse off without it. As the situation stands, the dilemma is indeed a cruel one. It is possible to have the greatest sympathy for those responsible for facing it. <u>To deny that it exists is, on the other hand, the acme of both intellectual and political irresponsibility.</u>[43]

There are many reasons for these Traditional societies' inability to make the crucial transition. In the midst of their aspirations and frustrations stands the gloomy but perhaps true prediction that "creating a viable system of states in most of the former colonial areas is going to be a painful process. We can only hope that the rest of the world can avoid being drawn into what promises to be <u>an endless round of coups, conquests, revolutions, and wars.</u>"[44] This tendency of Western observers to lump together all the political events in the Third World in characterizing their predicament is not only morally unfair but also intellectually and empirically unwarranted. The Third World rightly, and righteously, demands that there must be a distinction "between real revolutions, which have been relatively infrequent, and <u>putsches</u> or <u>palace coups</u> which have hardly affected the life of the countries in which they have occured."[45] The genuine transition from Traditional to Radical society parallels, at the same time, the distinction between world-historical events e.a., (real revolutions, revolutions-by-coup, etc.) and local-events (e.a., palace coups, one-shot attmepts, etc.)

The generally valid key determining a successful transformation of social and political structure is the extent to which the masses participate in the new regime's power maintenance, visions and plans, and permanently institutionalizing the new Radical ideology and its corresponding social character changes. It further depends on (1) whether the revolutionary leaders possess or claim to possess radically new programs for the masses that necessitate mass mobilization; and/or (2) whether the masses are psychologically, socially and culturally willing to be mobilized. Coercion need not be as drastic as it appears in some cases, such as in Russia and China, but a nationalist and at times even religious appeal can accomplish, as in Egypt, Korea and Cuba, a good measure of mass mobilization. The most traditionalist and populous segment of society, i.e. the rural population, however, tends to resist mobilization with the greatest force in the new regime. Their resistance to mobilization, a historically familiar phenomenon, may be due to (1) economic immobility (underemployment); (2) civil immobility (lack of political participation; (3) status immobility (caste system); (4) psychic immobility (traditionalist superstition), etc. It has been shown for instance that breaking through this barrier required the "notorious mass organizations and the endless action meetings " in Communist China and North Vietnam.[46] To a limited extent then Etzioni's generalization that social development depends on the struggle between "the mobilizers" and "the immobilized" may be considered valid in its conceptual definition:

> Collectivities are bases of potential power, but generally only a small fraction of these potentialities are actualized for purposes of societal action and change. The capacity of any collectivity to influence history depends to a considerable extent on its capacity to mobilize--that is, <u>on the outcome of the internal struggle between mobilizers and the immobilized</u>....Above all, the unit of action is not the collectivity per se, but that part of it which has been mobilized by organizations. Thus, history is not affected by the working class as such , which is a passive unit, but by labor unions, labor parties, social protest movements that mobilize a segment of the working classes. (The same sould be said about the civil rights movement and the Negro-Americans, national movements and colonial people,etc.)[47]

"The degree to which mass support or participation is forthcoming depends partly on the prior existence of a political community and partly on the consensus or dissension which emerges along with the efforts to develop the country." The drastic sacrifice and regimentation which characterized Russian mass mobilization since 1917 were steps to insure mass compliance in the massive industrialization process, although some degree of consensus was secured on the basis of improved material

conditions.[48] As noted earlier, India is a classic case of mass
immobilization caught between economic necessity and democratic
obsession, although it typifies D. Rustow's thesis of "dual
enforcement" of tradition and modernity in accomplishing
modernization as a gradual process.[49] On the other hand, David
Wilson recognizes the effectiveness of a tightly organized party,
a prototype of which would be Lenin's Communist Party, and a
dedicated cadre of propaganda and revolutionary workers.
Political revolution to Wilson. seems the shortest and most
effective road to nation-building and modernization, whose
success has been proven in many Communist-led uprisings and in
other similar events.

> The aim of the revolution is to annihilate
> constituted authority and substitute a new
> authority. The <u>simultaneity of these two
> aspects of the process may be critical in
> successful nation-building.</u> The process of
> annihilation is pursued by such actions as
> sabotage, terrorism, armed raids, ambushes,
> and the like which, on one hand, seek to
> demonstrate the ineffectiveness of constituted
> authority and, on the other hand, seek to
> destroy the concept of justice upon which
> constituted authority stands by such acts
> as propaganda attacks on land law and other
> economic relationships, on the honesty and
> integrity of officials (corruption), on the
> patriotism of officials (lackeys of
> imperialism), and on the justice of social
> relations and social opportunities (class
> struggle, education and literacy, unemployment,
> wages, rents).[50]

It has been generally acknowledged that the ineffective and
corruption of the old order is a necessary precondition for
successful revolutionary changes. This has also been pointed out
by de Tocqueville: in the case of the French Revolution, one of
the main contributing factors was the isolation of the French
nobility from social interaction with the middle classes and
peasantry, and from its traditional political and civic duties,
while its counterpart in Germany (where serfdom still existed)
and England fulfilled their obligatory duties. "The French
nobility had themselves exempted from most of their duties to the
community, fondly imagining they could keep their lofty status
while evading its obligations."[51] Generally, "the ruling classes
in the old regimes (were) markedly divided, markedly unsuited to
fulfill the functions of a ruling class," noted Crane Brinton in a
phenomenology of revolution. Further,

Some have joined the intellectuals and deserted the established order, have indeed often become leaders in the crusade for a new order; others have turned rebels, less because of hope for the future than because of boredom with the present; others have gone soft, or indifferent, or cynical. Many, possibly even most of the rank-and-file of the ruling classes, the English squire, the French and Russian Country nobleman, retained the simple faith in themselves and their postiton which is apparently necessary to a ruling class. But the tone of life in the upper classes was not set by such as these. Fashion had gone over to the intellectuals. The sober virtues, the whole complex series of value-judgements which guards a privileged class from itself and others, all these were out of fashion at Whitehall, at Versailles, at the old court of St. Petersburg.[52]

Brinton's study included the four classic revolutions, English, American, French and Russian, in which the ineffectiveness and moral corruption (except in America, possibly because no feudal nobility had ever existed) were omnipresent in all ruling classes. However, it seems that some measure of ineffectiveness and/or corruption of the constituted governments in even modern pre-revolutionary countries seem to invariably exist: China's Sun Yat-sen's highly democratic and enlightened but chaotic and ineffective Republic, followed by the equally trouble-ridden leadership by Chiang Kai-Shek's Kuomintang government until the Communist take-over in 1949; Egypt's upper class totally isolated from the rural population, about 80 percent of all, and its ostentatious life style, no less glamorized and pronounced by King Farouk's internationally notorious personal expenditure and liberal exercise of favoritism in political affairs until Nasser came to power in 1952; Cuba's highhanded but isolated dictator Batista who had no mass support and simply crumbled when in 1959 Castro marched in; Korea's too-liberal and too-lenient John Chang's second Republic that allowed many affairs settled on the streets and by demonstrating mobs, thus creating unprecendented freedoms but at the same time creating chaos and disorder, in 1961, just to name few obvious ones in our recent memory.

4. VARIETIES OF TRANSITION

The transition from Tradition to Radicalism takes a variety of means and modes under different circumstances, suitable for each society in a particular period of history. This political transformation can be observed in three major varieties, resulting in the same Radical ideology and its social character.

First, obviously the massive political revolutions that are familiar to us, i.e. the French and Russian Revolutions, with relatively clear-cut beginnings and endings, must be considered as the most epochal of all. Since there are other revolutionary regimes, i.e. Egypt and Cuba, that did not involve the masses in the beginning and during the affair, it is necessary that we conceptually recopitulate the two types of political revolution referred to earlier:

(1) "Classic" revolutions in which the masses are directly involved and much blood shed, i.e. the revolutions in America, France, Russia and China. Although our familiar images and slogans of revolution are fostered largely by these classic revolutions it seems that the Chinese Revolution is the last one of that kind in the modern world. Not only the passions and visions of popular revolutionary uprising have been neutralized into technical and administrative programs in many parts of the world, but also the formal declaration and the international recognition of independence have dimmed the passionate dedication in the revolutionaries without a visible and easily recognizable villain, e.a. the colonial imperialist. In those ex-colonies the imperial powers may continue their domination through intricate networks of diplomacy and economic monopoly, but their domination may not be clearly identified as such. With the now expanded means of the mass-media, virtually every member of the community can be reached and manipulated, backed up by nationalistic, traditional or religious appeal to the masses. The relatively high degree of armament for even an ancient Traditionalist society, equipped with modern electronic means of violence, renders any mass uprising in the classic sense not only impossible and futile but also unconceivable. Hence in the second half of the twentieth century we witness the other type of political revolutions;

(2) "Modern" revolutions in contrast with the classic ones. The crucial difference is that in the latter cases, the masses are mobilized only after, or toward the end of, the revolutionary movement, ordinarily initiated by few idealists or visionaries in and out of the military. The Egyptian Revolution by Neguib-Nasser, the Cuban Revolution by Castro and Company, the Korean Military Revolution by Park and his military officers are some of the text book examples of this type of "modern" revolution. Both in the aims and visionary effects the modern revolutions essentially share the similarities with the classic revolutions: old Traditionalist social structure is replaced by Radicalism of either an Enlightenment or Marxian variety; Radical revolutionary measures are immediately taken; new social institutions are created and the old ones destroyed or rearranged; and a Radical social

character is created for the masses. Since many military coup d'etat are attempted without any Radical programs or visions directed in view of the masses who may have legitimate reasons for condoning the efforts (as was the case in Egypt, Cuba and Korea) their failures in seizing power, or failures in political transformation of their Traditional lot into Radically new dimensions and structures only prove the weary Western observer's lamentation that the conductor may change but the music remains the same.

When successful, however, it must be noted, the modern revolution-by-coup ranks with the classic counterpart with only two differences that (a) mostly it is without bloodshed; and (b) the masses are afterwards successfully mobilized into maintaining the revolutionary regime and carrying out the massive transformational programs and reforms. The characteristic differences between the successful and unsuccessful modern revolutions and their attempts essentially lie in the fact that (a) the former have an alternative set of political programs, mainly geared to fulfilling the egalitarian ideals of the Enlightenment of a Marxian socialism of which the masses are considered to have been deprived; and (b) they succeed in their coup by succeeding in post-coup national mobilization. All three revolutions-by-coup in Egypt, Cuba and Korea followed these successful paths, while others like coups in Pakistan, Burma, Iraq, Peru, Argentina, Guatemala, Equador and other numerous members of the Third World failed because they either (a) secured power but did not change the Traditionalist structure which resulted in a mere change of the ruler but not in the rules; or (b) did not succeed in securing power in the first place. The import in modern coups is not only whether or not they succeed, but also whether or not they are "revolutionary." The inevitable high concentration of military weaponry in the armed forces, centuries ahead of the society's level in general, makes it a safe prediction that military coups will be the predominant mode of future revolutions in Traditional societies aspiring to be transformed into a Radical type. This theme will be rediscussed in the following section.

Second, a drastic social reform resulting in a power transfer from the monarch to the Parliament as is the case with the English Revolution of 1649 with very little or no violence.[53] The Scandinavian societies and the Low Lands in Europe too have actually undergone a theoretically similar transition without violence which involved a creation of constitutional monarchy and other reform measures gradually. As mentioned earlier, the Traditional-to-Radical transition in a gradual manner is essentially a pre-twentieth century feature of what is almost exclusively confined to European societies. This democratic gradual social reform is important in two ways: (a) that this "gradualist revolution" from Traditionalism (with divine monarchs) to the constitutional Radicalism (of the "sovereignty of the people") helps complete our analytical and conceptual model of ideology and social character namely, that the Traditional-to-Radical transition is an empirically generalizable historic phenomenon, although within it variations (like gradualism) do exist; and (b) that this gradualist reform must be viewed as the remnant of a historic past; there is not a single example of this kind in the twentieth century; such a gradual process is both objectively and subjectively impossible, given the material and social reality of the Third World nations which confront the task of transition today. Hence the paucity of gradualism in contemporary political practice.

Third, the acquisition of an independent nation had as a politically defined and internationally recognized entity must be listed as a special case in the transformation process--but not an exception. Theoretically speaking, the former colonies now made independent can turn this occasion of independence ceremony and the new formation of a governing body into revolutionary changes, both in ideology and in social character. None of the former colonies has made these changes, still clinging to the ideal of achieving parliamentary politics Western style while remaining under dictatorships or endless rounds of coups and civil wars.

In turning independence into Radical transformation, Israel is the case in point. Scattered around the world for two milleniums under all sorts of humuliation, persecution, and discrimination, desperately holding onto their cultural and religious heritage, the Jews before the 1947 U.N. partition of Palestine that made Israel an independent state were no better off as a collectivity than Gypsies or natives under colonial rulers. Although noted for a remarkable survival record,[54] Jewish consciousness in the modern Radical sense of the term hardly existed until the independence of 1948. The changes in ideology and social character among the newly independent Jews were so dramatic and world-historical that the full perspective of those changes were not felt until some time after the partition. Rarely in history was the birth of a nation more charged with emotion than when "the Hebrew state was restored in Palestine... eighteen centuries after the destruction of Jerusalem and only a half-century after Herzle's prophecy."[55]

> Outside the museum, crowds had assembled along with representatives of the press, only one of whom was permitted to enter. Inside, the future cabinet members sat at a long table. Facing them were two hundred people--the writers, the artists, the economists, the rabbis, and the

Haganah leaders who had played leading roles in
the struggle for independence. Ben-Furion,
usually in shirt sleeves and tieless, looked
unfamiliar in his dark suit. His voice even,
his eyes riveted to the paper he held, he read
the proclamation. In 979 Hebrew words, which
took less than twenty-two minutes to read, it
dealt with the unbroken connection between
the Land and the People. It announced that
Israel, which was the name chosen for the new
state, would be open to all Jews from all the
countries of their dispersion. It would
uphold the freedom of religion, conscience,
education, and culture, and would safeguard
the holy places. Israel would abide by the
UN charter and now called upon the UN for help.
Then Ben-Gurion read the final paragraph of
the proclamation: "With faith in Almighty God,
we set our hands to this Declaration, at this
Session of the Provisional State Council, in
the City of Tel Aviv, on this Sabbath eve,
the fifth day of Iyar, the fourteenth day of
May, 1948"....The traditional Jewish blessing
was intoned: "Blessed be Thou, oh Lord our
God, King of the Universe, who has kept us
alive and made us endure and brought us to
this day." His eyes moist, Ben-Gurion read
the first ordinances of the new government.
From a gallery upstairs, the Palestine
Philharmonic Orchestra played the "Hatikvah."
At exactly 4:37 1/2 p.m., he banged a gavel
and said, "The State of Israel has arisen.
This meeting is ended."[56]

Although from a different route, Israel's Radical
transformation shared the essential characteristics of
revolutionary (both classic and modern) regimes in its
ideology and social character changes. In common with
other revolutionary types (as will be detailed later)
Israel emphasized nationalism as a state ideology for
unity; its constitution broadly reflected the Enlightenment
ideals; collectivization was attempted; secularism gradually
made inroads into religiosity in many facets of Jewish life;
technological efforts were made in industry and agriculture;
the "new man" then emerged with the new identity; a radical
theme of struggle continued to dominate public as well as
private rhetoric; national defense demanded mass mobilization;
a certain collective spirit of brotherhood flourished; the
minorities who presented a clear and imminent as well as
suspected danger were severly dealt with in the name of the
security of the state. One thing that was absent in the Israeli

case was the usual sweeping reform in land-holding and taxation system, ubiquitous in all revolutions,[57] for the early Jewish settlers had been more or less collectivized from the start that rendered such a reform measure unneccessary.

The varieties of the pre-modern social system, which we have inclusively termed Traditional type, can be seen as composed in actuality of two main variations: (1) an outright feudal structure against which some classic revolutions were staged, i.e. England before 1649, France before 1789, Russia before 1917, China before 1949; in this of course other quasi-republics that resembled some sort of constitutional democracy, e.a., Egypt before 1952 and Korea before 1961, are also included, for despite the modernistic appearance their mentality and working structure of society were strongly feudalistic. And (2) colonialism: from this group we must consider a variety of deviations, some of which we have already spoken of, that is, (a) prototype colonies under imperialist mandate without any disguise of self-determination mainly in Asia and Africa; (b) semi-colonies, that is, independent nations that live on foreign investments and their entailed supervision on domestic as well as foreign policies; (c) ethnic colonies: Gypsy nomads and the Jews before 1947; and (d) colonialism as sub-culture: this last category refers to special ethnic groups that form in essence a colonial sub-culture, i.e. black Africans in white minority nations in Africa and the black population in the United States.

It is from this pool of Third World nations that we see the glimpse of inevitable political transformation to come as the stuff of future history-making. Let us now consider military coup d'etat as the most common path through which such transformation is likely to be attempted.

5. REVOLUTIONS-BY-COUP

Considering the curious coexistence of pre-modern social structure and its Traditionalist mode of thought and action in the general population, on the one hand, and the elite, conscious and relatively well-educated military officers and the modern equipment of violence under their control, on the other, makes military coup the most prevailing mode of transition attempt at the present and in the future. (A typical standard operation in a military coup follows this pattern: (1) a general-rank officer of some public esteem is joind by a field-rank officer in the initial plan to overthrow existing authority; (2) under the junior officer a small military unit swiftly occupies the capital and places key government officials under arrest; (3) all channels of mass communication, e.a. television, raido, newspaper, etc., are under the new Revolutionary Council's direct control, which immediately begins to broadcast the new plans and programs for the masses; (4) all airports, sea ports, and banks are ordered closed; and (5) the junta government now confronts the tasks of consolidating its inner power structure, punishing the old officials and politicians, and most importantly, persuading the masses to support the new regime. Mostly within a week or so, the relative success or failure of a military coup can be fairly well determined.) In the Northern-tier of the Middle East, i.e. Turkey, Iran, Afghanistan and Pakistan, for instance, military involvement in coups and politics have been one of the major political characteristics, although none of them is as successful in managing a complete Radical break as the Egyptian Revolution.[58]

D. Rustow draws a distinction between coups under the "command of the chief of staff and other top ranking officers" and coups "resulting from a colonel's conspiracy."

>The senior commanders, in short, have not spent their entire lives in the barracks and on the proving ground; even under the old regime, their most recent professional activity was largely political and administrative. Hence a junta of top-ranking generals and admirals may be expected to bring to the tasks of government more experience and sophistication than the conspiratorial colonels and majors. On the other hand, as military servants in good standing of the deposed regime, the top commanders will have a harder time justifying their coup to the troops and the citizenry, formulating a distinctive program for their own government, and rallying the opponents of the old regime around it.

>In contrast, the colonels' oppositional credentials are likely to be more authenic in inverse proportion to their previous political experience. As the victorious conspirators grapple with the old but unaccustomed problems of civiliam politics, moreover, they may find that their coup has created a number of new and thorny problems in the ranks of the military.[59]

These new and thorny problems generally are: (1) the chasm between those involved officers who wish to relinquish their new troublesome positions in politics to civilians and return to the barracks and those who desire to transform the coup into a radical social revolution. This struggle often determines the success or failure of a military coup.

In Egypt Nasser, the cololnel, outsted General Neguib, in Turkey the general expelled the colonel and his radical followers (therefore the coup could not consolidate its power hold after all), and in Korea in 1961 the younger general who led the coup from the beginning outsted the chief of staff who nominally represented the coup after its ascendency for the purpose of military unity; (2) middle rank officers taking charge of the affairs are likely to create displinary problems. The new head of the state was an adjutant yesterday in a division; and (3) consolidation of the military posts vacated by those who enter politics, and therefore, may face a few threats from those officers who occupy the new military posts.[60] In successful ones this did not happen to an unmanageable extent. For example, Egypt's President Sadat, the successor to Nasser, was forced to disband a commando unit after learning that the majority of the unit's man and officers favored a coup against the President.[61]

The most monumental task for revolutions-by-coup is thus turning the coup into a national-scale revolution of total change, including a change in ideology, institutional structures, and the old social character of the population. Hence D. Rustow's rather unsympathetic view on this task faced by the junta officers:

> Where loyalties among civilians have broken down, force can triumph; but unless some new principle of legitimacy emerges, force may continue to displace force in a steady succession of coups. Nor is there much profit in speculating about the sincerity of the soldiers' professions of democracy and reform, in tracing their "ideological formation" to their high-school textbooks or to the spare-time reading matter of their years in the staff college. To issue promises of reform is mandatory even for those who may not intend them; or to carry them out is difficult even for those who do. In the turmoil of the political contest, mere intentions count for little. A junta's desire to retire to the barracks after a brief stay on the political stage will lead to nothing but frustration.[62]

Rustow's cynical indictment unfortunately holds true in most coup attempts, but few have managed to roll through the mounting odds after their junta. The most essential point in their success or failure has been rallying the masses behind the revolutionary causes and aims, presupposing that the revolutionary force possessed clearly and radically defined causes and aims to begin with.

According to Rustow's phenomenology of military coups there are five sequels that might emerge afterwards: (1) the

officers who staged the coup will retain power for a minimum of
time and restore the civilian control of government. But their
voluntary return to the barracks would be as precarious as their
urge to seize political power, as has been shown in the cases of
Peru (1962-62) and Turkey (1960-61).

For the body politic as a whole,
military seizure of power is a symptom of
profound disorder. It takes more than a
casual difficulty to overcome an army's
inhibition in seizing power, and it takes
more than a casual set of decrees to effect
a remedy. For the members of a conspiratorial
junta, a brief tenure in office is hardly
a proper reward for the effort they have
expended and the risks they have run. A
truly new regime cannot be erected overnight,
and under a restored ancient regime the
conspirators would be criminally liable
for high treason. For any civilian successors,
the soldiers' rapid and voluntary withdrawal
hold little promise of stability. If
they depart for their barracks of their
own accord; what is to keep them from
reentering the arena at any time of their
choosing?[63]

(2) "The soldiers may stay in power permanently, (forming)
a stable military oligarchy." However, this situation is more
likely to exist in Traditional societies or ones in a similar
stage of historical development, e.a., Somona's seizure of
power in Nicaragua and his son's succession (1936-1956), and
Thailand's military rule (1932-1944 and since 1951). (3)
"Praetorianium" or an endless coup attempts will follow the
first one, mainly by other equally ambitious junior officers
who have seen the relative ease of military take-over. This
is generally true in slightly more advanced countries, e.a.,
those in Latin America and in the Middle East armed with
modern military hardware and personnel.

The junta's ardor and inexperience
may have done more to aggravate than to
resolve the political and economic problems
that gave rise to the initial coup. Meanwhile, popular enthusiasm has soured,
military discipline has been shaken, and the
key commands near the capital have passed
into new hands. Having seen how it was for
one group of colonels to seize power, many
majors and captains will now nurture the
same ambition. After breaking the spell

of loyalties that sustained the old regime,
the junta has found no new basis of legitimacy.
Might having become right, it remains for
some new group of conspirators to possess
themselves of greater might.[64]

(4) After a successful coup and the subsequent political purges the military forces may decide to return to their usual posts, but not completely. "The result is likely to be an ambiguous situation in which the military leave the political stage but continue to hover in the wings." Hence,

> The soldiers may entrust to a civilian
> president or cabinet the daily conduct of
> government while reserving to themselves
> a veto on certain decisions. They may
> allow elections while banning from parti-
> cipation or victory certain specified
> groups. In short, the soldiers, in one way
> or another, continue to assume the role
> of umpire of the political game, of guardians
> of the constitution, of guarantors of
> national unity.[65]

Examples of this "civilian-military twilight" abound in empirical reality: Brazil since 1945, Argentina after 1958, and Turkey since 1961. Generally what follows is not a democratic practice in the usual sense but a military tutelage, with the consequential demoralization and the blurring of civilian and military responsibilities in government.

Or (5) a military coup is turned into a total Radical transformation. Here Rustow remarks something akin to what has been described as revolution-by-coup when he observes that "all military revoultions begin as coups, and some coups develop into revolutions: the difference is not in the promise but in the performance."

> If a coup is to become the basis of a
> revolution, it must first meet a negative
> requirement. The military rulers must not
> be overthrown in short order; they must
> have time to carry out a program of basic
> reform. The initial contribution that a
> military junta or dictator can make in
> turning their coup into a revolution consists
> in preserving or reestablishing discipline
> within the army. The withdrawal of the
> military politics thus begins typically
> with the forced withdrawal of the soldier-

rulers' military rivals. If the head of the regime is a victorious general enjoying wide respect, the process becomes easier; soldiers who do not withdraw from politics out of conviction may do so out of loyalty to their commander.[66]

The revolutions-by-coup in Egypt (1952) and in Korea (1961) present almost identical cases in the person of the leaders, in the pronounced ideology, in the aftermath-power struggle and in the popular support they enjoyed. In order to make the transition less traumatic the more radical and idealistic Nasser chose general Naguib, a widely respected man for integrity, as the figure-head of the revolutionary regime. Within two years the general was ousted for his apparent reluctance for drastic reform measures that the younger officers were intent upon inaugurating. With colonel Nasser in power these reform measures were swiftly put into effect, enjoying unprecedented popularity.[67]

The situation in Korea was almost identical. General Park, known for rare integrity and honesty, led the junta sucessfully (1961) and retained general Chang as the chairman of the Joint Chiefs of Staff mainly to consolidate military support. Within a year the Chairman of the Joint Chiefs of Staff was charged with conspiring against the revolutionary regime's goals and visions. The Revolutionary Special Tribunal soon ousted him and sent him to "studying abroad." Soon thereafter Park formally resigned from the military. In the ensuing presidential election which was generally characterized as the "fairest election in Korean history," Park was elected to the Presidency. Now his legitimacy confirmed, Park's revolutionary government began to push programs for social reform and economic development relentlessly.

Among the gallery of coups and small scale power struggles, these success stories of Egypt and Korea are quite uncommon. Revolutionary purges were not rare incidents although surprisingly mild compared with those more massive and ruthless cases of Russia and China.

Finally, the question remains: What are some of the more significant-yet sociologically generalizable qualities that a Radical society displays which has just made the Tradition-to-Radical transition? It is in these general characteristics manifest in various examples for Radical ideology and social character that we observe the emergence of a truly modern state, now prepared to meet the challenge of economic welfarism. In the following chapter we shall deal with these characteristics which differentiate Radicalism from Traditionalism.

FOOTNOTES

1. Irving Louis Horowitz, *Three Worlds of Development: The Theory and Practice of International Stratification*, Oxford University Press, New York, 1966, p. 4. (emphasis original) The Third World nations that succeed in breaking away from tradition completely establish their Radical ideology and social character. Until the "Radical break" occurs, as elaborated in this and the next chapters, these Third World nations must remain Traditional societies with their appropriate ideology and social character traits as discussed in the preceding chapter.

2. Gustavo Lagos, *International Stratification and Underdeveloped Countries*, The University of North Carolina Press, Chapel Hill, N.C., 1963, p. 37.

3. Ibid., p. 23.

4. W.W. Kulski, *International Politics in a Revolutionary Age*, J.B. Lippincott Company, New York, 1968, p. 277.

5. Paul Sigmund, Jr., "Introduction," in Paul Sigmund, Jr., (ed.), *The Ideologies of the Developing Nations*, Frederick A. Praeger, Publishers, New York, 1964, p. 11.

6. Edward Shils, "The Military in the Political Development of the New States, in John J. Johnson (ed), *The Role of the Military in Underdeveloped Countries*, Princeton University Press, Princeton, New Jersey, 1962, pp. 9-12.

7. Uegene Staley, *The Future of Underdeveloped Countries*, Harper Brothers, New York, 1961, p. 6.

8. See, for example, Mark Selden, "Revolution and Third World Development: People's War and the Transformation of Peasant Society," in Norman Miller and Roderick Aya, (eds.), *National Liberation*, The Free Press, New York, 1971, pp. 214-248.

9. Brian Crozier, *The Morning After: A Study of Independence*, Methuen & Co., Ltd., London, 1963, p. 62.

10. Henry Bienin, "Introduction to Henry Bienen (ed.), *The Military Intervenes*, Russell Sage Foundation, New York, 1968, p. xiii. (emphasis original)

11. Ibid.; see Morris Janowitz (ed.), *The New Military: Changing Patterns of Organization*, Russell Sage Foundation, New York,

1964, pp. 339-362, for comprehensive bibliography on the military and politics.

12. Moris Janowitz, _The Military in the Political Development of New Nations_, The University of Chicago Press, Chicago, 1964, p. 26.

13. Henry Bienen, "Introduction," op. cit., p. xv.

14. Morris Janowitz, _The Military in the Political Development of New Nations_, op. cit., p. 29. Concerning Peru's military regime: "The military leaders (of Peru) do not believe elections are very relevant in a country where more than half the people are illiterate Indians living very much as they did five centuries ago, and where politicians and political parties have historically been corrupt and subservient to foreign economic interests. "Is Peru's Military Revolution Key to the Future?" _Los Angeles Times_, April 22, 1973, Part Three, p. 3.

15. Moris Janowitz, _The Military in the Political Development of New Nations_, op. cit., p. vii.

16. Paul Sigmund, Jr., "Introduction", op. cit., pp. 38-9.

17. David Apter, _The Politics of Modernization_, University of Chicago, Chicago, 1965, pp. 323-27.

18. William McCord, _The Springtime of Freedom: Evolution of Developing Societies_, Oxford University Press, New York, 1965, pp. 193-197.

19. Leon Trotsky in _The Permanent Revolution_, Pioneer Publishers, New York, 1931, states that "in semi-colonial or belated development of the bourgeosie, the proletariat and peasantry must be the advance guard representative of the social revolution." Any political leader after his ascend to power may represent the whole nation by claiming that he stands behind the poor and deprived masses and by actually carrying out programs to crush a handful of former ruling groups without seriously endangering his political position. In those Third World nations the size of the former ruling elite is practically negligible, a stable middle class not yet formed, and the size of the former ruling force constitutes the absolute majority.

20. C.B. MacPherson, "Revolution and Ideology in the Late Twentieth Century in Carl J. Frederick, (ed) _Revolution, Nomos VIII_, Atherton Press, New York, 1969, pp. 139-153.

21. Yehoshua Arieli, *Individualism and Nationalism in American Ideology*, Harvard University Press, Cambridge, Mass., 1964, p. 3.

22. *Ibid.*, p. 1.

23. *Ibid.*, p. 3.

24. David Wilson, "Nation-Building and Revolutionary War," in *Nation-Building*, (eds) Karl Deutsch and William Foltz, Atherton Press, New York, 1963, p. 84.

25. Joseph Tenenbaum, *Races, Nations and Jews*, Bloch Publishing Co., New York, 1934, pp. 50-51.

26. *Ibid.*, pp. 52-53.

27. *Ibid.*, p. 61.

28. Leonard Binder, *The Ideological Revolution in the Middle East*, John Wiley & Sons, New York, 1964, p. 14.

29. Joseph Tenenbaum, *Races, Nations and Jews*, op. cit., p. 57.

30. Dunkwart Rustow, *A World of Nations*, The Brookings Institution, Washington, D. C., 1967, p. 7. Note that this "dual revolution" is *not* actually simultaneous; the political transformation almost always precedes modernization through industrial technology.

31. The basic thesis of Rupert Emerson in *From Empire to Nation*, Beacon Press, Boston, 1964, is that the rise of national consciousness and self-assertion is the (benign) result of Western colonialism and the spread of Western civilization that accompanied colonialism. It is like saying that a cat experiencing the pain from jumping on a hot stove should thank the (benign) hot stove for the knowledge it has given the cat.

32. Rupert Emerson, *From Empire to Nation*, Beacon Press, Boston, 1964, pp. 380-384.

33. David A. Wilson, "Nation-Building and Revolutionary War," in K. W. Deutsch and W. J. Faltz (eds), *Nation-Building*, op. cit., p. 85.

34. Leonard Binder, *The Ideological Revolution in the Middle East*, op. cit., p. 85.

35. *Ibid.*, pp. 9-10.

36. Dunkwart Rustow, A World of Nations, op. cit., p. 120.

37. Ibid., p. 123.

38. Ibid., pp. 123-126.

39. Ibid., p. 127; See also Everett E. Hagen, On the Theory of Social Change, The Dorsey Press, Inc., Homewood, Ill., 1962, pp. 310-352; and Robert E. Ward, "Political Modernization and Political Culture in Japan," in Claude E. Welch (ed.), Political Modernization, Wadsworth Publishing Co., Inc., Belmont, Calif., 1967, pp. 88-104.

40. Barrington Moore, Jr., Social Origins of Dictatorship and Democracy, Beacon Press, Boston, 1966, p. 314.

41. Ibid., p. 314.

42. Ibid., p. 330

43. Ibid., p. 410 (emphasis added)

44. Joseph R. Strayer, "The Historical Experience of Nation-Building in Europe," in K. W. Deutsch and W. J. Foltz (eds.), Nation-Building, op. cit., p. 26.

45. J. Halcro Ferguson, The Revolutions of Latin America, Thames and Hudson, London, 1963, p. 7; Reinhard Bendix, Nation-Building and Citizenship, op. cit., p. 213.

46. David A. Wilson, "Nation-Building and Revolutionary War," in K. Deutsch and W. Foltz (eds.), op. cit., pp. 89-90; see also Karl Marx, The 18th Brumaire of Louis Bonaparte, International Publishers, New York, 1963, pp. 123-8, for remarks on the reactionary character of the French peasantry as a class-in-itself, that sided with Louis Bonaparte's coup on December 2, 1851.

47. Amitai Etzioni, "Introduction: A Theory of Societal Guidance," to J. P. Nettl and Roland Robertson, International Systems and the Modernization of Societies, Faber & Faber, London, 1968, p. 14. The order of the two paragraphs has been reversed for a clearer summary. (emphasis original). For a fuller treatment of this "societal guidance" theory, see A. Etzioni, The Active Society: A Theory of Societal and Political Processes, The Free Press, New York, 1968. See also David A. Wilson, Politics in Thailand, Cornell University Press, Ithaca, New York, 1962, for the structural obstacles in mobilizing the rural masses in Thailand as a good example of the "immobilized." We shall see in the next chapt-

er, however, how mobilization, among others, is successfully deployed by revolutionary regimes.

48. Reinhard Bendix, Nation-Building and Citizenship, John Wiley & Sons, New York, 1964, p. 215.

49. Dunkwart Rustow, A World of Nations, op. cit., p. 124. This observation was made before the authoritarian attempt by Indira Gandhi. However, the Gandhi experience only proves the difficulty of achieving democracy and mass mobilization in India.

50. David A. Wilson, "Nation-Building and Revolutionary War," op. cit., pp. 89-90. Of course, the tactics here described as the revolutionary methods cannot be taken as a generalized form applicable to all types of revolutions, although they may be true with older revolutions. (emphasis added)

51. Alexis de Tocqueville, The Old Regime and the French Revolution, Doubleday & Co., Garden City, New York, 1955, p. 135.

52. Crane Brinton, The Anatomy of Revolution, Vintage Books, New York, 1965, p. 55.

53. Charles I was beheaded and a few parliamentary members were purged, which was of course a traumatic experience being the first real revolutionary uprising by the "sovereignty of the people" against the Divine King. When compared with the later events, i.e., the French or Russian Revolution, the violence involved in the English Revolution was negligible. However, the revolutionary violence involved is described in S. R. Gardiner, The Constitutional Documents of the Puritan Revolutions, Oxford at Clarendon Press, London, 1889, and David Underdown, Pride's Purge, Oxford at Clarendon Press, London, 1921.

54. See for a very exciting account of this Jewish survival throughout history in Max I. Dimont, Jews, God and History, The New American Library, New York, 1964.

55. Jacques Soustelle, The Long March of Israel, American Heritage Press, New York, 1969, p. 202.

56. Rinna Samual, Israel: Promised Land to Modern State. Golden Press, New York, 1969, p. 116. Ben-Gurion wrote in his diary: "At 4 p.m. the Declaration of Independence. The people are profoundly happy. I am filled with foreboding." p. 117.

57. Although many students of history, Crane Brinton for example, include the American Revolution as one of the classic world revolutions, we will follow the European conception of revolu-

tion which treats it as a War of Independence rather than as a revolution in the classical sense. For its unique beginning, we shall hereafter consider America as having started as a Radical type whose Traditional period had already been terminated in Europe. It will follow from this simplification that much of what happened during and after the independence process in America somewhat parallels the characteristics of Radical changes we are presently attributing to independent Israel.

58. For the military involvement in coups and politics in the northern-tier, see George M. Haddad, Revolutions and Military Rule in the Middle East, Robert Spellers & Sons, Publishers, New York, 1965. A "successful" revolution-by-coup must be judged ultimately by some "objective" measures of political and economic changes; for an extended discussion on this topic, see Jon Huer, The Military and Organizational Rationality in Emerging Nations, (unpublished Ph.D. Thesis), University of California, Los Angeles, 1975, especially Part I and III.

59. Dunkwart Rustow, A World of Nations, op. cit., p. 188.

60. Ibid., pp. 188-9.

61. "How To Lose a Regiment," Newsweek, August 28, 1972, p. 9.

62. Dunkwart Rustow, op. cit., pp. 185-6.

63. Ibid., p. 190.

64. Ibid., pp. 193-4.

65. Ibid., pp. 194-5.

66. Ibid., pp. 199-206.

67. Nasser's popularity was evident in his election as President and in the union of Egypt and Syria into the United Arab Republic (short-lived) by the fact that fewer than 300 negative votes were cast out of a total of 6 million votes. Don Peretz, The Middle East Today, Holt, Reinhart, Winston, New York, 1963, p. 229.

CHAPTER FOUR: RADICALISM AS IDEOLOGY AND SOCIAL CHARACTER

1. NATIONALISM

Nationalism plays an important role in all revolutionary transformations, be it guided by the Enlightenment ideals or by Marxism. An appeal to nationalism in one form or another is the safest and surest way of directing the citizenry's attention to the aims and the visions of the new regime. Many writers view the nationalist rhetoric as the road to nation-building, but the revolutionary appeals need not be oriented to that end for the society may have already attained nationhood even before this Radical transition. Societies that have experienced the Radical transformation have invariably used nationalism in their slogans and platforms. Take for instance the case of Russian nationalism. Russians in general had a profound awareness of their nation as one culture, and cultivated a broad base of national attachment, which served as a fairly comprehensive basis of national unity. This Russian tendency toward national identity had been made especially acute in the series of foreign invasions and national crises concerning internal security.

> The practical significance of Russian national feeling was made evident to the Soviet regime during the period of foreign intervention after the Revolution; and by the mid-thirties the Party leadership revealed a determination to transform it into an asset of the regime. The force of this feeling was made apparent by the reaction of Russian troops and peoples both before and after German policy in Russia had defined itself in 1941-42. The large-scale defections in the first phase of the war and the initial reaction of certain nationality groups were matched by the profundity of the nationalism (and notably Great Russian nationalism which asserted itself as Hitler identified himself as perhaps the most ruthless in the long succession of foreign invaders.[1]

During the critical outset of World War II the Party was now depicted as a "national leadership rather than that of a social class. And the forthcoming battle for the very existence of state and nation was no longer primarily a communist struggle." It was as if the nationalist outcry of 1812 had reemerged, this time under Stalin.[2]

Similar use of nationalism is observed in other Radical societies, e.g., China, France, Egypt, Cuba, Korea, during the transition from Traditional states despite the ideological differences among them that may appear significantly divergent. National identity either as a method or as an end in itself serves a crucial function in the Radicalization process.

Genuine Chinese nationalism did not begin until Sun Yat-Sen's "three people's principles" the first and foremost of which was "thorough development of Nationalism (the First principle), the Chinese people were to build a free and independent nation, which would take the place in the family of nation on a basis of equality."[3] This coupled with the other two Principles, Democracy and Industrialization, became the future blue-print for the Kuomintang. It failed in obtaining mass support, however, by enlisting the old ruling landowners as its main supporters, which rendered any attempt at land reform virtually impossible.[4] On the other hand, the Communists skillfully exploited the potential power of nationalist appeal in both opposing the Kuomintang forces and fighting the Japanese. It was indeed a brilliant feat of strategy that killed two birds with one stone.

> The Communists temporarily relegated their agrarian revolution to a secondary place and pursued a new plan in an effort to avert the new series of anti-Communist campaigns initiated by General Chiang Kai-shek. Accordingly, they greatly exploited the issue of resistance to Japan and the need for a united front against foreign aggression. Prior to this the Communists had gone on record with a token declaration of war against Japan (1932); a manifesto on an anti-Japanese united front (1933); and a call for an all-class stand against Japan (1934). But now from Yenan, a new drive was launched to magnify the issue of a united front. In August 1934 a declaration was issued calling for the establishment of an anti-Japanese National United Front. The slogan: "<u>Chinese do not fight Chinese</u>," sent its echoes throughout the four corners of the country.[5]

With this united effort against Japan, and with the bitter memory of the old Western imperialist exploitation that plundered the country's economy, China's militant nationalism became "the fundamental force motivating Communist China's new role in international affairs."[6] "In place of the ineptitude of the last thirty years, Chinese nationalism has forged a determination to restore greatness to the new nation and to make it the leading power in Asia."[7] Hence

> The central thread of development, however, has been the powerful drive to win big-power status.... A great complex of psychological and emotional reactions, driven by a new nationalism, has spearheaded this great upheaval in her international relations. Among these reactions, one notes especially a strong

sense of emancipation from oppression and an eagerness
to overcome past humiliations, a great outburst of
national pride, tinged with frequent shows of arrogance,
a tendency to saber rattling and demagoguery, and a
plain xenophobia.[8]

The same author observed that Mao's revolutionary ideas mobilizing a peasant proletariat was a hybrid product of Marxism-Leninism and Chinese nationalist heritage.

> A great part of Mao's thinking as well as his methods of organization are no doubt inspired by Marxist and Leninist teachings. But equally important as sources of Mao's inspiration as been the stream of proletarian literature handed down through the ages in China and the doctrine of the People's Livelihood of Sun Yat-sen himself. Mao's thorough and shrewd understanding of the temperament and needs of the Chinese masses and his downright ruggedness in championing the cause of the underdog or the social outcast are traceable to such popular novels as the Shui Hu Chuan (<u>All Men Are Brothers</u>). It is this stream of popular literature that helped to develop in Mao's thinking a particular pertinence to the realities of Chinese society. On the other hand, if Sun Yat-sen's doctrine of the People's Livelihood ever had a thorough convert, that convert was Mao Tse-Tung himself. More than anybody else, Mao took Sun's exhortations to heart. It is interesting to recall in this connection that it was Sun Yat-sen who declared that <u>the economic and social objectives of the Chinese Revolution were not unlike the objectives of Communism</u>, but, given the unique conditions of China, the Chinese revolutionaries "should follow Marx in general principle but must not slavishly copy his methods." If Mao is the inventor of a new Asian version of Communism, as is often maintained nowadays, Sun Yat-sen certainly was the harbinger who blazed the trail for him. Mao is thus the greatest eclectic among the world's revolutionary leaders.[9]

The Communist leaders since the seizure of power, therefore, have been singularly preoccupied with emphasizing not only making the imperialist evils appear ever unforgivable but also with their intention to "turn the table" and "punish the imperialists." In foreign policy, for instance, Chou displayed "vitriolic blasts his roughshod strategy, his skillful blending of threat, suspense, and cool calculation, demonstrated repeatedly in diplomatic duels with the West," indicating that "the fortunes of the nations have come full circle in China."

In the wake of their successful seizure of power,

the Communists have also displayed an unrestrained
national pride and arrogance. This has been notable
in all the major diplomatic events involving China
since 1949. In the violent anti-American campaign,
facts and merits have been ignored in order to give
free play to the nations ego. The reason that the
United States has been butt of such bitter hatred is
not that she is the real culprit, but rather that attacking a great nation like the United States seems
the best way to meet China's own pretensions. When
Great Britain extended diplomatic recognition to Peking,
the latter treated it with a studied indifference, the
inference being that she cared little for the favor of
a great Western power. Peking's approach to the United
Nations when branded the aggressor in the Korean War,
she quickly upheld the visit of the Secretary-General
to Peking in connection with the case of the American
airmen as proof of China's growing international prestige. Peking also has made capital of the fact that
on every important state occasion an impressive assemblage of leaders from foreign countries pays tribute
to the new government. Never before in China's past
periods of imperial greatness has the sense of a national pride and prestige been raised to so high a point.[10]

In Castro's Cuba nationalism has a similar record of having
been utilized as the basis of its revolutionary ideology in the form
and rhetoric of imperialism, notably against the United States.
Before Castro publically embraced socialism, Huberman and Sweezy
observed in 1961 that the reform measures that were "vastly superior
in performance to (their) predecessors," were basically multi-ideological, i.e. capitalistic, socialistic and/or communistic,
which, at the same time, could not be characterized by any single
ideological orientation or definition.

> This question cannot be answered on the basis
> of any programmatic or ideological texts. Fidel's
> speeches are replete with advocacy of specific reforms
> of precisely the kind that have been adopted, but nowhere, so far as we have been able to discover, has
> he attempted to characterize the social order which
> either he personally, or the July 26th Movement which
> he heads, hopes to see created. Measures are adopted
> either because they seem obviously to be in the interest
> of the masses or because they are needed to complement
> other measures that have already been adopted, never
> because they fit logically into a theoretical framework.[11]

Similarly, J. P. Sartre observed that

> In Paris I questioned a certain number of Cubans, but was never able to understand why they refused to tell me if the objective of the Cuban Revolution was or was not to establish socialism. Now I understand why they could not tell me. That is, that the originality of this Revolution consists precisely in doing what needs to be done without attempting at defining it by means of a previous ideology.[12]

By 1963, however, Castro made it clear that the ideological basis of Cuban future was socialism Russian style, although in many fundamental and methodological respects they differed considerably from each other.[13] Opposing the influence of the United States was perhaps one of the most important immediate motives for the Revolution, for anti-Batista rhetoric was ultimately based upon its supposed imperialist oppressor, the United States, which was seen exploiting Cuba aided by Batista. Sensing the need for institutionalizing the revolutionary momentum, socialism might have been the only alternative for Castro which had already been clearly articulated, and coinciding with his drastic reform measures.

> Fidel Castro voluntarily embraced the Soviet Union and Communism. The State Department during the Kennedy and Eisenhower administrations was not directly responsible for this realignment of Cuban diplomatic and economic policy. Obviously, one cannot gloss over the historical impact of American foreign policy on Cuban thinking...that Castro turned to the Communist bloc without either having requested or having been refused aid by the United States. But whether or not Castro ever requested American aid is peripheral. Because of the strident anti-Americanism of his revolutionaries, any request by Castro for such aid would have been totally inconsistent. Cuban leaders could not accept aid from the United States <u>because achieving the radical reforms aspired to in 1959 required the repudiation of a Cuban society that had relied on such support</u>. In the minds of the rebels, indigenous ills had resulted from Cuba's close ties to the United States. Therefore, Castro's integrity as a leader, and that of the Revolution he symbolized, depended on the extent to which he remained free of former commitments of America.[14]

What Castro and his fellow revolutionaries rebelled against was essentially two-fold: one, the feudalistic backwardness of the Cuban economy; the other, the corrupt social and political structure that remained quasi-colonial with heavy American invesments, which could be characterized as both colonial and backward capitalist. Since they repudiated both, and succeeded in the overthrow of Batista by repudiating them, the most articulate alternative ideology that coincided with revolutionary nationalism had to be one variety or another of socialism. Whether Castro himself had been an ardent, and latent, communist before the takeover is thus entirely academic; but the import is that he is a nationalist, and will embrace anything if that aids his dreams and ideals in rebuilding Cuba in its Radical transformation.

This is also true in Nasser's Egypt. On the eve of the 1952 coup, there was virtually no national identity among the majority of the Egyptian population, the rural masses, who "had identified central authority with tyranny and had accordingly viewed it with suspicion. Primary loyalties were to the family, to the village, to Islam--not to the nation-state. In urban centers, society was divided by different educational systems, economic and social classes, and minority viewpoints. There was no homogeneous national ideology, or national loyalty."[15] In part, modern nationalism in Egypt and in other areas of the Middle East is a reaction to the religion's failure to cope with political crises, aggravated by the foreign dominations, by the Ottoman Empire and other Western powers. The mainspring of Egyptian nationalism was, however, fostered and expressed mainly by the military, especially acute after Egypt's bankruptcy in the hands of Ismail. Against foreign intervention the nationalism-conscious young Egyptian officers revolted along with other nationalist movements, which characterized the Egyptian political scenes for the following century.[16]

> The Egyptian army, which was largely of rural origin, became an important link between the peasantry and the top echelons of society, especially since officers from peasant families could rise to fairly high ranks. A national awareness thus began to emerge in rural as well as urban areas as such army officers, imbued with patriotism, brought an "Egyptian" consciousness back to their native villages. The need for compromises between Islam and the modern world was increasingly acknowledged by these young Muslim officers, who had received a Western education.[17]

Nasser, after the 1952 coup, observed that "the revolution marked the realization of a great hope felt by the people of Egypt since they began in modern times, to think in terms of self-government and to demand they have the final word in determining their own future. But if that is so, and if what happened on July 23rd was neither a military mutiny nor a popular uprising, why then was it entrusted to the Army, and not to other forces, to bring it about?"[18] The primarily nationalist strain in the 1952 coup is clearly seen in the way the Free Officers Club, the organization that enacted the junta, restricted its members. That is, very few, if any, FOC members could be labelled either religious or political fanatics. It was mainly composed of those motivated chiefly by patriotism and the nationalist calling against corruption and imperialism. Egyptian Radicalism was thus based on almost purely nationalist sentiments. As a political form the revolution strived for creating a suitable democracy for the ex-colonial people of Egypt; as was the case with many far-sighted leaders of the third world this national interest in governing ideology found neither communism nor capitalism totally fit for the Egyptian conditions. Hence, since the revolution

> Nasser had taken the position that democracy must be established not just in parliaments and slogan, but in the life of the people, and that the Egyptians were in fact not yet ready for the Western parliamentary institutions that the old regime had introduced only to pervert for its own ends. Before the revolution, he contends, the so-called democratic institutions, such as political parties and the parliament, were centers of political corruption and degradation. A transition period is therefore necessary, a period in which Egyptians can be educated to understand and use effectively such institutions. Rather than political freedom, accordingly, the revolutionary leaders in Egypt have chosen to emphasize "social democracy", by which they mean destroying the class distinctions of wealth and privilege.[19]

This "guided democracy" doctrine was also adopted a decade later in a very similar situation in Korea by Park's revolutionary regime,[20] in which the nationalist interests rather than the ideological forms were seen as the matter of collective importance. Nationalism in various areas and at various times played the most significant role in revolutionary social changes, although socialist formulas may have been the articulated guidelines for actions and policies. Especially in the twentieth century Radical revolutions which have taken place in mostly backward nations, feudalistic remnants in one form or another, this nationalist tendency has been an indispensable mover and molder of the revolutionary forces.

It is in this sense inevitable that the Radical new regime must take on an authoritarian character in order to "educate", to "guide" and to "administer" the process of nationalist re-shaping, without which there is no Radical transition to speak of. The Russian Duma before the Bolshevik Revolution was notoriously powerless and ineffective as an intermediate parliamentary form of government; so were the Sun Republic in China before Mao, the constitutional monarchy of King Farouk in Egypt, and John Chang's Democratic regime in Korea before their respective transitions, and in Cuba Batista's dictatorship was without any of the above aims in its totalitarian governance. The following observation is a most lucid summary of the type of governing policies in Egypt in terms of its nationalist goals:

> The Egyptian constitution has its full complement of political and social rights limited by law or by their gradual extension as adequate means are found. The executive, legislative, and judicial branches of government are separated, and popular elections are provided for. But only a single party which includes almost the entire nation is permitted to campaign, and many candidates have run unopposed. Moreover, the President himself was elected by a plebiscite which offered no real alternative. Evidently it is the purpose of the Egyptian government to awaken and mobilize the people to an awareness of their interests... Clearly the people are not to be consulted but directed. Eventually a system of democracy, nationalism, constitutionalism, and socialism (or "antifeudalism" (sic)) will be justified by the absolute coincidence between the wills of the individual and the group. <u>Until that time radical nationalist governments will disregard individual wills in order to serve what they know to be the wider nationalist interest.</u> They know this because they are the vanguard of the nationalist movement.[21]

This purely non-ideological (in the conventional sense) character of nationalism in Egypt's revolutionary regime is best evidenced in the criticism by a Marxist theorist, Anour Abdel-Malak. He argues that mere state-control and nationalization do not automatically render the regime a socialist brand. More specifically, (1) "it is impossible to build a modern state in the absence of a 'political class' in the Gramscian sense of the term; yet this is precisely what the military regime has tried to eliminate since 1952;" (2) "it is impossible to initiate a socialist revolution and to build a popular state in the absence of socialists, without a mobilization of the popular masses, rural and urban,[22] and the revolutionary intelligentsia; certainly not by relying on a political apparatus committed to a fight against the Left,[23] and by that fact open to all forms of penetration."[24]

However, despite the "impurity" of Egyptian quasi-socialist political style,

> Egypt since 1954 (the year of Naguib's exit) has been an integrative society rather than a competitive society. The leader's team has been rather stable since 1952; the same head, the same hard core of officers.... The Free Officers originally wanted to avoid any political involvement discovered that their socio-economic choices, such as land reform, nationalization and the

general ideological trend of the regime, entailed political choice. They changed the balance of power in favor of new classes, prompted the emergence of a new opposition, gave rise to claims, and led to the adoption of certain methods to the exclusion of others. The group's initial options did not relate to internal politics. The Free Officers' only aims were modernization and independence. They remained stubbornly faithful to these principles.[25]

In viewing the Radical revolutions, from Russian to Korean, and specifically in their historical aims and the methods by which such aims have been attempted, it is not difficult to conclude that in each of these revolutions the ideological and policy pronouncements have turned out to be almost identical with one another's, which may alter our conception of ideology and political revolution.

The role of nationalism was also vividly illustrated by the Russian Revolution, too. As mentioned earlier beginning with the twentieth century Russian nationalism that had been rather loosely defined by the diverse cultures and peoples within Russia was gradually being channeled into an awareness by the earlier revolutions of this century and their slogans. When the Revolution of 1917 took place the loose basis of the general Russian national character became the major factor that facilitated the success of Communist ideology and creating appropriate revolutionary social character in the new generations.[26] The uniquely ideological character of Russian Communism, however, was gradually turned under Stalin into methods and instruments for Soviet interests. Having no illusions about a world-wide proletarian revolution, Stalin managed to strike a balance between retaining a verbal loyalty to the world-historical coming of proletarianization and skillfully exploiting by omission and commission in domestic and foreign policies the advantages that were made available by communist ideology. After all, communism-in-one country meant the supremacy and priority of Russian interests. "No risks were to be taken in the pursuit of impossible (world) revolutionary tasks."

If in practice this often meant consigning Communist Parties in the West or in developing countries to the mercy of capitalist governments, then this was no worse than the treatment these parties had received before the war. Stalin was just skeptical after the war about communists changes abroad as he had been in the 1930s. He hardly expected the resurgence of communism in western Europe which resulted from the communists' control of a large part of the resistance movements in France and Italy; when Togliatti returned from Moscow to Italy in 1944, his colleagues were staggered by Stalin's sealed instructions--recognition by

the communists of the monarchy, and service under
Badoglio, no less! Stalin underrated the alliance
between communism and nationalism in countries like
India and the Middle East. Above all, he sold the
Chinese communists short. While he certainly expressed no public enthusiasm for capitalist forms of
government, his analysis of the world situation as-
signed the new wave of left-wing radicalism even less
chance of success than it had had after the First
World War. In any case he was not going to risk Soviet interests on its behalf.[27]

Russian patriotism during World War II inspired by nationalist slogans and historical recollections of common bonds remains the most spectacular example of the role Russian nationalism played. Russian resistance against the invasion of Hitler recalled the historical valor and legend of 1812 against Napoleon, now offi- cially identified as the menacing foreign invader along with Hitler. Nationalist fervor was stirred up and patriotic sacrifice inspired, in which Communism stood much less in evidence both in the minds of ordinary citizens and in the language of official pronounce- ments. The military failures in the initial phase of the German invasion brought mass purges of high ranking officers, and subse- quently the Party interference with military affairs was lifted; new morale was brought into the military by promoting younger of- ficers en masse and introducing new uniforms. "Ideologically the interpretation of the war turned increasingly into a Russian- German dichotomy. Love of the Russian motherland was matched by hatred of the German invaders....Party was now subsumed under the nation in an entirely new way, and the old priorities were reversed."[2] During the period between 1941-44 the Party members rose from 2 to 6 millions.

On 24 June 1945 Stalin attended the victory parade
in Red Square and thanked the Russian people for all
they had done. It was the last time that he appeared
in the role of great military leader of a united nation.
Communist perspectives had been played down during the
war. There were no narrowly political purges; the
criteria were loyalty to the state and efficiency in
executing allotted tasks. The special sufferers had
been national minorities of doubtful loyalty, especially
in the newly liberated or annexed territories in the
south and west. Religious and class differences were
pushed into the background. Indeed the war witnessed
a substantial religious revival in the Soviet Union,
both Greek Orthodox as well as Jewish.[29]

In Russia as well as in other countries since then, nation- alist interests served their functions. Being essentially a mod- ern phenomenon, anti-thetical to all that feudalism represents, nationalism has rallied the masses behind revolutionary slogans, has called for nationalist patriotism and sacrifice in times of national crisis, and in the course of time has become almost the sole preoccupation of nation-building through radical measures of social reform.

2. THE EGALITARIAN SPIRIT

The official constitutions and pronouncements that abound during a Radical transformation remarkably reflect the basic ideals of human equality. Human equality and dignity are emphasized against the background of feudal absolutism in governance and social relations. The Radical political transformation, as has been observed earlier, is then a visionary attempt of what the Modern Era offers as alternative to the existing absolutist traditionalism. This idealistic reflection on human equality has been remarkably uniform throughout all Radical revolutions up to date. The sense of egalitarianism bears its mark on every major modern political transformation, from the English Revolution to the latest revolution-by-coup in the third world. It is only natural that the intolerable social conditions against which a Radical revolution is set must include a certain measure of real as well as imagined inequality among the population. When the revolution is successfully carried out and a new constitution proclaimed, the latter abounds with copious references to egalitarian ideals that seem to have originated from the same prototype declaration.[30]

One of the most common elements in the emergence of the Radical character from the feudal Traditional type has been the egalitarian articulation embodied in the ideals of the Enlightenment. Egalitarianism either as a sole ideological proclamation or as a method against feudalism has figured prominently in all political revolutions since 1649, but the articulation of the spirit of equality-among-men historically has taken two distinctive forms and contents, although in their anti-Conservative order they both fulfilled essentially similar purposes.

The first type of egalitarianism was voiced in the form of "naturalist" rights of man, which implied that the absolutist traditionalism as defined and sanctioned by tradition at times imbued by Divine Rights was against human nature. The classic revolutions, the English and French, for instance, were basically the product of this ideal on the natural and inalienable rights of man, as Locke, Montesquieu, Voltaire, Didroit, Rousseau and other Enlightened philosophers and scientists arduously advocated. The rhetorical formulations of the English, American and French Revolutions were studded with the defense of natural rights of man, which was undoubtedly functional in destroying the feudal order that was viewed "unnatural" in view of Enlightened human reason. (See the next chapter for a detailed discussion.) Even Hobbes who stood by the king during the English Revolution by no means supported the feudalistic monarchical structure; although the monarch was the head of his sovereignty it was conceived of as a matter of convenience rather than as superhuman sanction.[31] On the other hand, by the end of the Civil War in England the king's authority was resoundingly denounced by the left-wing radicals, the Levellers, who told the House of Commons that:

> As we conceive all Governors and Magistrates, being the ordinance of man, before they be the ordinance of God, and no authority being of God, but what is erected by the mutual consent of a people: and seeing this Honourable House alone represents the people of this nation, that therefore no person whatsoever, be permitted to exercise any power or authority in this nation, who shall not clearly and confessedly, receive his power from this House, and be always accountable for the discharge of his trust, to the people in their representatives in Parliament.[32]

"In the English Revolution, it was of the essence of the movement that the authority of the King should be restricted."[33] As early as 1628 the curtailment of the King's authority was clearly voiced in the grievances in the Petition of Rights which declared illegal the exaction of "any gift, loan, benevolence, tax, or such like charge, without common consent by Act of Parliament," for

> ...by the statute called, "The Great Charter of the Liberties of England," it is declared and enacted, that no free man may be taken or imprisoned or be disseised of his freeholds or liberties, or his free customs, or be outlawed or exiled; or in any manner destroyed, but by the lawful judgment of his peers, or by the law of the land: And in the eighth and twentieth year of the reign of King Edward the Third, it was declared and enacted by authority or Parliament, that no man of what estate or condition that he be, should be put out of his lands or tenements, nor taken, nor imprisoned, nor disherited, nor put to death, without being brought to answer by due process of law.[34]

This drastic transition of social character from Traditional to Radical social types has been viewed as one phase of dialectical struggles between classes in history by Marxists, which will be treated in later pages. However, suffice it at the moment to say that in this Radical transformation one element was certain--the old order was replaced by a totally different one.

The English Revolution of 1640-60 was a great social movement like the French Revolution of 1789.

An old order that was essentially feudal was destroyed by violence, a new and capitalist social order created in its place. The Civil War was a class war, in which the despotism of Charles I was defended by the reactionary forces of the established Church and feudal landlords. Parliament beat the King because it could appeal to the enthusiastic support of the trading and industrial classes in town and countryside, to the yeomen and progressive gentry, and to wider masses of the population whenever they were able to free discussion to understand what the struggle was really about.[35]

The old order was brought to obsolescence through the enactment of the Tonnage and Poundage Act, abolishing the Court of Star Chamber and other numerous declarations during the Revolution, and finally in 1689 the Bill of Rights completed the Glorious Revolution, a transformation from feudalism to a modern state.[36]

No doubt, the ideas that fundamentally motivated this history-making change were made a landmark, more prominently, in the French Revolution, another birth-place of the "natural" rights of men to equality, freedom and fraternity. In this Radical transformation, also, the king was executed and the hereditary privilages of the ancient nobility abolished. On the night of August 4, 1789, in the midst of riot, distress and fear, the National Assembly declared the end of an era: "The National Assembly abolishes the feudal regime entirely, and decrees that both feudal and censuel rights and dues deriving from real or personal mainmorte and personal servitude, and those representatives thereof, are abolished without indemnity, and all others declared redeemable....All citizens may be admitted, without distinction of birth, to all ecclesiastical, civil and military employments and offices, and no useful profession shall entail forfeiture."[37] The drive toward human equality contradictory to all that was feudal and traditional, continued to press a complete extinction of the nobility although the August 4 decree had reduced it to an aristocracy of name only. On June 19, 1790, however, a decree abolishing the feudal hereditary nobility and titles was finally enacted: "Hereditary nobility is abolished forever; accordingly, the titles of prince, duke, count, marquia, viscount, vidame, baron, knight, messire, squire, noble, and all other similar titles shall neither be accepted by nor bestowed upon anyone whomsoever. A citizen may assume only his real family name; no one may wear liveries or have them worn, or have coats of arms; incense shall be burned in the churches only to honor the Divinity, and shall not be offered to any person whomsoever. The titles of monseigneuer and messeigneuers shall not be bestowed upon any group or individual; likewise, the titles of excellency, highness, eminence, grace, etc...."[38] Considering the long standing tradition of feudal era in France this unprecedented decree of demolishing the ancient structure entirely justified Mirabeau's characterization of the decree as "sheer insanity." The ideals of the Enlightenment that men are naturally born equal to one another, however, did exist as fact and the rise of industrial technology (and its scientific tenets contradicting scholasticism) made anything less than total equality unacceptable. The basic cause of modern political revolutions can thus be attributed to this simple fact that (1) the ideas of intolerability become powerful psychological motives for human action, and that (2) technical means render this human action possible in reality. Never in history these ideals were so clearly formulated under so dramatic circumstances as in the French Revolution.

Examining the Declaration of the Rights of Man and Citizen of August, 1789, the following significant aspects appear pronounced:[39] (1) Man's natural equality; (2) acceptance of capacity, talents and virtues as criteria for public service; (3) transitions from "traditional" authority to "legal" authority, using Weber's terms; (4) supremacy of legal transaction over arbitariness; (5) free expressions of opinions; and (6) establishment of collective identity through the nation-state. The Constitution of 1791, the first written constitution entirely based on the Enlightened human reason to which every man and woman of the age aspired, was the most daring expression of the Radicalization process.

> The National Assembly, wishing to establish the French Constitution upon the principles it has just recognized,[40] abolishes irrevocably the institutions which were injurious to liberty and equality of rights. Neither nobility, nor peerage, nor hereditary distinctions, nor distinctions or order, nor feudal regime, nor patriomonial courts, nor any titles, denominations, or prerogatives derived therefrom, nor any order of knighthood, nor any corporations of decorations requiring proofs of nobility or implying distinctions of birth, nor any superiority other than that of public functionaries in the performance of their duties any longer exists. Neither venality nor inheritance of any public office any longer exists. Neither privilege nor exception to the law common to all Frenchmen any longer exists for any part of the nation or for any individual. Neither Jurandes nor corporations of professions, arts, and crafts any longer exist. The law no longer recognizes religious vows or any other obligation contrary to natural rights or the Constitution.[41]

The Revolution summoned the masses into the crusade, offering state aid "to all peoples who wish to recover their liberty... (and) who might be harassed for the cause of liberty."[42] In December of the same year a more extensive decree, but essentially based upon the previous declarations, was proclaimed which was primarily aimed at the new territories annexed by the French Army. "Peace," "aid," "fraternity," "liberty," and "equality" still appeared predominantly, which culminated in this remarkable "liberation" pronouncement to the citizens of the annexed territories:

> Brothers and friends, we have gained liberty and we shall maintain it. We offer to help you enjoy this inestimable good which has always belonged to us, and of which our oppressors have not been able to deprive us without crime. We have expelled your tyrants: show yourselves free men, and we will guarantee you from their vengence, their designs, and their return. Henceforth the French nation proclaims the sovereignty of the people, the suppression of all civil and military authorities which have governed you up to the present, and of all taxes which you sustain, in whatever form they exist; the abolition of the tithe, of feudalism, of seigneurial rights both feudal and censuel, fixed or contingent, or banalities, of real and personal servitude, of hunting and fishing privileges of corvees, of the gabelle, of tolls, of octrois, and generallly of every species of contributions with which you have been burdened by your usurpers, it proclaims also the absolution among you of every corporation, coble, sacerdotal, and others, of all prerogatives and privileges that are contrary to equality. You are henceforth, brothers and friends, all citizens, all equal in rights, and all equallly summoned to govern, to serve, and to defend your Patrie....[43]

Having seen the classic origins of "natural" human equality in the modern world, now we can consider the other path by which the anti-feudalistic efforts of egalitarianism were articulated and practiced. We may call this "socialist" equality as distinguished from "natural" equality. There are no doubts that both natural and socialist equality of men has been formulated in an effort to dismantle feudalism, but there are several important points by which the socialist conception of equality differs from the other: (1) "Naturalist" rights of man assert that all men are "naturally" born equal thereby implying both in theory and practice that in whatever lot a man is born into, be it economic, social or biological, it is there to stay. The reason that this essentially Enlightenment conception of human equality was congenial to the rise of industrial technology and capitalism, while it ideally supported abolishing feudalism and proclaiming human equality, was this dual function of that idea itself. When the fate of all men is contingent upon the random, and fair, work of nature whatever a man is endowed with by nature he has no recourse but accept it as the God-given lot. Although the work of nature is fair by definition, in reality it is not so symmetrical, for the social structure into which one is born is already established in such a way that a man's natural endowments entail different adaptations and accomodations by society. It is in this theoretical and practical consequences that enabled the emergence of the socialist conception of equality; that is, that <u>men (born naturally inequal) must be made equal by artificial (social) means.</u> Elaborated and articulated, this is the major characteristic distinction between capitalism and socialism.44 (to be discussed in greater detail in the next chapter.)

(2) The coincidence between the articulation of natural equality and the growing industrial processes rendered so apparent the distinction between those naturally equal and those naturally "more" equal, i.e., with better "naturalist" endowments in forms of property, mental and/or physical capacity, etc. Borne of this incongruency of the Enlightenment idea for equality, Marxism gave clear and logical reasons for the historical contradictions that again had to be abolished. For the defenders of natural equality, the job was essentially finished; all that was necessary would be improving everyone's lot in society, now that feudalism is gone and the king's authority a thing of the past. In historical retrospect, Marx's conception that the new form of human inequality was merely a succeeding stage of traditionalist inequality and hence was bound to be destroyed stands essentially valid. Our formulation of the Liberal stage, however, attempts to modify the thesis that the change must occur through revolution, for the Liberal state is a gradual evolution from the Radical state characterized by industrial technology, which is gradualist rather than revolutionary. The confusion is compounded by the fact that later Marxist revolutionaries were mostly from those societies which were still feudalistic regimes in one guise or another, which brings us the last point to consider.

(3) The conception of "natural" equality was formulated and practiced mostly when the political and social structure was visibly feudalistic both in form and in content. If there was little confusion in their theoretical and practical opposition to feudalism it was mainly due to this clear-cut manner in which the revolutionary objectives were presented. In the course of time, two major factors made the distinction between the friend and the enemy rather blurry: one was that Marx saw the "natural" inequality as a logical successor to feudalist inequality, and rendered the class struggle conceptually inevitable; and the other factor was that many feudalist societies changed their essentially feudalist form into a guise of a modern "legal" state, retaining at the same time the unchanged essence of feudal content.

Significantly, the second factor above made any direct ideological attack upon the state for being feudalistic almost irrelevant and superfluous, for in Russia and China prior to the irrespective Revolutions, for instance, the surface structure of political system and articulated governmental formula was not feudalistic. In form at least, the Tzarist Russia before 1917 resembled the constitutional monarchy of England, which had passed the feudal stage long before. Hence attacking the constitutional government of Russia, with the Duma as the representative of the sovereignty of the people, would have been tantamount to killing a dead horse, theoretically speaking. The same condition was also true in China; Sun Yat-Sen's Republic and its successor the Kuomingtang regime was at least in form no feudalist system by any means, for the Traditional Manchu Dynasty had already been destroyed. Yet in essence, the feudalist content still prevailed even more oppressively this time, for the people's expectation was now filled with buoyant hopes for a better life which never came. In this dilemma of having the enemy but not being able to locate the exact target, Marxism was utlized in solving the theoretical difficulties. Instead of conceiving the quasi-modernistic guise as another form of feudal absolutism, the revolutionary leaders interpreted it (as Marx had done) as the next logical step in the historical dialectic which, in reality, did not develop at all. The Marxist formulation, however, fulfilled one function as the Enlightenment ideology had done before, that is, the abolition of the latter-day feudal order.

This contention can now be substantiated by considering the actual workings of the revolutions in the twentieth century in which mainly "socialist" egalitarianism was the proclaimed program and vision. The first observation is that in none of the societies in this century where socialist (sometimes "guided" or "administrative") ideology was the predominant force and aim did any transformation from feudalism exist as it had earlier in England or in France. If there were any symbolic changes existing on the surface level at least, it was either through a benign consignment of the monarch who granted some measure of parliamentary participation (as was the case in China, Cuba and Korea). In actual mentality and the socio-political relations and manifestations they differed very little, if any at all, from the Traditional feudal structure. Whether they outright embraced the Marxist version of socialist equality (Russia and China), or they reluctantly accepted one or another dubious version of socialism (like Egypt and Cuba), or they attempted to carry out the nationalist reforms under the existing quasi-capitalist system (like Korea), their overriding concern was how to provide the masses with some measure of social equality. This concern with equality (whether "naturalist" or "socialist") is by definition contradictory to feudalism, and in the twentieth century revolutions in which this concern was manifest in one form or another, the characteristic perspective may be summarized in that they were all after destroying the feudal system, however it disguised itself in modernist form, and whatever ideological theses the latter-day revolutionaries adopted methodologically.

The conclusion that both the Enlightenment and Marxism served the essentially identical functions in history, namely, overthrowing feudalism and establishing the Radical order in ideology and social character, is based on historical facts and reflections upon those facts: (1) the classic revolutions of England and France destroyed the feudalist traditional order (or the Traditional ideology and social character) directly inspired by the ideals of the Enlightenment; (2) human equality was then based upon natural equality as opposed to the "unnatural" feudal arrangements; (3) Karl Marx identified the development of another "unnatural" inequality subsequent to the "naturalist" conception of equality as the next inevitable stage of history to be ultimately overthrown; (4) none of these societies where the "naturalist" formulation of equality was to be destroyed by its own contradiction has actually been overthrown in history, nor is this event likely to occur in the future; (5) in many socieities the traditionalist feudal absolutism continued to prevail in quasi-parliamentarianism, -constitutionalism, -republican forms of government in colonialism and in authoritarianism, not by hereditary authority but by means of coercion; (6) given the articulated formula of both the Enlightenment and Marxist ideology, many revolutionists took up the latter, for (a) Marx had already predicted the fall of the old anti-feudalist forces as inevitably as the feudal order itself which they had destroyed, and (b) this interpretation of historical development was compounded by the fact that beginning this century there were very few outright feudal structures left, except those colonial territories, which made the adoption of Marxist socialism much more congenial, if not inevitable, to the visionaries and the revolutionary leaders; hence (7) future revolutions occuring in those modern versions of feudalism will likely to follow the socialist line, in which the socialist rhetorics will be mixed (as have been in the past) with the older formulations by the Enlightenment ideals.

As a matter of historical fact, the expressed egalitarianism both by the Enlightenment and Marxist socialism is strikingly similar to each other's. Their difference is either ideologically exaggerated or distorted by intentional misreading. A third factor, a significant one, is that the socialist or quasi-socialist revolutions in this century have been attempted and carried out when many advanced societies are already enjoying the harvest of industrial technology, thus making a strict adherence to the more gradualist and liberal-democratic reform much less attractive. Methodologically speaking, socialist methods and techniques of revolutionizing a society may yield much greater and faster results, than through the liberalist method of persuasion and appealing to human reason.

"The constitution of the Russian Socialist Federal Soviet Republic (RSFSR) of July 1918 preceded by the 'declaration of the rights of the laboring and exploited people' which had been adopted in January 1918. The title of this declaration served at the time, as at present, to establish an immediate connection between the Bolshevik Revolution and the French Revolution with its declaration of the rights of man and of the citizen, not to mention the earlier American declaration of independence...."[45] Although "none of the many guarantees of the 'natural and imprescriptible rights of man' 'to liberty, property, security, and resistance to oppression' to quote from the French declaration, is to be found in the Soviet declaration,"[46] by making the oppressed masses the sole sovereignty over all other strata, the Soviet declaration of 1918 was no less inspired, at least in expression, by the classic formula for egalitarianism than that of the English, American or French declaration. The "exploited and laboring peoples" after all the masses who suffered under the Tzarist regime and the ineffective Duma, not fundamentally different from those Frenchmen or Englishmen who revolted agaisnt their monarchs and declared themselves free and equal men. The langauge differences, e.g., in class, contradiction, exploiting and exploited classes, historical contradictions, etc., between the Enlightenment and Marxist socialism should not obscure the essentially homogeneous spirits and aspirations that the two great anti-feudalist forces express. Consider some passages from the 1918 Soviet Declaration of the Rights of the Laboring and Exploited Peoples:

> The Russian Republic is a free socialist society of all the laboring people of Russia. All authority within the boundaries of the RSFSR is vested in the entire working population of the country, organized in the urban and rural soviets.
>
> In order to secure for the laboring masses genuine freedom of conscience, the church is separated from the state and the school from the church, and freedom of religious and anti-religious propaganda is acknowledged to be right of all citizens.
>
> In order to secure for the laboring masses genuine freedom of expressing their opinion, the RSFSR annuls the dependency of the press upon capital and hands over the working class and the poor peasants all the technical and material resources necessary for the publication of newspapers, pamphlets, books, and all other printed matter, and guarantees their free circulation throughout the country. In order to guarantee to the laboring masses complete freedom of assembly, the RSFSR, recognizing the right of the citizens of the Soviet Republic freely to organize meetings, processions, etc., places at the disposal of the workers and of the poor peasantry all premises fit for public gatherings, together with their furniture, lighting, and heating.
>
> In order to insure for the laboring masses effective

access to education, the RSFSR undertakes to provide
for the workers and poorest peasants complete, universal, free education.

Recognizing the solidarity of the laboring masses
of all nations, the RSFSR extends all political rights
enjoyed by Russian citizens to foreigners working within the territory of the Russian Republic, provided that
they belong to the working class or to the peasantry
working without hired labor. It authorizes the local
soviets to confer upon such foreigners the rights of
Russian citizenship without any difficult offences.

The RSFSR grants the right asylum to all foreigners
persecuted for political and religious offences.

The RSFSR, recognizing the equality of all citizens,
irrespective of race or nationality, declares it contrary to the fundamental laws of the republic to institute or tolerate privileges, or any prerogative whatsoever, founded on such grounds, or in any way to limit
their rights.[47]

It could easily be recognized that some passages might have
been taken straight from the French Declaration, although the nuance
differences do exist. The basic tenets are decidedly anti-feudalistic and -traditional absolutism. One passage recognizing no special
privileges and/or prerogatives has the ring of the French counterpart abolishing the hereditary nobility. Although Batsell objects
that "in the soviet declaration there is no mention of human liberties or rights, the fundamental considerations in most constitutions since the seventeenth century,"[48] it must be recognized that
the Russian Revolution followed the Marxist socialist ideology
and that this declaration was not only the ideal expression of
a new order but also a methodological program for carrying out
the ideal. The differences between the Russian and other Enlightenment declarations are either artificially exaggerated or confused by historical myopia. That the Russian Revolution was more
concerned with the practical aspects rather than the theoretical
import is apparent in Lenin's words written in 1918:

Democracy means equality. The great significance
of the struggle of the proletariat for equality, and
the significance of equality as a slogan, are apparant,
if we correctly interpret it as meaning the abolition
of <u>classes</u>. But democracy means only formal equality.
Immediately after the attainment of equality for all
members of society <u>in respect of</u> the ownership of the
means of production, that is, of equality of labor and
equality of wages, there will inevitably arise before
humanity the question of going further from formal equality to real equality, i.e., to realizing the rule,

"From each according to his ability; to each according to his needs." By what stages, by means of what practical measures humanity will proceed to this higher aim--this we do not and cannot know. But this is important to realize how infinitely mendacious is the usual bourgeois presentation of Socialism as something lifeless, petrified, fixed once for all, whereas in reality, it is only with Socialism that there will commence a rapid, genuine, real mass advance, in which first the majority and then the whole of the population will take part--an advance in all domains of social and individual life.[49]

In opposing the Traditional feudal order, human equality thus proceeded from the two paths as we have discussed, from the "naturalist" conception (each according to his ability) and from the "socialist" conception (each according to his needs). In the last analysis, however, their historical aims and functions were essentially identical, except the differences in rhetoric and methods, and the genuine misreading of history for all involved. That the Traditional-to-Radical transformation is prevalent in this century must be viewed with the practical significance of the transformation in mind, not with the historical short-sightedness that our events indeed change from "ability" to "needs," or from "naturalist" to "socialist" conception of human equality, or still in the Marxist term from "bourgeois" to "proletarian" stages. Historically speaking, whenever there is a political revolution, whether classic or modern, the dichotomies blend immediately, and when the contemporary Liberal stage is reached the distinctions often become obscure within the unique ideology and social character of Liberalism itself.

The reactions involved in a revolutionary process in this century are divided generally into two groups. One is those that declare their ideological intentions and methods clearly e.g., Russia and China; the other those that do not have a clearly perceived ideological position, e.g., Egypt, Cuba and Korea; for the latter group ideological concern seems entirely secondary, and this creates a great deal of confusion between the dichotomous distinctions. Is Egypt a socialist regime? Is Cuba really communist? How can one characterize the drastic reforms by military regime in Korea, an avowed anti-communist state? Considering the discussions that preceded any recapitulation of the same thesis is entirely redundant. Suffice it to say, however, that there are various ways to Radicalism as ideological and characterological antithesis to feudalist Traditionalism, and that they take place at various times of history, which lies in the midst of all the stage-minded interpretations of history. The first abolition of feudalism was accomplished in the seventeenth century, and it is still to be abolished today and tomorrow; but that (1) the feudal order is under various guises today; (2) which leads one to believing that the world has indeed been modernized, therefore feudalism no longer exists; (3) what we have today is at least in form different from the typical feudal order, or its next logical development of history, (4) which has been evident in our historical examinations that <u>all</u> political transformations have been made in the form of Traditional-to-Radical transition.

3. RADICAL SECULARISM AND THE DECLINE OF RELIGION

Secularism is planted in the educational aims and plans of the new regime, one of the peculiar character traits of Radical society. Religiosity as the basis of the statecraft is sharply de-emphasized and directly attacked in many cases, where necessary, although discrete attempts to dismantle its influence are by no means rare. Among other ideological and characterological facets of Traditional society, religion ordinarily figures prominently, and the new Radical regime's attack is only a natural reaction, for the egalitarian proclamation is almost always incompatible with religious predominance in society. Now the new education is firmly secular and "political" based on the pronounced Radical ideology and its corresponding social character. In Cuba, for example, "political socialization and the transformation of culture are first-order goals of revolutionary education."[50] In the Middle East "it is not difficult to discern the change from Islamic political perspective toward a nationalist-democratic preference in matters of political legitimacy."[51] This tendency is true in other equally religious regions as well, i.e. Israel and Egypt.

Although secularism is one of the modernizing characteristics it is more pronounced in revolutionary than gradualist societies. Even nearly two decades prior to the French Revolution La Chalotais observed that:

> To teach letters and sciences, we must have persons who make of them a profession. The clergy cannot take it in bad part that we should not, generally speaking, include ecclesiastics in this class. I am not so unjust as to exclude them from it. I acknowledge with pleasure that there are several...who are very learned and capable of teaching....But I protest against the exclusion of laymen. I claim the right to demand for the Nation an education that will depend upon the State alone, because it belongs essentially to it, because every nation has an inalienable and imprescriptible right to instruct its members, and finally because the children of the State should be educated by member of the State.[52]

Within 20 years from this observation the French Catholic Church faced a threatening competition with the secular rationalist attempt by the Revolutionary regime which declared decrees on religious liberty and on establishment of a new calendar which intentially aimed at a de-christianizing effect.[53] This secularism was also liberally tried both in Russia immediately after the Bolshevik takeover which ended with Stalin's ascent to power, and in China in 1956; Mao briefly allowed a "hundred contending schools of thought," that soon proved to be an unpredictable interlude in the revolutionary ideology. In the course of revolutionary transformation the most dramatic shift from religiosity to secularism is generally observed, expectedly, in societies predominantly religious. This tendency is, of course, worldwide with the advent of technological mobility and communicational facility that help render religion less omnipotent in general. But since feudalism is based in part on a religion compatible with the Traditional authority system, an outright anti-religious or at least an indirect persuasion agaisnt religious emphasis is common place as one of the first actions in all transformed societies from England to Russia and to Israel. In the case of Israel or to some extent Cuba there is no overt anti-religious tendency, to be sure, but the overriding preoccupation with national priorities force religious practice to be either harmonious and cooperative with or at least unobstructive to those national priorities. In addition, Radical leaders tend in general to be more nationalist and secularly idealist than ardently religious in any particular faith. Let us now consider this secular tendency in some concrete historical context.

Among the intellectual influences of the English Revolution secular liberal ideas and religious toleration were some of the more prominant features, and scientists like Bacon, Raleigh and Thomas Smith in general supported the parliamentary cause.[54] "There was to be a public profession of the Christian religion 'reformed to the greatest purity of doctrine,' and the clergy were to be maintained 'out of a public treasury,' but 'not by tithes.' This public religion was not to be 'Popery or Prelacy.' No one was to be compelled to conformity, but all religions which did not create disturbances were to be tolerated."[55] Religious tolerance was the first step toward secularism, and in 1650 an act "repealing several clauses in Statutes imposing penalties for not coming to Church" was declared by the Parliament.

> All and every branches, clauses, articles, and provisoes expressed and contained in any other Act or Ordinance of Parliament, whereby or wherein any penality or punishment is imposed, or mentioned to be imposed on any person whatsoever, for not repairing to their respective parish churches, or for not keeping holy days, or for not hearing Common Prayer, or for speaking or inveighing against the Book of Commom Prayer, shall be, and are by the authority aforesaid, wholly repealed, against any such person or persons as aforesaid, shall be fully and wholly superseded,

made void and null.[56]

In France, Article 6 of the Declaration of the Rights of Man and Citizen had already laid the foundation of secularism by declaring that "Law is the expression of the general will; all citizens have the right to concur personally, or through their representatives, in its formation; it must be the same for all, whether it protests or punishes. All citizens, and employment, according to their capacity, and without other distinction than that of virtues and talents." It was only a logical next step that in December, 1789, a decree was enacted that granted religious liberty to non-Catholics: "Non-Catholics who have fulfilled all the requirements...may be elected to all governmental offices, without exception, (and) non-Catholics, like other citizens, are eligible to all civil and military positions."[57] In July of the following year, the Civil Constitution of the Clergy completely subordinated the Church to the State by making it a governmental department, and several other decrees were declared soon either to supplement the previous ones or to meet the opposition that arose from this liberalization of religion.

With the tide of secularization and control of religion by the State the strict moral burdens associated with religious sanction also relaxed, notably concerning illegitimacy and divorce. "The syllogism lay already: All men are created equal; bastards are men; therefore bastards are the equal of other men."[58] The law of 12 brumaire made the illegitimate children equal to legitimate ones, although understandably the opposition from the local courts and the minister of justice almost nullified it in practice.[59] Symbolically, the secularizing tendency reflected in decrees denouncing the old ways of moral behavior was already significant as groundwork for further liberalization. Similarly, the decree of September 1792 regulating divorce made the matrimonial affair entirely a civil contract that belonged to the State. In a startlingly modern tone it declared that "Marriage may be dissolved by divorce, (and) divorce shall take place by mutual consent of husband and wife." The secular spirit is well summarized in the preamble:

> The National Assembly (considers) the importance of enabling Frenchmen to enjoy the privilege of divorce, a consequence of individual liberty, which would be doomed by indissoluble engagements; considering that already a number of married couples have not waited, in order to enjoy the advantages of the constitutional provision according to which marriage is only a civil contract, until the law had regulated the manner and consequences of divorce....[60]

(It matters very little that the provisions in this enactment were considerably modified in practice, and finally abolished in 1816 only to reappear in 1884.)

This secular tendency reached its peak with a force of terror and frenzy when between 1793 and 1794 a host of dechristianization decrees were declared, among them the famous establishment of new calendar by the National Convention. In the same period, enactments of other matter, mostly secular affairs, were also made reflecting the ideology and character of a revolutionary regime, among which education was declared "free (and) public" to all citizens.

Between September, 1792, and July 1794, the National Convention somehow managed to find time to discuss and enact numerous items of legislation pertaining to social and cultural matters. In fact, if judged by the amount of legislation, this is perhaps the most prolific period of revolutionary social and cultural achievement. Encouragement of artist and scientists, protection and preservation of works of art, development of the metric system, establishment of a "revolutionary" calendar, and abolition of Negro slavery in the colonies constituted the substance of many decrees; while the postal services, theatres, beggars, inheritance rights of illegitimate children, and charity and public relief were the subject of others. As is frequently the case, especially during revolution, much of this legislation progressed no further than the statute books. Yet, even in the form of abortive laws, it is of value as a reflection of the aims and hopes of the people who produced it. That such things could be given serious consideration under the conditions which prevailed in France at the time is, in many respects, one of the most significant facts of the history of the Revolution.[61]

One article in the Russian Constitution of 1918 was already devoted to religious freedom, in a language that is remarkably similar to that of other decrees concerning secularization. Outright religious repression was not in full force until after industrialization had begun. Instead, anti-religious movements were left to Party persuasion rather than to direct state action, and good Bolsheviks were all rigid atheists. Varying modes of persuasion and reconciliation were attempted and experimented in an effort to incorporate the church into the flow of state actions and programs. With the general momentum of revolutionary stability the secularizing tendency gradually became a target in which the state machinery was fully utilized.[62] For a while a strangely liberated mood swept across Russia, giving birth to something akin to a Russian version of the Renaissance in literature, the arts, philosophy, and notably in the "experimental" education, a completely liberated educational system that ended in disaster for the qualitatively inferior results. However, religion gradually gave away to revolutionary causes and slogans. As early as 1929 one observed:

> The feature in the religious disintegration of Russia that is especially provocative of reflection is the defiant atheism of the youth. Everywhere so-called advanced youth is openly and hilariously atheistic, and this youth is sucking into its fold the other youth of the land, save possibly that of the Protestants. I say possibly, because, while the Protestant youth has hiterto held to its faith more firmly than the other youth of the land, it is still a question whether in the end it will not break away from the religion of its fathers.
>
> There are religious leaders who smilingly dismiss the notion that atheism can remain a permanent condition in Russia. They argue that religion, Christianity especially, has survived all attacks in the past, and it will as surely survive the opposition of the Bolshevists. In reply I must emphasize the consideration that never in its history has any religion, and Christianity in particular, faced a foe as formidable as it is now encountering in Russia--a foe so determined, so energetic, so intelligent as the Bolshevists are.[63]

Although soon after the revolution an effort was made to liberate Russia from the feudalist remnants of the Tzarist regime, as in France it became obvious that religiosity was incompatible with the highly progressive and positively-minded revolutionaries and their visions. In the beginning at least the philosophy of educating the youth closely resembled that of the West, especially that in the nineteenth century. "The child, inherently good, was to be shaped by a natural reaction to his environment; and in general, the life of the new socialist society would itself, without elaborate institutional intervention, educate its citizens appropriately."[64] Liberal education and secularism go hand in hand, and this is certainly the case in most revolutionary eras. One of the most interesting aspects in the Bolshevik Russia at least before Stalin's ascent was this dual development of liberal education and secularizing tendency. Thus,

> Perhaps the most exciting experiments were introduced in the educational field. In the city schools particularly there was a drastic revision of curricula. An attempt was made to integrate children's work around one large theme, known as the complex method, instead of dividing it into separate and distinct subjects. Group work among students was encouraged. Above all the traditional and disciplinarian relationship between teachers and pupils tended to give way to new forms of collarboration; 'the teacher must be an organizer, an

assistant, and instructor and above all an older comrad, but not a superior officer.' Indeed in some cases pupils were invited to demonstrate and report any attempt to impose excessive discipline. Pupil self-government in the schools was encouraged....Visting factories, museums, theatres and other places of public entertainment became an essential part of the school curriculum and remained so even after the reimposition of orthodoxy after 1929.[65]

In this vein of optimism and liberation from the traditional shackles, one Soviet philosopher of some eminence observed that:

> There will be no school in the future communist society. The child will go immediately into social work. There he will find no pedagogues, but a work director, who will be a sufficiently cultured person, and one who knows how to handle children. More correctly, we will all be pedagogues. The child will go directly from social work to industrial work, and from there to the library, where he will find answers to all the questions which interest him. We are approaching closer to this all the time.[66]

"Once the Civil War was over, many old, long-buried anarchic desires and ideas burst to the surface and found concrete expression in education, literature, the arts, and in the morality of the personal relationships. The Bolsheviks themselves constituted almost a conservative force regarding the latter. Madame Kollontoi, a leading communist and a member of the workers' opposition, had been a staunch advocate of free love; in 1919 she had stated that under socialism 'the family is no longer necessary.' Lenin and the official Party institutions disagreed with this completely." In spite of official efforts to tame the outburst of liberated spirits Russia immediately after the Civil War was of considerable licence.[67] One contemporary observed not without indignation that:

> Abuses of the new freedom in sex and marital life have been rampant in Russia....In several cities men have told me of abuses to which they are subject which are truly novel. Servant girls who find themselves with babies on their hands often fix responsibility for fatherhood on the men who employ them, and only because, if the girls win, they obtain a higher allowance from their employers than from the guilty parties, who may be only proletarians. That is why men prefer older women as servants. They may be spies of the dreaded GPU, but they cannot set alimony traps for them....The court, baffled by the tes-

timony adduced, will often make all the men charged with guilt shoulder the burden of supporting the child, and thus inadvertently foist on it a multiple father or fatherhood....Indeed, this attempt to reforge sex morality and family relations, not with palliatives but with a drastic discard of old standards and old sanctities, old fears and old shames, old restraints and old taboos, has whirled to the surface of Russian life a host of monstrosities. Tragedy and travesty follow hard on one another, and darken more often than they illumine the inner nature of man.[68]

Egyptian secularism, a far more arresting example, dressed in nationalism arose out of the religion's failure to meet the political changes, and the 1952 revolution gave a distinctive impetus to the secularizing tendency in Egypt. From the outset, the Free Officers led by Nasser were remarkably free of religious fanaticism and this was intentional, not accidental. The ensued conflict between the military revolutionary regime and the Muslim Brotherhood, a religious organization that commanded a considerable influence among its religious followers, was not just a power contest between two rival factions involved; it was a direct confrontation between a revolutionary force that based its ideology on the futuristic progress and no less on secularism, a distinctively modern outlook, and a group whose general tenets and principles were more or less looking to the past glory and grandeur. To the revolutionaries religion was as irrelevant, if not outright antagonistic, to the radical reforms and reorganizations of society as the glorification of the medieval splendor. The Free Officers thus carefully excluded from their inner circle those who were in any sense fanatically religious before and during the coup of July 1952. For instance,

> Colonel Rashad Muhanna, who organized the abortive army revolt of 1947 and was later one of the three members of the provisional Council of Regents (established by the Revolutionary Government in 1952 to represent the infant King Ahmad Fuad II), was probably a Muslim Brother, although he denied being one. He co-operated with the Free Officers, but he was never a member of the executive committee (which became the Council of the Revolution). Colonel Muhana was dismissed as Regent, in October 1952, for working against the Revolutionary Government. In January 1953, he was arrested for plotting a counter-revolution, and in March he was tried in camera by the entire Council of the Revolution, and sentenced to life imprisonment.[69]

The reason given by general Naguib was that Colonel Muhanna "chose to conspire against (the revolutionary regime) on the ground that a secular republic would be inimical to Islam."[70]

Considering the impact of religious influence in Egypt, the revolutionary regime sought to incorporate the Islamic domain into the radical programs and modernizing changes rather than to directly antagonize it. However, the religious sphere came gradually under government control, and sermons on "health, education, foreign affairs, and matters" about which the leaders desired to educate the masses took precedency over the traditional religious preaching.

> Abolition of all religious courts in 1956 was a major step toward secularization, although removing marriage, divorce, and other personal status matters from religious jurisdiction deeply antagonized non-Muslim leaders, especially Christians, who felt that the loss of control over personal status threatened their hold over their flocks. Since the religious courts were closed, their functions have been taken over by civil courts, which apply religious law in personal status matters. Christians complain that this is not harmful to Muslims because most civil judges are Muslims, but that the latter are not qualified to interpret Christian ecclesiastical jurisprudence.[71]

Of course, the revolutionary leaders have made full use of religious unity throughout the Muslim world, but this has been so strictly as an ideological device as in other pan-Arabic slogans and proclamations that have virtually no religious bearing. (Religious repression, on the other hand, may be thought of as proportional to the religion's threat to the revolutionary causes and plans. The reason for Castro's ambivalence towards religion in Cuba is because there is no organized religious opposition to the nation-building attempt by the revolutionary regime.)

Ironically general Naguib was himself forced to resign in a confrontation with the revolutionary officers, who had regarded him merely as figurehead, on the vital issue of reform vs. revolution. Naguib favored a democratic, liberal form of constitutional government and withdrawal of military forces from politics, while Nasser and other officers strongly insisted on a total social and political transformation. The former was also sympathetic toward maintaining a religious (Islamic) republic as opposed to a totally secular one.[72] In a final showdown in February 1954, Naguib resigned, which was followed by a host of trials for those who "supported" Naguib to incite a counter-revolutionary plot, including breaking up the entire organization of the Muslim Brotherhood which had attempted to assassinate Nasser at the end of the same year.

The aims of the Revolution Command Council, now under Nasser's exclusive leadership, were primarily nationalist, secular and progressive whereas those of the Muslim Brotherhood were narrowly partisan and myopic. The Constitution of 1956 guaranteed all Egyptians the freedom of worship, and all Egyptians were declared "equal in respect of rights and obligations without discrimination on account of race, origin, language, religion or creed."[73] "By contrast the Muslim Brothers were principally concerned with the rights and equality of Muslims, rather than those of all Egyptians. By implication at least, the Christian and Jewish minorities would have played the role of second-class citizens under any government established by the Muslim Brotherhood."[74] Hence,

> In 1952 the Muslim Brotherhood had only themselves to blame for their exclusion from the new government. That exclusion was based on the one great ideological barrier that separated them from the leaders of the Revolution (who warned against "fanatical Islamism" and "proposed to weld a united Egypt, wherein all Egyptians, Muslims and non-Muslims alike, should exercise the full rights of citizenship"). The Brotherhood had never ceased to demand the establishment of a wholly Islamic government--and this was the issue on which the two groups split irretrievably....Late in 1955[75] the government announced its decision to transfer the administration of all religious laws to the state civil courts. Current Muslim and non-Muslim religious laws were to be upheld in cases that did not contravene Egypt's modern codes of civil and criminal law...But in the interest of social unity and equality of treatment for all Egyptian citizens, the traditional autonomous religious courts, with their obsolete practices and procedures and their conflicting jurisdictions, were to be abolished. Justice was to be efficiently centralized under the supervision of the civil courts.[76]

By 1964 the Muslim Brotherhood was completely shattered so that one observed "it will be given no opportunity to become again a powerful movement above ground, unless the Egyptian people repudiate the Revolution and its achievements" which is highly unlikely.[77]

Religiosity and Radicalism are neither necessarily incompatible nor inevitably antagonistic to each other. In many cases, however, their co-existence is a precarious one, for there is no doubt that those revolutionary leaders who consider Radical nation-building and social reconstruction their fundamental objectives will not tolerate any obstacle, even a religious one, in the way. Since religion that is the dominant spiritual force of a given society commands a considerable social influence the revolutionary regime's effort is ordinarily directed to re-channelizing the potential of religious devotion to the Radical causes. Conflict arises between the two forces only when the religious content contradicts the essentially secular revolution and its vision, as was the case in Egypt. Many Egyptian leaders were devout Muslims themselves and had friends in the Brotherhood, and they generally sought its cooperation in the State's new course rather than outright rejecting it. This failed, and given the ideology and behavior of revolution they decided to directly intervene with the religious life. Is it possible that the religious and revolutionary-secular aims could coincide and eventually blend into one monolitic national ideology and social character? The case of Israel may be an appropriate example of this development.

> Jewish religious institutions within Israel are continually subject to opposition and criticism. Many Israeli Jews insist that they are a nation in reality no different in kind from any other people. There is no guarantee that secularity will not become the dominant way of the future in Israel, as is happening throughout much of today's world. Attention is often directed, for example, to the alleged turn among Israeli youth away from traditional spiritual interests. On the other hand, Jewish religious observance is a massive fact in Israel, and this applies to many young people as well as to older persons. Judaism has always been marked by its devotion to human concerns and values. Because of this, any final division between secular existence and the life of faith is untenable, just as is any attempted divorce between Jewish peoplehood and Jewish religiousness. Nevertheless, a contrast and even a certain conflict between secularity and religiousness is a truth of experience in Israeli society today.[78]

In the last instance, in the development of a Radical society and its possible move toward Liberal and post-Liberal states, secularity will predominate and religiousness consequently will have to give way to this historical tide.

4. SOCIAL REFORM

Every successful Radicalization, whether classic or modern, accompanies a sweeping measure of social, political and economic reform. Conversely, often the yardstick of revolutionary success and significance is thought to be the magnitude and nature of the reform measures, from the abolition of the Court of Star Chamber, the Court of High Commission and the Common Prayer Book in the English Revolution to the land redistribution in the Cuban Revolution. The import is not so much that the measures resulted in the immediate increase of income per capita or of GNP in general as that such measures were taken at all under the given conditions which are totally antithetical to such measures sweeping reforms.

There are many similarities in the reform movements among the Radical nations. Many of these sweeping changes have been mentioned in terms of egalitarianism, secular tendency and liberation movement, and consequently very little recapitulation may be necessary. However, these characteristics of reforms are one constant in understanding the revolutionary events, and further the epochal changes from a pre-modern to a modern era for those involved in the process. It is therefore important to think of these changes, both rhetorical and real, as constants of human events in history rather than in terms of how much gain they have actually accomplished on numerical scales. Drastic historical changes especially through a political revolution is difficult, if not impossible, to measure other than through a synthesizing mind and perception.

In Egypt, for instance, the "Liberation Province" movement, a Kibbutz-style cooperative, failed as far as its actual economic gain is considered. Nevertheless, it displayed the aspirations and hopes of the revolutionary leaders to modernize Egypt against all odds and difficulties, and with this attempt at collectivization Egypt entered a totally new era in its long history of traditional repression and sameness. Egypt's land reform stands pronounced more for its symbolic significance than for its actual effect on the peasants as individuals. "Land reform became the first dramatic social measure seized on by the RCC after coming to power, perhaps because it was the most obvious need. In the first weeks of the revolution, the RCC thought of land reform as one way of destroying the political power of the large landlords. Another objective of land reform was to divert investment from land speculation to much needed industry. Traditionally, investors preferred the safe and immediate returns from farm investment. However, this prevented creation of new wealth by concentrating capital in existing hands."[79] The actual changes were far smaller than promised. Only about 10 percent of the cultivated areas in Egypt actually changed their owners; fewer than one million farmers (less than 6 percent of total) received new holdings, and the hope of creating a small-peasant class evaporated immediately. "The most important political significance of the legislation perhaps was to lessen the power of some 2000 individuals from whom land was requisitioned."

> The greatest effect of the land reform on the peasant was psychological. The harsh agents of the absentee landlords no longer controlled the village police, the local tax collectors, or the municipal authoritites, nor could they continue to manipulate local elections. Today, employees of the government's agrarian-reform department have replaced the agents of

the former owners, and the peasants no longer live in fear of being dispossessed from their farms.[80]

"The landed aristocracy no longer dominated political life.... The tightening of the military dictatorship, followed by the creation of the Republic of Egypt in 1954, the promulgation of the Constitution of 1956 and the election of Gamal Abdel Nasser as President of the Republic, marked the end of the landed aristocracy's power."[81] So the feudal order in Egypt that characterized its socio-political life since time immemorial was once and for all disappeared and a new era entered the ideology and social character of the Radical Egypt.

The Cuban experience is somewhat similar to that of Egypt, that is, shattering reform measures and very little actual effects, other than symbolic ones. Lack of experienced technicians and managers and the attitudes of the general population, among others, seriously crippled the revolutionary aspirations and visions.[82] The agrarian reform in Cuba took up the form of "state farm" rather than the Soviet styled "collective farm". The criticism that the difference is purely verbal notwithstanding, there are both structural and psychological differences, stemming from the unique characteristics of Cuban conditions. In the Russian collective farm, the farmers' individual holdings are pooled together,[83] and the profits are shared among the member workers. In theroy, at least, the Soviet collective farm is an autonomous body which decides and executes its own policies and management. On the other hand, the Cuban state farm belongs to the state and the management is appointed by the state; the workers are paid wages and the remaining profits go to the State. There is no workers' control in the state farm in Cuba.[84] The Cuban version of cooperatives is neither orthodox Communistic nor precedented anywhere in the past, which "the Communists regard as heresy." But the underlying reasons for the establishment of state farm cooperatives were deeply rooted in the realities and needs of Cuban situation:

    1. The distribution of many large estates, including sugar and rice platations, would probably have led to a fall in production. Large agricultural units, which <u>if well run</u> are often superior to small holdings, predominated in Cuba.

    2. Most of the Cuban rural population were agricultural laborers rather than peasants.

    3. There was no tradition whatsoever in Cuba which might have helped the establishment of free, uncontrolled cooperatives. There was nothing corresponding to the Mexican ejidos, the Russian mir or the Bolivian syndicates.

4. The formation of independent cooperatives would soon have led to a division into rich and poor cooperatives, and probably also to increased exploitation of the rural proletariat working for the cooperatives.

5. The revolutionary government planned to develop a new communal life in the countryside—with new villages, schools, hospitals, clubs and so on. This could most rationally be achieved through collectivization.

6. Most country dwellers lacked any knowledge of modern methods and did not have either the capital or machinery needed to increase agricultural production.

7. If the new individual owners had been given absolute possession of the land it might easily have led to the creation of minifundia or new latifundia.[85]

It has been observed that Cuba traditionally lacked the sense and skill of local self-government in the past to implement the ideal of self-determination. "Now it seems quite possible that the cooperatives will change this, not via some lofty constitutional pronouncements but by virtue of the fact that it is the agency which is lifting the Cuban guajiro out of his traditional poverty and illiteracy and integrating him into a thoroughly civilized community life."[86] Further,

> The members (of the cooperatives) *feel* like members of an organization that belongs to them in a direct and intimate sense, not like employees of an entity as distant and abstract as the "state". If this is so, and if it is not simply a temporary phenomenon connected with the enthusiasm which the early stage of successful revolution always generates, then we think it likely that the peasants themselves will *make* the cooperative into something quite distinct from the Soviet version of the state farm. Given the fact that the cooperative is completely reshaping their physical environment, raising their cultural level, and transforming their whole way of life, it seems reasonable to expect a degree of involvement and participation far beyond that which characterizes the relationship of the industrial worker to the plant in which he is employed. And as literacy increases and new skills are mastered, it would indeed be surprising if the members of the cooperative did not find themselves assuming increasing responsibilities for its affairs--including, in addition to the management of its productive and commercial operations, also the government of the new community to which the

cooperative is giving rise.[87]

Very few would indeed object to, much less criticize, the pessimism and caution expressed by the Cuban sympathizer Rene Dumont that mere state control and ownership--Quasi-socialist-- would not necessarily entail development. Yet even fewer would doubt the exhilarating sense of rebirth and spirits as authentic in Cuba created by the agrarian reform, although the true content of such exaltation may be more symbolic than substantial, more epoch-making than production-raising and more rhetorical than realistic. The following is one example of this kind:

> It (the cooperative) was smashing the ancient feudalistic chains, and in this astonishingly short time since January 1, 1959, the land was going to the peasants--the Government expropriating, as is its inalienable right, the holdings of foreign corporations and native exploiters, turning these over to the people's good and the national welfare. Everywhere you saw this truth-- that big cooperatives were arising even as the individual peasants were working their newly won lands with the aid and solicitious care of the new government. Cooperatives in a land where the peasant hungered, traditionally, for his own patch of land.[88]

Other reform measures have also been enacted and progressed impressively. One observer, while criticizing Castro for failing to fulfill his pledge of democratic reinstitution in Cuban politics, acknowledged this massive fact of social reform.

> Social welfare aspects of Castro's program have likewise been initiated since he took power. In the first months of his regime an extensive housing program was begun which aimed at providing every Cuban with the opportunity to own his own home. Health and medical facilities were extended to the rural areas, rental rates were reduced by 50 percent, and utility costs were drastically lowered. Large-scale school construction was started, and great efforts have been made to eradicate illiteracy. Recreational facilities, which had been available to only a minority of Cubans, were opened to all Cubans, and many new facilities were provided. A campaign was launched to eliminate racial discrimination, and new opportunities for employment were extended to non-whites. Thus, a start has been made to carry out that part of Castro's program aimed at giving all Cubans a better chance in life.[89]

Sweeping socio-political reforms that characterize a successful "quasi-socialist" revolution are necessarily incompatible with democratic liberal procedure which aims at gradualist improvement, for (1) the modern version of feudalism in many guises and variations appear more intolerably oppressive today, especially given the anti-feudal ideology of the Enlightenment and Marxist historical logic, than ever before; and (2) modern technological facility for nationwide communication and instruction makes it possible for a revolutionary regime to indoctrinate and mobilize the entire population behind its aims and plans within a relatively short period of time. The classic defense of liberal democracy, mainly a product of the nineteenth century, is as obsolete in containing the fervor of Radical movement of the still-feudal contemporary world as the scholacistic argument is in countering the rising tide of modern science.

For the sake of world peace, the best one can hope for is that (1) the big powers will actively encourage the overthrow of the feudalist remnants in underdeveloped Traditional societies that still suffer from the economic backwardness and no less from the fascination with the unworkable Western democracy; (2) the revolutionary process will be swift in execution, bloodless in aftermath, and clear in its ideological commitments; and (3) the "guiding" and "administrative" period will be as short and thorough as possible before the society strives toward stability and development with the full use of industrial technology.

5. INDUSTRIALIZATION EFFORT

Industrializing efforts are one of the many typical facets of the modern nation-buidling processes. What is so striking about this especially among the revolutionary nations in the twentieth century is their almost obsessed frenzy with industrialization and the high priority that it imposes on human and material resources. Spartan discipline and hard work is both physically and ideologically emphasized and enforced, with the constant stress on the good life for future generations. In no other social type is there so much demand for discipline and hard work for industrialization as in a Radical society. In Egypt Nasser's inflammatory speeches emphasize the importance of industry in general and the Aswan High Dam in particular.[90] In Israel even the Kibbutzim are turning into industrial factories,[91] boasting a 700 percent increase in industrial output in the first two decades since independence.[92] Korean President Park envisions that without industrialization no democracy is possible.[93] In Cuba, the Schools of Revolutionary Instruction shift their emphasis from doctrinaire teaching to technological training.[94] However, it is the Soviet Union which paved way to massive industrialization as a single-minded national effort.

The frantic effort at industrialization is nowhere more pronounced and better epitomized than in Russia under Stalin mainly between 1929-40. Big or small, all later revolutionary regimes were inspired largely by the techniques and planning methods of Soviet Russia that had been totally unprecedented. The relationship between the contemporary Radical state and controlled industrialization that is peculiarly proto-typical and characteristic of revolutionary Russia is, thus, of vast historic significance for future world development, and, more specifically, as a model for the Third World (more on this in the next chapter).

The importance of industrialization was clearly stated by Lenin who had characterized Communism as "Soviets plus electrification." Despite this urgency, however, the first 4 years after the revolution still saw industrial productivity fall far below that of the pre-Revolutionary era. And it was not until after the venom of economic crises had been staved off through the New Economic Policy that true industrialization began to take shape. In the meanwhile, the disparity between the fantastic notion of American perfection in scientific management (of Frederick Taylor) and traditional Russian workmen's mentality that defied the precision and exactitude required by modern industry plagued and frustrated the revolutionary leaders.[95]

The major thrust of Russian industrialization that began in 1928, which witnessed the first of the Five Year Plans, was perhaps the greatest human engineering ever attempted in history since the Great Pyramids. In an effort to create surplus in food and capital, vital to industrial investment, the whole nation was put under rigid control in terms of production and distribution. The sacrifices imposed on the rural peasants demanded almost super-human endurance and will to survive, upon which the industrial projects depended. The purges that rolled off in the early 30's created extra labor force in addition to the working population that had already been sufficient. Natural resources were abundant. Almost endless repetitions of indoctrination, supervision, the threat and exercise of force, differentiated ranking and human mechanization followed, by which Russia was eventually to emerge as an industrial power. "In the next few years the achievements of the Five Year Plan provided the main content of news in the Soviet Union. Production statistics became the thought and life of Soviet society." "Rapid industrial development became the main goal of Soviet society, its attainments justification for everything else." This "second revolution" under Stalin perhaps stamped Russia with its enduring mark of cruelty, staggering achievements, and legacy of terror and stupidity.

In effect the second revolution transformed the whole of the Soviet Union into a single enormous firm. The management of the economy merged with the government of the country: managing director Stalin, the Politburo his board, and everyone else managers, technicians, public-relations men and workmen. The plan figures of 1929 had been merely indicators of what production levels were desirable, as was the practice during New Economic Policy; they now became overnight legal norm--by statute. This did not make the figures any more attainable; it took many years of hard struggle and the dismantling of an already outdated Stalinism before the technique of planning could finally be made to accommodate economic criteria of balance and preference instead of a set of behavioral rules which incessantly spurred and threatened. Many competent economists have devoted much time to exposing the irrationality of Soviet industrial plans, as well as measuring reality against expectation and propaganda. In a sense all this is beside the point. What mattered was the obsession with _more_. At the level of production of the USSR in the late 1920s there could hardly be a serious danger of over-production in physical terms, and the problem of balance was solved, at least for the next decade, by concentration on heavy industry as a first priority. So everything was ploughed back into more production. The bottlenecks came mainly in distribution, and these were tackled, if not always solved, by the institutionalization of permanent crisis. Almost overnight the Soviet Union became 'plan conscious'; as children learn the Ten Commandments in Christian countries, so Soviet children learned the importance of fulfilling plans.[96]

This strictly scientific and impersonal character of production-orientation necessarily resulted in having to sacrifice some fundamental tenets of Bolshevism which had promised a basically egalitarian "socialist" distribution of economic proceeds, by introducing a differentiated reward system. Consequently, competition for producing more, or fulfilling more than the quota became the criterion of heroism and patriotism.

In 1935 a coal-miner called Stakhanov, under the full glare of publicity, succeeded with two assistants in producing 102 tons of anthracite in a work shift of five and three-quarter hours at the Irmino Coal Mine in the Ukraine. Stakhanovism had arrived: the perpetual pressure to overfulfill work norms and plans, with rewards of public esteem and material benefits in money and kind for success, and public condemnation or punishment for failure. Within a few months similar records were reported from many other industries. In spite of its unpopularity--during the mid 1930s shock-workers ran the risk of being killed by their workmates--the Stakhanovite campaign was never abandoned during Stalin's life, and was even copied in some of the People's Democracies in eastern Europe after the war. It may seem a heavy-footed, even absurd approach today, but it dominated the attitude to work of an entire Soviet generation.[97]

Its secondary impact was felt in the cultural and social-psychological realms; the free-spirted experimental nature of liberal expressiveness and search for the right methods of governance, which had characterized Bolshevism under Lenin, were permanently over. Under the punishing circumstances which demanded mechanization and conformity, personal initiatives and criticisms could in no way co-exist with the industrializing efforts and coercion. The Soviet society, within and outside the Party, was put under thorough thought control in which no dissension was allowed. It was in this period, mainly between 1928-40, that the gray, terrifying and shocking image of the Soviet Union was created and permanently stamped on the Russian social character.

However, this effort bore fruit. By 1940 Soviet industrial output trebled; the annual growth rate was registered at 9 percent compared to the 3 percent of England in the same period, and the productive rate in the United States fell by almost a third during the Depression. By 1940 the Soviet Union was a major industrial power. Though impressive these figures may seem, however, the growth rate during the rigid regimentation between 1928-40 under Stalin was not much higher than during the period of New Economic Policy, a considerably relaxed practice for socialism. Based upon this fact, Western historians have argued that a similar progress would have been made had the NEP recovery been channelized into industry without the totalitarian process of monolithic national organization. Of course, Soviet historians consider such arguments irrelevant to the socio-political facts of Russian historical development.

While the Western observers approach the Russian phenomenon with quantitative measurements and GNP rates, the Soviets view the development of Russian industrialization as an historical "constant" that is self-evident and inevitable. Choosing the right methods for the Soviet Union is a matter not only of expediency but also of principle. "Socialism requires this order of priorities, the transformation of the economy from individual small-scale procedures to collective and integrated large-scale production....Only fully controlled industrialization justifies planning; and vice versa--only full-scale planning can solve the problems of socialist industrialization."[98]

6. THE EMERGENCE OF A NEW EPOCH

The most striking impression of the aftermaths of a Radical transformation is the emergence of a new order, a new ideology and a new social character. The making of a new era becomes evident to all who observe the changes. One observer was struck by the similarities between new China and Israel of 1948:

> In both countries the awareness of a totally new start seems to me to have made new people from old. This is what lies behind the new honesty, and partly also behind the anxiety of officials to act "correctly" at all costs. True, the admixture of terror, narrow-mindedness, and fanaticism frequently distorts these positive features to the point of making them unrecognizable. But, for all that, one cannot escape the feeling that underneath all the depressing things there lies the bliss of a new start.[99]

D. Rustow similarly observed that in the post-revolutionary France, "after a quarter century of riot, terror, coups d'etat, and convulsive wars, the country retained a more orderly system of law and of administration, and the welter of traditional weights and measures had been replaced by a uniform decimal system."[100] Among the most evident is the definite historical testimony that one era has ended and another has just begun. In the French Revolution, for instance, it was

> Not the execution of Louis XVI, nor the taking of the Bastille, but the night of August 4, when feudal privileges were thrown to the winds, was the central fact of the French Revolution. It was a secondary consequence that the King's authority was restricted or his person misused.[101]

It was also this sense of a rising new epoch with the masses as the central characters, which was something entirely new to them, that determined the fate of Russian Revolution against the almost insurmountable odds present at the outset.

> They succeeded, first and foremost, because they brought to the common people of Russia the first hope, in a century of misgovernment, of power over their lives. No one can analyze the decrees of the Bolshevik government in that first momentous year of its history without something akin to awe for its leaders. It is not only the depth of the insight they displayed into the wants of the governed; it is not only the largeness of the conceptions with which they operated. It is, even more, the width of the avenues they opened to talent--here the resemblance to 1789 is remarkable--and the genius with which they appealed, again as in 1789, to the highest creative impulses they encountered. They did not seem apart and aloof from those over whom they ruled; they were one with and of them. They had the insight to associate with their adventure those nouvelles couches sociales, the workers and the peasants, who in field and

and factory, in army and in soviet, both learned responsibility for the exercise of power and acquired an interest in the regime from participation in its governance. The break-up of the large landed estates, moreover, and the wholesale expropriation of the capitalist class, gave peasants and workers a sense of mastery over their own fate they had never previously possessed. Amid all the ruin of civil war and famine in the early period of the October Revolution, it is noteworthy that observers consistently report an immense exhilaration among the people. They feel that they are living in a great epoch; they feel they are dying for great ends. Not even the coming of dictatorship, after the attempted assassination of Lenin, seems to have deprived them of the conviction that a new and wider freedom was theirs.[102]

Out of this exhilarating awareness and participation, aided by iron discipline and sustained ideological indoctrination emerges the Radical "new man." His fate no longer depends on the Divine whims nor on the sacred past, but on himself and others exactly like him who face the new world collectively. In every revolutionary rhetoric and pronouncement this theme of new man is omnipresent, obsessive and overwhelming; a new era, new order and new man are the most totalizing changes in Radicalization.

As the defining characteristics of a revolutionary epoch, thus converge the themes of "new man," "new thought" and "new social order." In reality, the new man is molded by the new thought formation, which in turn generates and gives identity to the new social order as one whole process. The implementation of this Radical character requires time, yet its structural changes are almost always overnight, and no less clear-cut in the most literal sense.

No revolutionary changes, however, are as astoundingly epoch-making in a short span as those made by the French Revolution, as most historians agree, although many of the changes were obviously more formal than substantial and more symbolic than actual. But "never in human history, or at least never prior to 1799, had so much been achieved by one people in such a short span of time!"[103] Never in human history the distinction between feudalism and post-feudalism was so sharply established by the revolutionary ideals of the Enlightenment, at least not until Marxist socialism would perform the identical function in the Soviet Union more than a century later. This dichotomous distinction, pre-modern (feudal or Traditional) and modern (Radical and thereafter), would more or less characterize successful revolutions and revolutions-by-coup in later stages of history.

We might do well, therefore, by examining the most marked,

and obvious, contrasts of a new epoch in France established by the first decade after 1789. Politically in 1789,

> France was a monarchical state, with a long tradition of divine-right absolutism. It lacked anything approximating the "free" parliamentary institutions of England--even the existence of recognized constitutional foundations was a matter of controversy. Liberties, such as they were, were conceived principally in terms of the old Latin "libertas," i.e., "privilege." "Liberties of the subject" were unknown, and there was no official statement of either "rights" or "duties" of citizens. The remark attributed to Louis XIV might still explain the relation of the king to his subjects: "I am the State" was as applicable, in many respects, as it had been a century earlier. Little that might be identified as political democracy or political liberty existed. The people were governed by the king and his bureaucracy mainly for the benefit of the privileged classes.[104]

Execution of local political and judicial affairs was strictly centralized,[105] and the manner in which justice and taxation were administered, for example, was arbitrary without consistency; virtually no local autonomy existed. The State and Church were mixed in matters secular as well as ecclesiastical, and provincialism rather than nationalism prevailed throughout France. What today's world takes for granted--the ideals articulated by the Enlightenment--were just hopes and wishful thinking of few men in 1789. After 1789, however, the hopes and wishful thinking of few began to be viewed as a materializable reality. Within a decade, by 1799,

> Divine-right, absolute monarchy had yielded to a republic, with at least a quasi-democratic form of government, and with popular sovereignty widely accepted in principle. By that time France not only possessed a constitution, and written one at that, but she had <u>three</u> such documents, had tried two of them, and was about to experiment with a fourth! For the most part these constitutions were the work of regularly selected constitutional conventions, three of them carried declarations of right of the individual, and one included a statement of <u>duties</u>.

> New standards of political life had become known-- freedom of action, security of property, protection of persons. Codes of law had supplanted the chaos and confusion of an earlier day. An elected judiciary, the principle of habeas corpus, trial by jury, humanized

> penalities all had come into being. Law had come to
> symbolize the general will, and equality <u>before</u> the
> law had taken the place of privilege. In local affairs
> a decentralized system, likewise with elected officials,
> and with a high degree of local autonomy, had taken
> the place of the intendants. And everywhere much ex-
> perience had been gained in voting for candidates,
> running for office, discussing public issues, and par-
> ticipating in the affairs of government.[106]

Nationalism in place of provincialism emerged from counter-revolutionary and foreign wars, which further contributed to the egalitarian practice of citizen participation.

Economically, the France of 1789 was primarily an agrarian state.

> The economy rested upon an outmoded manorialism,
> one of the holdovers of the feudal regime, characterized
> by burdensome and inflexible features. Land was still
> very much a monopoly of privileged classes and corpora-
> tions; and there was a vast gap--political, economic,
> and social--between those who owned it and those who
> worked it. The system, moreover, tended to perpetuate
> archaic agricultural techniques which, combined with
> natural conditions, frequently left France desperately
> short of food.
>
> In commerce and industry France was the leading
> continental state. But those activities were hampered
> by numerous internal duties and customs, which added
> greatly to the cost of land transport of commodities;
> and so far as foreign trade was concerned, there was
> little in the form of a regular tariff system. In in-
> dustry, progress was impeded by the outworn methods and
> tradition of guilds, a survival of the middle ages.
> And in all phases of the economy everyone suffered from
> the lack of a uniform system of weights and measures.[107]

By 1799, however,

> Manorialism and all that it represented (the so-
> called "feudal regime") had been abolished, never to
> return, and "free" agriculture had taken its place.
> Land had ceased to be a monopoly of the few, and, al-
> though it was not redistributed as some would have wished,
> at least it was made available to all who could afford
> to buy it. Internal duties and customs had been dis-
> established, and France had become domestically what
> Colbert had tried to make it in the seventeenth century--
> a free-trade entity. On the frontiers a national tar-
> iff now provided protection to local industry and revenue

for national government. The guilds had fallen along
with other corporations, and industrial activity had
received a mighty impetus from its connection with the
war effort. In place of diversity and confusion in
weights and measures, by 1799 the now universally used
metric system had come into being; and its significance
far transcended the limits of things economic. Socialism,
however abortive, had raised its head to indicate the
inevitable and inseparable relationship between the e-
conomic and social activities of the community. Bud-
gets and civil lists had become commonplace. Taxes had
been reduced in form and number, and serious efforts
had been made to assess them equitably and collect them
efficiently. Control of finances, in so far as there
was any, had passed from the upper classes to the middle
class. And the franc had replaced older standards of
money for the nation as a whole.[108]

Socially, France was also divided in sharp contrast between pre-
1789 and 1789-99 periods. Before 1789,

> France was a class society; moreover, it was a
> class-<u>conscious</u> society. The privileged minority en-
> joyed most of the benefits and prerogatives, while the
> unprivileged majority shared but little in those fea-
> tures of life. The upper class rode high; the middle
> class waited, impatiently, for their chance to rise to
> power; the peasants kept on working. Slavery existed
> in the colonies, but perhaps that was to be expected
> at the time. The common man counted for little, and
> whatever social reform there was usually took place un-
> der the aegis of the Church.[109]

But by 1799,

> Classes had given way to equality, an equality more
> pronounced than that in politics--though some were "more
> equal than others." The bourgeoisie were coming into
> their own, while the lower levels of society, both urban
> and rural, were slowly rising, although they still had
> a long way to go. In any case, labor was presumably
> a free commodity, and laborers relatively free people.
> One of the most significant developments of the decade
> was the revolutionary idea of "careers open to talents."
> This meant that one's natural gifts could enable one
> to cross all lines of caste, wealth, inheritance, and
> family. Humanitarianism had taken form in many ways,
> notably in the improvement of conditions in prisons
> and in the abolition of slavery in the colonies. The
> common man had been recognized as a human being, as
> an individual. And social reforms of very considerable

consequence had been undertaken by the State. In the social sphere may be seen, perhaps more clearly than in other, one of the major features of the Revolution, the revolt against privilege.[110]

We have already seen the changes that took place in the religious sphere after the Revolution, in which legislation was enacted to subordinate the Church to the State bureaucracy, to protect Protestants as well as Jews, and to liberalize civil matters that had been hampered by religious sanctity in one way or another. Between 1789 and 1799 the State virtually took over many of the church functions in civil and educational functions and consequently reduced it down to an official department. And the general tides of the secular tendency, symbolized by civil marriage, liberalized divorce and equal status accorded illegitimate children, took away a great deal of power from the Church, although France continued to be, nominally at least, a Catholic nation.

The changes were also manifest in the intellectual sphere as well. Before 1789,

> France suffered from widespread restrictions, and the fact that she *had* a most vigorous cultural life was a triumph for the intelligentsia. Education, as already indicated, was under the hand (sometimes a dead one) of the Church. A periodical press scarcely existed. Few opportunities were available for obtaining educational or other cultural advantages. And what encouragement existed for arts and letters was usually of a limited variety dispensed by the kind and the aristocracy.[111]

But by 1799,

> Frenchmen had had the experience of enjoying, at least in theory, freedom of speech and freedom of the press. Education had been reorganized along the lines which it still follows in most modern states—free, compulsory, universal, and secular. The Revolution had given rise to an extensive, if not always great, periodical press. Lack of opportunities had yielded to the "careers open to talents" already mentioned, and such talents were encouraged and brought to fruition through public prizes, state patronage, and similar devices. Moreover, while there had been few museums and libraries prior to 1789, the revolutionaries established many more, planned still additional ones, and endeavored to integrate them with the education system.[112]

In classic revolutionary transformations, such as the French

Revolution, many of these dramatic changes did not move beyond the statute books. In the twentieth century revolutions, with the improved technological means of supervision and communication, most of what were introduced to change thoughts and control the behavior of citizens in order to implement the Radical causes were actually and promptly carried out. We have just seen, for instance, how rigid collective efforts in industrialization were achieved in Bolshevik Russia. Controlling and remolding human thoughts and behavior in order to create an ideal generation of revolutionaries has been one of the greatest and most significant obsessions of the Radical regimes in their making of a new historic epoch.

Characteristically, Russia has symbolized this emergence of a new epoch in many remarkable ways. Lenin from the outset had emphasized the rigid disciplinary approach within the Party, although in his ultimate aim he remained faithful to Marxist egalitarianism.[113] By necessity and in obsessive aspiration, however, the Soviet attempt at establishing a new historical era, with a new generation of perfected men and women, has become a classic framework of revolutionary totalitarianism. And in many respects, as one of the most significant defining characteristics of Radicalization, the attempt has displayed a spectacular success not only in Russia but in later communist and non-communist revolutionary societies. "The Bolsheviks by drastic measures did, indeed, succeeded in making an almost complete clearance of the remanats of the old spirit wherever it lurked."[114] The Bolshevists attempted at not only altering the aesthetic feeling, eye, ear and taste, but also at the "revolutionizing of man in his everyday life, his manners and customs, his faith; all his feelings and thoughts had to be adapted to the fact that henceforward a new type of man was to populate Russia."[115] However, it was with the launching of the first Five Year Plan that required active participation by the workers in fulfilling their work quota, and excelling it whenever possible that the true legacy of the new man--the Stakhanovite--in the Soviet Union took shape.

> The conception of the new man in Soviet society can best be understood by analogy with Stalin's conception of his own role in relation to history. Stalin viewed himself and the state he commanded as the instrument for driving history in the right direction, at the right place, at the right time. The flow of Soviet policy was the reflection of this correct and purposeful interpretation of what should be done, in the light of Marxist-Leninist-Stalinist science of society. Within this gramework, the function of each man in Soviet society was not simply to respond passively to his environment, but, rather, consciously to govern his actions so as to fulfill his part in the execution of the correct historical line. Theoretically, within his own narrow orbit for action, the New Soviet Man

would choose the alternative which could correctly fulfill his role in history.115

Hence, "conscious, purposive action" and "conscious understanding" became the basic tenets of pedagogy in Russian psychology in developing a new variety of human beings appropriate to the new historical epoch. Soviet psychologists point out that the materialist conception of voluntary action lies in recognizing "the necessary," whereas the idealist conception can only group voluntarism as "free will."

> Soviet psychology has explicitly fostered the theory that consciousness is the highest most specifically human level of development of the psyche, and has indicated the dominant role which conscious influences play as compared with unconscious influences. In this regard, Soviet psychology is hand in hand with Soviet pedagogy. Soviet pedagogy maintains as the basic principle of didactics the doctrine of conscious understanding. And, in questions of training, Soviet pedagogy holds the principle that it is the conscious personality of man, his conscious behavior, and his conscious discipline that are to be molded.117

Purges of the universities followed essentially this pedagogic line; "in order to protect the next generation, the communist youth, from the 'spiritual poison of the old philosophy,' it was decided to make a complete reform of the universities. To the Bolsheviks all idealistic doctrines were as false and dangerous as religion." Soon the Main Committee for National Education, headed by Lenin's widow, damanded the removal of some 134 books from the educational institutions, which included the works of Kant, Plato, Schopenhauer, Herbert Spencer, Ernst Mach, Nietzsche and others.118 The underlying purpose of thought control and remolding of behavior was of course turning the mentality of every man and woman in Russia, formed and sanctioned since time immemorial, into what true socialism required in fulfilling the historical demands and their logical development. The revolutionary ideology thus ultimately turned to a remaking of social character on an unprecedented massive scale.

After more than two decades of extensive remaking of social character the test came during the German occupation of some seventy million Soviet citizens in World War II. "The majority of the population in German-held territory were either people who took little interest in politics or were sincere anti-communists. Yet in most respects they reacted as Soviet people! They had typically Soviet ideas about the primacy of politics over everything else, and nearly all of them had the 'organizational' mentality that distinguishes the Soviet citizen. Their reactions indicated that although the regime had not created a generation of convinced communists, it had created a solid 'Soviet' mental pattern that was hard to change."[118] This was clearly observed in an episode during the war years:

> A former teacher at a Soviet secondary school near Moscow...prepared to contribute his share to the liberation of Russia in the last war. When he was convinced that military defeat would topple the Stalin regime, he and the director of the school decided to draft a constitution for a liberated postwar Russia. After two weeks of work they met secretly to compare their drafts. It turned out that the two drafts were almost identical and differed only slightly from the Soviet Constitution. They were unable to conceive of anything outside their experience and knowledge, and independently they had come to the conclusion that all that was wrong with the Soviet regime was that there were too many "bad people" on top.[120]

Although it may be true that many in Russia are not totally convinced of the regime's official ideology, and may even be cynical about it, this does not implicate, much less prove, that the "Bolshevist method of thinking" itself has ceased to be the influencing factor in Russian life. "Despite changes in the formal ideology and in concrete policy goals, there has been a high degree of continuity in Bolshevik behavior, stemming from the persistence of certain 'core' ways of thinking and acting."[121] Further,

> The Soviet system lays enormous stress on ideology both as a doctrine and as a practical instrument. The "operating ideology" of the leadership at any given point in time is kept remarkably consistent. The more formal total theoretical system has, in fact, undergone change through time, but much effort is expended to rationalize these changes and preserve the appearance of continuity and consistency. There is good evidence that Communist ideology affects the thinking and the acts of leaders and other intelligentsia who grow up under the Bolshevik regime.[122]

In this ideological sustenance by the Soviet regime, both negative and positive functions of propaganda, in addition to other material and psychological incentives and/or threats, are held to be vital. On the one hand, propaganda persuades and deceives the population by misgiving or withholding certain information, and, on the other, it simply blunts the critical mind both physically and intellectually.

> The system of Soviet propaganda is apparently designed, in part, simply to exhaust the intellectual and political energies of men. Almost all levels of

Soviet (and satelite) life appear to provide
for special required forms of indoctrination.
These take an important part of the time of
hard-working people after their work hours
or otherwise in their free time. Whether or
not these propaganda dosages are meant to convince men, as that term is normally understood
in the West, they certainly have the effect
which is undoubtedly known, of exhausting their
intellectual and political energies. Propaganda
carried to surfeit helps produce, within the
whole enviroment of Soviet life, a political
apathy which, with this generation of Soviet
rulers, may be judged as useful as or more
useful than political enthusiasm.[123]

This dichotomy of apathy-enthusiasm should not obscure
the fact that the new historical epoch from which the Soviet
Union emerged must be viewed more or less in its own terms
of merits and significance. The result of official indoctrination since 1917 on the minds of the Soviet population
has produced neither clear apathy nor distinct enthusiasm
as such; rather a certain measure of harmony has been
achieved between the State apparatus, bureaucracy, diverse
institutions and the Party, on the one hand, and the
occupational and professional groups of ordinary citizens
who have grown up with Bolshevism and its long institutionalized thought-control, on the other. Public matters
are no longer overwhelmingly political, but technical
and realistic. Since 1917, Russia (the State and its
people) has gradually grown into one gigantic corporation
whose main function is to provide social welfare for its
members. It may be postulated at this point that Russia
is passing through the mature phase of the Radical stage,
with its mastery of industrial technology. Therefore it
can be summed up that

The professional and technical aspirations
of the educated strata who really run the complex
industrial society of the Soviet Union strongly
influence the overt policy formulated and carried
out by the Party. Though the Communist Party
in the Soviet Union is and will continue to be
an essentially political instrument, and the
top leadership is still recruited from among
those pursuing a full-time political career,
the days are over when political considerations
simply overrode all technical ones. Social
consensus is therefore no longer created by a
small and autonomous political elite enforcing
its own views and decisions on and through the

Party, but is rather a two-way process generated within the Party which in turn effectively permeates and organizes every walk of life. In this respect the withering away of the state can now be considered a long-term possibility rather than a utopian dream. Already a number of activities like sports have been "socialized" into self-administration. More important is the growth since 1959 of socialized law enforcement—Comrades Courts and Volunteer Squads to take over the problems of controlling social delinquency. The Party will gradually take the place of the retreating state organs of enforcement---but the Party as an institution of popular participation, not of political control from the top. Administration and regulation, hitherto considered the classic perserve of the state, of its institutions and its bureaucracy, will increasingly be carried out through a form of self-regulation expressed by this consensus, which in turn finds expression through the organized Party. When we consider the promises that Soviet society will move, within a finite period, towards a state of full communism, we must assess this not in terms of any disappearance of regulation and control, but of their institutionalization in an even broader form---that of a growing Party made up of all the leading elements of an entire society.[124]

Many revolutionary states have attempted at imitating the Soviet "success"; and China comes close to the Soviet Union in the expressed official ideology and method of transforming the greatest human masses into a totally different variety within a short span of one generation. Considering the immobile, indifferent and politically unconscious rural masses of the traditional past, the complete transformation of their thought and behavior into an appropriate form for the new epoch may be judged even more staggering than the Russian experience. Mao expressed the directions and aims of reform in the following terms: "The principle of land policy of the Soviet is to wipe out completely feudalistic and semi-feudalistic oppression and exploitation....Our class line in the agrarian revolution is to depend upon the hired farm hands and poor peasants, to ally with the middle peasants, to check the rich peasants, and to annihilate the landlords. The correct practice of this line is the key to the success of the agrarian revolution and the foundation for all other policies of the Soviet government in the villages."[125] After the existing system had been destroyed, the expropriated lands were redistributed to the poor and landless peasants who were given a major voice in decision-making and were organized into the Red Army. With the land reform by the revolutionary regime, there emerged a new epoch in China; the feudal order was destroyed beyond recognition, and the sweeping (and stupifying) Cultural Revolution that had started late in 1966[126] completed the destruction of whatever remnants of feudalism in China. This process, too, demanded the grueling toil, sacrifice and constant pressure on millions of human beings, a pattern essentially similar to that employed by the Soviet Union.

The rigid Party control over the masses through persuasion and force in this epoch-making process became a unique feature of the new China that thoroughly defied precedency:

> What (has happened)...then, is that there is a new alignment of social classes in government. Under the old pattern, the alignment was the monarchy plus the landlord-scholar class against the peasantry. When the peasants revolted, they often succeeded in upsetting the monarchy but they almost always lost their leadership to the landlord-scholar class, who would line up with the new monarchy to oppress the peasantry. Now, for the first time, a new force has emerged to champion the cause of the peasants, but the rest of the process is not to be repeated. Not only have they overthrown the equivalent of the monarchy, but they have liquidated the landlord-scholar class, so that the usual spectacle of the latter usurping the leadership and transferring it to a new monarchy cannot occur. Instead, the new force (that is, the Communist Party) has kept the leadership for itself. In other words, between the governing and the governed, there is no longer an intervening class. The Communists deal directly with the peasant masses, with no brokers, as it were, between them. The development of China thus will differ radically from the development of the Han or other dynasties. There exists no force that can dilute the control exercised by the Communists. This is why the Communist leaders of China practice no tolerance and make no compromises with other groups. They are determined to make themselves masters of the new China.[127]

Hence, despite Mao's description of Chinese democracy as "democracy under centralized direction," it is one under tight autocratic totaliarianism, without which the making of new men, of a new social reality and of a new historical epoch is utterly difficult, if not impossible. Although the freedom of speech, of the press, etc., is denied in China, the stability of Communist leadership is not fostered by coercion alone. Strongly reminiscent of the Soviet methods of "active, conscious participation," Mao "spares no pains in fostering the cohesion of the team around him....It is for this reason that power is highly concentrated at the top of the Chinese Communist Party, and yet the whole government apparatus in Peking works with remarkable smoothness. What makes the giant dictatorship tick is the democratic spirit at the top of the regime."[128]

The new theme of the revolutionary regime places a particular emphasis on the educational institutions and processes, as part of its thought-formation and thought-control processes. Making a new epoch in China demands a total loyalty from the new generation, and the perpetuation of the revolutionary causes must be sought in institutionalizing the revolution itself. Therefore,

> To cope with situation, Peking has been focusing its major attention on the training of youth. Feverish programs of education and indoctrination are now going on in Communist China, the aim of which is to turn all the young people into ardent followers of Communism. The Communists openly state that they have no use for people over thirty. Instead, they concentrate their efforts on those below that age, who, they belive, can still be shaped to the Communist mold and thus turned into faithful supporters of the new regime. In the Ideological Remolding Campaign of 1951-52, agitations were deliberately fomented on college campuses and among professional groups.[129] In these high-strung agitations, students were incited to rise against their teachers, younger members of the staff to rise against the older ones. Peking's over-all purpose is to recast the educational system, giving the lead to the young people who are more prone to carry out the wishes of the Communist Party. Not only are young people taught the Communist creed, but they are made to understand that all branches of learning must have a useful function for the state. They are taught that the individual exists for the sake of the state, that learning is not for learning's sake, but has to be utilitarian and patriotic.[130]

Consequently, those Party members who held key positions in

the institutions of higher learning in China yeilded power in decision-making over the educational faculty and staff, and in most instances the department heads "merely rubber-stamped the decisions made" by the Party personnel. The dominant mood at the controlled institutions was characterized as fear: "fear of offending the Party commissioners, fear of saying the wrong thing, fear of being reported to the Party leadership by activists and informers in their midst. To avoid suspicion, most people cautiously avoided close contacts with one another. A person who had casually remarked that 'one must be careful what one says these days' was reported by an unknown informer and confronted with the question whether he was planning a revolt."[131]

The best means of enforcing collective thought-control in China was stamping out individuality and "selfishness" by subjecting one to the criticisms of his friends, relatives and general comrades, in addition to regular Party members. Group enforcement of collectivism has been practiced to its fullest effect, especially effective in a society where close personal ties are one constant formed in its past social history. As in any socialism, "the Communists want a collective society; they preach collective living. The individual must submit to the group, and obey the 'organization.' Consequently a specific target of thought reform is the individualism of the intellectuals, as expressed in their personal ambitions, in seeking fame and personal gain, in the desire for individual freedom, in various forms of 'selfishness.'"[132]

> As long as intellectuals retain their individualism, they will be independent in thought and behavior. Individualism is therefore a central target of attack. The new way of life is the collective life. The methods of thought reform utilize group pressure. To the group the individual bares his thoughts in self-criticism and confession. He must tell all without any reservations. He must not have any secrets. Inasmuch as the 'group' is always directed by capable manipulators and the acme of group life or collective life is the Party or the state, the replacement of individualism by collective means in the last analysis the total surrender of the individual to the Party and the state. Once this has been accomplished, thought reform will have been complete.[133]

The group pressure method is as subtle and irresistable as it is effective. "The worst that can happen to a Chinese (especially under the new regime) is to feel outside his group, different, not concerned about others." "They usually put pressure on people to make them feel selfish if they do not conform."[134] Individuals are taught through official ideological indoctrination and group pressure to think in terms of others and to discard whatever self-oriented thoughts they might personally espouse. The result is one of the most terrifying varieties of alienation of individual citizens from one another, eyeing one another with suspicion and mistrust.

  The (collectivist) system demands of all citizens that <u>they supervise their nearest and dearest, that they keep a stern watch over all his actions and conversations</u>, and bare him to public accusation if he has sinned in the moral and ideological sense. And finally, those who do not denounce such faults are declared equally quilty. Those who try to avoid denouncing their friends and relatives must fear that they will be denounced because they have failed to expose faults known to them. The harshness of this system is apparent.[135]

  One of the characteristically Chinese techniques of collective behavior control is the process of "confession" among peers and group members. These confessions especially among the intellectuals serve many functions in the development of the new man in China: (1) they are used as evidence of what remains to be done about one's ideological "impurity," and by forcing open, written confessions, one's own thoughts become clarified along the collectivist line; (2) the unique "arrogance" of the Chinese intellectuals that dominated the feudalist era by siding with the monarchy is destroyed by public "self-abasement" and "abnegation," and further they publicly acknowledge the authority of the Communist Party and accept its pronouncements and policies; (3) public statements confessing one's sins, and endorsing the regime's aims, mostly in written form, binds one to his commitments. With repeated and more articulated, restatements of confession, the line between what is real and what is politically expedient invariably becomes obscure; (4) the confession makes the process an intimately personal affair, by repeated questions and criticisms from the audience. One is unable to state his confession in mere generalized terms. "Every person must dig up his own past and expose his own personal failings, mentioning specific times and places;" (5) public confessions by renown intellectuals are used to reinforce public sentiment behind the revolutionary objectives, now that they "embraced the new ideology of the proletarian revolution and had placed themselves in the service of the leaders of the proletarian revolution--the Communist Party.[136]

For the majority of the intellectuals, to co-operate with the new rulers is not a matter of choice, but of necessity. To live in China they must accept the conditions which they cannot change. They join the mass campaigns and participate in thought reform as the only way of making peace with a situation which may stay for quite a while. To some it must be very hard to resolve their inner conflicts and find some measure of inner peace. In doing so, a number may bring themselves to see the logic of the Marxist mode of thinking and to agree that the proletarian-socialist revolution is the only 'way out' for China.[137]

For ordinary citizens group pressure and public confessions are not the only means by which the theme of the new men and the new epoch is forged. "Re-education through labor," a euphemism for hard labor, is another commonly used means in molding and reshaping the mind and behavior of the masses. This reeducation through labor "can take place in prisons, camps, penal communes, on irrigation projects, railroads and dams, and probably in mines; perhaps today mainly in the remote, inhospitable parts of the country," which accompanies ideological training and often physical punishment in addition to hard labor. As a result of such a punishing remolding of thoughts and behavior appropriate to the new historical epoch and its social character and institutional structure, nearly 700 million Chinese people have cast away their old habits and adopted new ways of life in an astonishingly short time span.[138]

Within a decade after the revolution a travelling observer reported that "people who knew the old China and the old sceptical, quick-witted, highly intelligent Chinese are all horrified at what a few years of the new education have made of the younger representatives of this race: robots incapable of independent judgement, filled with stock phrases which they automatically produce in response to a definite cue, as a slot-machine produces a bar of chocolate."[139] He also reported that in the revolutionary China the citizens were thoroughly conditioned to the new ideology and social character that even honesty, for instance, is "practiced to a point of absurdity, where it almost becomes a surrealist nightmare,"[140] for "one can leave money practically lying in the street and never see anyone pick it up except (and then only before witnesses) to take it to the police."[141]

The majority of the Chinese--who are rightly known throughout the world for their diligence and willingness to work--have undoubtedly submitted to the decrees of the government and the Party. The slogans of the communist did not fall on deaf

ears when they appealed to the Chinese people
to help make China once more great, mighty, and
the equal of other nations. Chinese nationalism
is so strong, particularly in view of all that
happened to China in the nineteenth and twentieth
centuries, that the people voluntarily endured
many sacrifices to reach this goal. Nevertheless,
there must have been millions who did not readily
submit to the harsh discipline and the exorbitant
demands of the regime. That the Chinese people
have been totally disciplined can best be explained
by the law for "education through labor."[142]

An interesting point that emerges from the rhetoric
and techniques of the revolutionary regimes utilizing the
expressed ideology of Marxist socialism: the more the regime
embraces socialist ideology, the more thorough results. This
can be observed in the revolutionary processes of quasi-
socialist Egypt, and socialist Cuba and non-socialist Korea.
Although some political purges and token punishments have
properly frightened the citizens these latter regimes have
not practiced the methods and ideology of Russia and/or China
to the letter. The desire to create a new historical epoch
is evident in the revolutionary regimes in their political
pronouncements and economic policies, yet for one reason or
another their methods and attitudes toward the task have not
been modelled after those of their more "successful" predecessors. Nevertheless, the essence of the new epoch, the new
men, and the new social character still remains their expressed
program as well as implicit vision.

Among the late comers in the revolutionary stage of
development, Cuba stands out as the paragon of all in its
dramatics and impressionism as well as in its unique position
in Latin America, a region heavily dominated by the Traditional
character types. This fact fits the remark that the Cuban
Revolution "is the most radical in the history of the Americas."[143]
The new age in Cuba is thus characterized by a Radicalism
"that has given rise to the many interpretations of the revolution
for socio-political transformations of this magnitude can be
neither ignored nor evaluated with equanimity by those whose
lives they affect."

To answer the question "What is the Cuban
Revolution?" we must first examine what might
be called the evolution and content of Cuban
radicalism—those fundamental changes in the
structure and operation of society and politics
that define the revolutionary experience. A
preliminary checklist is easy to assemble: in

ten years Cuba has seen the advent of Leninist politics, agrarian reform, education reorganization, economic transformations, and international realignments--all force-drafted at a rate that leaves outsiders as well as many Cubans bewildered. But it is not just the magnitude and pace of the transformations that makes the Cuban experience radical; the manner in which change is effected is also important. For although the Cuban elite makes the decisions and dictates their belief systems and their lives in the service of the revolution. Thus there arises a pervasive and continuous effort to mobilize the people and enlist their energies, loyalties, and skills which are found wanting by the revolutionaries, they have taken upon themselves the job of creating new ones.

It is (the) effort <u>to create a new Cuban man</u>, a man equal to the tasks set for him by the revolutionary elite....The transformation of Cuban man into revolutionary man is at the core of Cuban radicalism; it is seen by the leadership as requisite for the success of the new institutional order, and the regime spares no energies in its pursuit. In the Cuban view, there can be no successful and lasting Leninist politics, agrarian reform, economic transformations, or international realignments <u>without the education and re-education</u> of the Cuban masses. As Castro has said, "All revolution is an extraordinary process of education....Revolution and education are the same thing."[144]

In this process of reeducation the whole of Cuba is involved as one stream-lined workshop. The creation of a new man in a new historical epoch involves various institutions, i.e. the family, the church, the mass media, schools, peer groups, youth organizations, religious and social clubs, and political parties. The resulting changes in Cuban society through this transformation effort have come to rival many other similar events in history.

The overriding theme of the Cuban Revolution is change. Its leaders seek a new society, one organized from the ground up <u>on principles different from and often diametrically opposed to those of the preceding regime</u>. One need not concede either the morality or the workability of the new order to admit that the social, economic, and political bases of Cuban life have been fundamentally transformed.

The pre-Castro system of land ownership is
gone; private enterprise has been destroyed;
education has been nationalized and restructured;
the politics of Batista have given way to the
politics of Castro and the Cuban Communist
Party; dependence on the United States has
been replaced by a special relationship with
the Socialist countries; more than 5 percent
of the population--including many of the most
highly skilled--have fled; and the pre-Castro
system of status and economic rewards has been
almost completely replaced.[145]

The agrarian reform and other economic transformational
measures had been formulated and carried out against a strong
opposition "with astonishing speed and spectacular political
success."[146] Indeed, "few nations have ever undergone such
massive transformations in so short a time. Certainly no
non-Communist system has been changed at such a pace."[147]

On the theme of the new men, the Cuban revolutionary
regime resorts more to voluntary enthusiasm and participation
and less to a direct exercise of coercive power: the
environmental settings of the masses are manipulated by the
leaders so as to make the masses voluntarily want to participate
in the revolutionary causes. The reeducation of the Cuban
masses lies essentially in their efforts to create this new
mentality and behavior.

Attitudes, values, and beliefs leading
to both extensive and diffuse behavioral change
are best shaped by participation in those
revolutionary institutions where direction, social
suggestion, and peer group pressures are greatest.
Futhermore, in revolutionary institutions where
participation in a wide range of activities is
encouraged, behavior is frequently modified
even when there is no initial change in attitude.
Such behavioral changes may lead in turn to new
ways of perceiving and evaluating the world, and
thus a permanent nexus for relating two types of
change is established. In short, participatory
activity--not in itself dependent on the
internalization of new norms-- may eventually
lead to very basic changes in the value and
belief systems of those who are swept into
participation. In this manner, easy formulas
such as "attitudes shape behavior" or "behavior
shapes attitudes" give way to a system that is
organized to sustain a dynamic relation between

behavioral change and attitudinal change.[148]

The defining characteristics of a new "political man" in the new order of Cuban society, e.a., "Cooperation, egalitarianism, sacrifice, service, hard work, self-improvement, obedience, and incorruptibility," serve both as the general framework of a Radical ideology and as the specific formulas for behavior in specific instances. The core of the Cuban cultural transformation is thus the aim of creating a new breed of citizens, like those of the Soviet Union and of China, appropriate in both thought and action to the new historical age in Cuba, which is, in Castro's words, "the task of creating a new consciousness, a New Man, on the basis of ideas that prevailed in our society for centuries."[149] While the revolutionary process was still under way with struggle and opposition, the New Man theme continued to occupy the main attention of the leaders, as the Party paper put it: "it is impossible mechanically to separate the building of socialism and communism..., they should, in one sense, be built at the same time. A fundamental implication of this is the education of the New Man, the Communist man, beginning new. "Hence,

> The Revolution saw selfishness as one of the toughest "old ideas" to be uprooted so that the New Man could emerge. Fidel Castro said in 1967, "It was impossible to advocate the concept of human brotherhood when the cardinal condition for survival was that of getting things away from others...." To put it another way: under the old economic setup, life was a rat race and Man an object at the expense of others. Talk of brotherhood could have reality only on an individual or parochial level. But the New Man--the twenty-first-century man or woman--would be a person, for whom work is a function of one's interdependence with all beings in a society where wealth is created and shared communally.[150]

One of the most striking instances of this new man campaign is reflected in the institutional destruction of racism in Cuba, now achieved at the institutional level and to affect the most stubborn and resistant psychological residues in a near future. Although there was no official policy in the previous regime under Batista the colored population in Cuba had suffered discrimination and exploitation along with the poor people; the colored were barred, for instance, from public places lest the tourists should be affected. Before the Revolution,

> The blacks and mulattos of Cuba endured
> the same types of exploitation as poor whites,
> but the added oppression of racism. They
> formed a colony-within-the-colony of cane-
> cutters, maids, shoeshine "boys", and news-
> paper vendors, plus a small black bourgeoisie
> of doctors, lawyers, politicians....A young
> black woman might be in high demand as prostitute
> or cabaret dancer, but little else. Blacks,
> in short, did the dirtiest work and for the
> least pay....Housed in ghettos at the sugar
> centrales, treated like lepers by everyone,
> they received even lower wages than other
> blacks and experienced a brutalization unmatched
> since the original enslavement of Africans.
> At the parks, whites sat on benches while
> black people had to stand along the sides;
> in Santiago, there were separate clubs for
> white, mulatto, and black. Luxury hotels,
> restaurants, beaches, social and sporting
> clubs were closed to blacks. Interracial
> marriage led to ostracism.[151]

But after the Revolution, all this changed, at least structurally:

> All overt forms of racism came to an
> end. Not only did social segregation pass
> away but, more important, racism in work relations.
> The first and second Agrarian Reform Laws
> changed life for thousands of black agricultural
> laborers and farmers. The Urban Reform Law
> put blacks into decent housing. Education
> opened up totally; the successful campaign
> against illiteracy was particularly important
> for black Cubans who were previously the
> largest group of illiterates. Thus the vicious
> circle of institutional racism (access to
> decent work, education, housing, and health
> facilities denied to blacks because of their
> poverty, which arose in turn from those denials)
> was broken once and for all....Racism in the
> sense of subordination of one racial group
> by another for the benefit of the oppressing
> group did not exist in Cuba in 1967. It was
> over, finished; socialism ruled out any such
> form of oppression. The Revolution had put
> the impoverished masses in power--and most
> blacks belonged to that class. The basic
> needs to which the state addressed itself
> were the basic needs of black Cubans. Conflict

of interests along a color line was a thing
of the past. Not only a decent life but a new
dignity had become available to black Cubans
for the first time. And whites began to be
freed from whiteness....Where the previous
society's institutions and authority had all
stood behind racism, the Revolution stood against
it. Fidel Castro established an equality based
on fact and backed by moral force; more, he
unified Cuba's people for the first time in
history.[152]

These drastic changes have preoccupied many revolutionary
leaders, both socialist and non-socialist. Their ideological
differences aside, both express essentially similar aims and
desires for their new revolutionary epochs. Korea's military
junta leader Park followed the fundamentally similar theme
when he proclaimed that:

The Revolution (of 1961) is designed to
establish true democracy in this nation.
Toward this goal, the general public must be
thoroughly trained in social education. Such
social training of the public should take the
course of increasing the sense of responsibility
and duty in each individual. Through public
organizations for community development works,
the pan-national movement and the public information activities, various evils of the nation
such as the easy-going, time serving, do-nothing,
"flunkeyism," and the habit of depending on
others should be corrected. To enable the
people to understand and exercise their democratic way of life and the principles of constitutional government will be carried on throughout
the country, utilizing all media of public
information.[153]

Further, he points out that "privilege conscious' is one
of the most serious obstacles to the common welfare and
prosperity of our people and our national unity."[154] On
economic equality necessary to furthering justice and freedom
in this new revolutionary order:

The key problems facing a free economic
policy are coordination and supervisory guidance
by the state of mammoth economic strength.
Neither state nor society can be the victim of
the private greed of powerful interest groups.
It should not be inferred, however, that what

I mean here is the refusal to private ownership
of the means of production. Rather, private
ownership of production should be unconditionally
encouraged except in instances where it is
necessary to control it to stimulate national
development and protect the interests of the
people in general. In other words, private
ownership is entitled to protection, which
must be expanded for the ideological requirements
of a free society, unless it operates against
the construction of a sound social order.[135]

Note the remarkable absence of Marxist phraseology in
these quotations from one who is one of the staunchest anti-
communist leaders today and also note the equally remarkable
similarities between Park's aims and visions, and those of
other more avowed socialist revolutionary leaders. The form
of the rhetoric matters little, for the essential content
of all revolutionary characters remains the same: The
creation of a new historical epoch.

Finally, something must be said about institutionalizing
the revolutionary regimes and their causes and momentum.
This is a problem made acute by the fact that the fate of
the whole revolutionary movement often hinges upon a leader
or an elite group possessing extraordinary talents and
opportunities for the task. The problem has perhaps been
less acute among the expressed socialist regimes that have
chosen the Marxist-Leninst lineage as the guidance for state
ideology and social character at present and in the future,
thus more or less stabilizing and perpetuating the new
institutional arrangement. Nasser's and Castro's often
dubious and belated embrace of socialist ideology (in
Marxist form) may be viewed as the solution to meet the
problem of institutionalizing the revolution. The Soviet
Union has succeeded in perpetuating the original Bolshevist
ideology (at least in its fundamental substance) by decades
of incessant indoctrination and rigid control on thought
and behavior. The Communist China is now facing the problem,
and probably will follow the Russian precedency. Sadat in
Egypt was one of the elite Free Officers with Nasser, and
consequently Egypt is still in its first generation of
revolutionary epoch. Castro chose Communism as the perpetuating institution of his revolution. Park, the only non-
communist revolutionary leader who has almost matched his
communist counterparts in Radical social reforms, has
fended off this problem by being constitutionally elected to
the presicency for three consecutive terms, and during whose
time some measure of institutional permanence for the May
Revolution must be established. This issue may be compounded

by the fact that Korea's close ties with the United States
hinder any more drastic social reforms (which may, after
all, resemble a socialist measure), which the latter is
obviously very reluctant to see taking place in one of its
allies. In the end, however, each revolutionary regime
must devise its own means of countering the possible lapse
into the pre-revolutionary state of affairs on its own
resources and ingenuity be they Marxian-socialist or
Enlightenment-libertarian, toward the universally desired
economic development.

7. THE THEME OF STRUGGLE

It is not only the initial success but sustaining
that success and its momentum in the following phases of
revolution that gives prominence to the theme of struggle,
mainly through the revolutionary rhetoric, ideological
pronouncements and visionary slogans. Endless meetings
are arranged to explain, to persuade and to communicate;
omnipresent in this process is the attack on the real or
imagined enemy, both internal and external. The rhetoric
may lack substance to a trained and analytically skeptical
mind but they are powerful and galvanizing to the masses,
and the purpose of the theme of struggle is just that.
Castro's speech in this context has the ring of an impending
crises and of inspiration:

>   Imperialism wants to do battle, mobilize
> its nest of worms, promote subversion, it
> doesn't matter. There is also virtue in this;
> it invigorates the revolutionary, it excites
> him, it quickens his fighting spirit. We
> have seen this a thousand and one times:
> A unit is doing nothing, the enemy has
> scarcely arrived and then it acts differently,
> it reacts differently. The Revolution needs
> the enemy, the proletariat does not flee
> from the enemy; it needs the enemy.[156]

Ho Chi Minh's rhetoric to the French negotiators in
1946 still has freshness into our own time especially in
the light of the recent Vietnam experience: "If we have
to fight, we shall fight. You will kill ten of our men,
and we will kill one of yours, and in the end it will be
you who will tire of it."[157] This sort of high-sounding
determination is found in no other social types; this is
the unique brand of Radicalism in the making. Lenin wrote
on the eve of November 6, 1917,

> The situation is extremely critical.
> It is as clear as can be that delaying
> the uprising now really means death. With
> all my power I wish to persuade the comrades
> that now everything hangs on a hair, that
> on the order of the day are questions that
> are not solved by conferences, by congresses
> (even by Congresses of Soviets), but only
> by the people, by the masses, by the struggle
> of armed masses....It is necessary that all
> the boroughs, all regiments, all forces
> should be mobilized and should immediately
> send delegations to the Military Revolutionary
> Committee, to the Central Committee of the
> Bolsheviks....History will not forgive
> delay by revolutionists who could be victorious
> today (and will surely be victorious today),
> while they risk losing much tomorrow, they
> risk losing all....Seizure of power is the
> point of the uprising; its political task
> will be clarified after the seizure...To
> delay action is the same as death.[158]

Very often this theme of continous alert and struggle has characterized a revolution in simplified slogans and battlecries, and it will continue to do so in future revolutions for Radicalization.

In this section we shall examine the relationship between the rousing proto-typical revolutionary rhetoric and the actual process of Radicalization.

Mao once said: "Death is only the physical exit from life. And if a man, the more so a Communist, can bring some good by dying, by his brains and his courage, then he should not think twice about it. He must boldly and proudly fulfill the will of the party and the people. A party that lives for the interests of the people, which suffers with them and fights to make them happy, is an invincible force. There is no force that can conquer the party of the Communists--the militant vanguard of the toiling masses."[159] In order to tighten the Party's control over the masses around the revolutionary regime, Chinese Communists fired constant alarms and ringing proclamations of struggle against their supposed enemy. The Anti-Three and Anti-Five Campaigns between 1951-52 were typical cases of the theme of struggle. The target of anti-three were "anti-corruption, anti-waste, and anti-bureaucratism," and citizens were asked to "help expose cases of violation so that the offenders might be duly punished and the 'three evils' might be stamped out;"

for "corruption and waste are the big enemies of production and economy" and " bureaucratism is the breeding ground of corruption and waste."

The 'struggle' became another 'mass movement' in which the 'progressive elements' took the lead and the not-so-progressive had to participate in order to show their devotion to the people's cause. While people of all walks of life were 'mobilized" to join a 'mass investigation campaign', persons in positions where any of the three evils might have flourished were asked to examine their own records and to confess their wrongdoings. Offences, either confessed or exposed, ranged from personal luxuries to unnecessary public expenses and embezzlement of public funds. Accusations and confessions filled the air; 'public trials' and swift punishment in the form of dismissal or fines or imprisonment or even summary execution were given wide publicity; and all 'patriotic citizens' were urged to take up 'tiger hunting', i.e. to expose specific cases of corruption, waste and bureaucratism. To be a member of a 'tiger-hunting team' was considered a mark of progressiveness.[160]

The five 'evils' in the Anti-Five Campaign were identified as "bribery, tax evasion, fraud, theft of state assets, and leakage of state economic secrets." "The entire nation was urged to cooperate in launching a vast counter-offensive to repel the ferocious attacks of the bourgeoisie," which had supposedly "infiltrated the ranks of the labor unions as well as government and Party personnel to bribe and corrupt them."

The five-anti campaign was an even bigger mass movement than the three-anti. It was a broadside attack on the city bourgeoisie. The 'five-evils' were so broad in scope that one or several of the evils could be pinned on any merchant, industrialist, or businessman the Communists wished to persecute. This campaign turned out to be the urban counterpart of the land reform. While the land reform sought to eliminate the landlords as a class, the 'five-anti' broke the back of the city bourgeoisie and its influence in Chinese

society. Those were months of extreme
terror for the city bourgeoisie; they were
marked by harrowing accusations, public
trials, forced confessions, confiscatory
fines, even summary executions. Wives
were encouraged to report on their husbands
and children to expose the 'reactionary'
activities of their parents. The pressures
exerted were so great that many were driven
to suicide.[161]

This campaign, the Party noted with satisfaction, "had paved way for the first five-year plan and the subsequent 'socialist transformation' of private enterprises into state enterprises."

The theme of struggle is more or less a standardized slogan in both socialist and Enlightenment revolutions. It abounds with colorful phraseology and rousing appeal to patriotism and sacrifice; the enemy is depicted as evil that must be destroyed, for history and human justice side with the oppressed and deprived. Cuba's Castro, among the leading revolutionaries, has been noted for emotional slogans and candid appeals. One typical example is the rousing statement issued by the government on the Bay of Pigs in April 1960. It reads in part,

> Our troops are engaged in combat in
> defense of our sacred country and of our
> Revolution against the attack of mercenary
> troops sponsored by the imperialist Govern-
> ment of the United States. And our troops
> are already advancing towards the enemy,
> sure of their victory. The people of
> Cuba are already mobilized in fulfillment
> of their oath to defend their country....
> Onwards, Cuban people! Let us answer
> with iron and fire the barbarians who
> despise us and want us to go back to
> slavery. They come to take away the land
> that the Revolution has given to the peasants
> and the co-operativists. They come to take
> away from our sons, our peasant girls, the
> schools that the Revolution has opened for
> them everywhere....They come to take away
> from the Negroes, men and women, the dignity
> that the Revolution has given back to them....
> They come to destroy our country and we
> fight for our country....Onwards, Cuban people!

>Everyone to his own job; work and fight....
>LONG LIVE FREE CUBA! FATHERLAND OR DEATH!
>WE SHALL WIN![162]

Win they did. The invading forces were bottled up in the Sierra Escambray, and the masses rallied solidly behind Castro. On certain disputes over reform measures which strained the revolutionary unity, he stressed that there would be no middle road or halfway measures.

> At times one asks oneself if there are any Cubans....who do not understand that in a revolutionary process as deep as this one that there is no middle road. Who do not understand that revolutionary process like this one reaches its goal or the country sinks in an abyss. Who do not understand that we advance a hundred years or we go back a hundred years; that a relapse would be the worst fate, the most unworthy that could happen to a country like this. I ask myself whether or not they realize the damage they are doing the country. Whether or not they realize that after the blood that has flowed and after the enormous damage done to the country by the criminals who have robbed it there can be no possible middle way between the triumph and the failure of the revolution.[163]

Some historians have observed that the Cuban Revolution is one historical example of what many men and women of the world aspire to achieve. In this century, however, the specific means and rhetoric of achieving the ideal ends have become increasingly transformed from Enlightenment to socialist.

> Now the leaders of the Cuban Revolution are ideal representatives of this large and historically decisive sector of the human race. Their whole program derives from and conforms to its own common sense. <u>In Cuba they are actually doing what young people all over the world are dreaming about and would like to do</u>....Not only does it enable us to view the reforms being enacted in Cuba in proper perspective, but even more important it explains why the Cuban Revolution, which at first might appear to be a local incident in a small Caribbean Island, is in reality an event of world-shaking significance.

Dreams have ever been the stuff of which history is made, and when they are turned into reality their power is multiplied manyfold. We see no reason to doubt that the achievements of the young people of Cuba will fire the imagination and steal the will of young people throughout Latin America--and far beyond.[164]

If there is a historical logic in believing that revolution is inevitable in many regions of the world, as many do today, we must first examine what type of men and women believe in this logic and how they have obtained the combination of idealist aspiration and logical inevitability. Next, then, we discover that (1) the aspiration-and-logic aspect is directly traced to the historical inheritance of Marxist and/or Enlightenment conception of justice, equality and freedom; (2) where this world-ideology functions as the actual force of transforming social order and reformulating social character, we note that the ideology and social character type to which they aspire is fundamentally and definitely anti-feudalistic in one variety or another, the differences in phraseology and slogans of each revolution notwithstanding; and therefore, (3) in those regions where the anti-feudal struggle has definitely been done away with, the youth may be fired up by romantic ideals and attempt at staging revolutions, convinced in their logical coming, thus creating confusion, misunderstanding and disillusionment; they do not understand that what they aspire to may essentially be a thing of the past, done away with at one point or another of their historical past.

Political revolution, if successful, occurs only once in any given society, in which the Traditionalist feudal order gives way to a Radical society. The only antagonistic forces in history, and its ensuing ideological and characterological ramifications, are between the conception of reality and human relations which derive from Tradition and Divinity, on the one hand, and those which derive from Marxist and/or Enlightenment doctrine on the other, in which the line of demarcation is becoming increasingly blurred.

The theme of struggle in revolutionary regimes, once established as part of the new era's ideology and social character, continues to be the guiding force of society even after the crises and struggles have long since passed, as in Russia.

It can be maintained that, in its ultimate values, Soviet ideology has not

changed since 1917 or, in fact, since the
turn of the century when the Russian Communist Party was shaped by Lenin. At its
core, the basic element in the ideology
derived from the notion of a single, correct,
and, therefore, good course of history,
capable of appropriate interpretation only
by him who is the best Marxist. This was
Lenin's moral sanction as leader of the
prerevolutionary Party; and it was on this
basis that Stalin sought to create the
legitimacy of his succession to Lenin.
From this concept of the correct interpreter
of history in Marxist terms arose also the
rationale for the absolute unity of the
Communist Party and the inviolability of
the Communist Party line.[165]

Thus, the theme of constant struggle fulfills its function
before, during and after the revolution both as rhetoric and
as actual means of administration. In Russia, China, Egypt,
Cuba as well as Korea and Israel, constant attention is called
to the both imaginary and real existence of threatening
forces against their new society. Alerts are called, martial
laws proclaimed, and, not infrequently, "exemplary" enemies
destroyed. New devices in creating a constant sense of
impending crises and sustaining the revolutionary momentum
are incessantly sought by the regime. The government issues
numerous directives, announcements and warnings, lest masses
should relapse and abandon the revolutionary causes.

8. MASS MOBILIZATION

Mass mobilization guided and implemented by a collective
spirit of fraternity and common destiny is an imperative
condition for a Radical revolution. As noted earlier, mass
mobilization and creating collective support ordinarily
determine the success or failure of any attempt at abolishing
the Traditional absolutist order, utilizing both coercive and
persuasive methods. The elite must enlist the masses for the
revolutionary regime's sustenance of power, activation of
plans and creation of new social order.[166] Making this
drastic transition possible, the masses must be organized at
all levels and in all social institutions.[167]

For example, with the fall of the Manchu Dynasty in
1911 and the birth of Sun Yatsen's Republic, the Kuomintang,
its rightful heir, could have become the truly revolutionary
force that might have made another attempt, i.e. Mao's
superfluous.[168] Instead of carrying out Sun's unfinished

social reform measures, the Kuomintang, pressed with internal as well as external urgency, rallied with the landed class to patch up the status quo, thus leaving the peasantry virtually untouched by the revolutionary mobilization. There was neither popular representation in the Party nor willingness among the Party members to push any notable reform movements.[169] On the other hand, Nasser's disillusionment with the masses's failure to be mobilized has been a famous episode in the revolution:

> Before July 23rd, I had imagined that the whole nation was ready and prepared, waiting for nothing but a vanguard to lead the charge against the battlements, whereupon it would fall in behind in serried ranks, ready for the sacred advance towards the great objective. And I had imagined that our role was to be this commando vanguard. I thought that this role would never take more than a few hours. Then immediately would come the sacred advance behind us of the serried ranks and the thunder of marching feet as the ordered advance proceeded towards the great objective. I heard all this in my imagination, but by sheer faith it seemed real and not the figment of imagination. Then suddenly came the reality after July 23rd. The vanguard performed its task and charged the battlements of tyranny. It threw out Farouk and then paused, waiting for the serried ranks to come up in their sacred advance toward the great objective.
>
> For a long time it waited. Crowds did eventually come, and they came in endless droves--but how different is the reality from the dream! The masses that came were disunited, divided groups of stragglers.... I felt, with sorrow and bitterness, that the task of the vanguard, far from being completed, had only begun. We needed order, but we found nothing behind us but chaos. We needed unity, but we found nothing behind us but dissension. We needed work, but we found behind us only indolence and sloth.[170]

As Laski noted earlier, the success of Bolsheviks is in great part measured by the mobilization of the trade unions that held key to the imperative needs for industrialization in the crucial decades following the revolution. In Joseph Schumpeter's observation,

The trade unions were not suppressed. On the contrary they were fostered by the government: membership increased by leaps and bounds and was nearly 17 million as early as 1932. But from exponents of group interests and obstacles to discipline and performance they developed into exponents of the social interests and into tools of discipline and performance, acquiring an attitude so completely different from that which is associated with trade unions in capitalist countries that some western laborites refused to recognize them as trade unions at all. They no longer opposed the hardships incident to the pace of industrialization. They readily stood for extension of the working day without additional remuneration. They dropped the principle of equal wages and espoused a system of premiums and other inducements to effort, Stakhanovism and the rest of it. They recognized--or submitted to--the manager's right to dismiss workmen at will discouraged "democratic meetingism"--the practice of the workmen's discussing the orders received and executing them only after approval--and, cooperating with "comrades' courts" and "pure commissions," adopted rather strong lines against the slacker and the subnormal. Nothing was heard any more of the right to strike and to control production.[171]

In agriculture, the local level resistance of the peasantry may be engineered towards consensus "by the totalitarian Party and synchronized with regular directives and tests of performance in order to remove bureaucratic bottlenecks and reduce to a minimum all attempts to maximize personal advantage at the expense of official plan-goals."[172] Understandably, one of the first order businesses of a revolutionary regime is to organize the masses, combining many different segments of the population into a broad popular basis in the new order.

Among the revolutionary regimes effort at mass mobilization, Cuba stands out as its most massive and impressive case. The revolution-to-social mobilization conception in Cuba runs along the following line:

(1) The social, economic, and political institutions inherited from the old regime are

fundamentally unjust, immoral in practice, and
unequal to the tasks of national development. (2)
It falls upon the leadership to seize the
instrumentalities of power, define the content
of the new order, and then use the full resources
of the state to bring the new order into being.
(3) It falls upon the masses to follow the
dictates of the leaders, to participate fully
in the building of the new order (which is,
after all, for them), and to endure willingly
the many sacrifices that must be made during
the period of national reconstruction.[173]

This line of reasoning is neither exclusively Cuban nor Marxist-Leninist, for many successful as well as unsuccessful revolutions-by-coup tend to follow this argument. "The argument is elitist in spirit and populist in rhetoric," and certainly pragmatic in aim. As a mass movement and mobilization the Schools for Revolutionary Instruction, and the Campaign against Illiteracy, the Committees for Defense of the Revolution involved practically every Cuban directly or indirectly in their peak.

The (illiteracy) campaign represented
a mass mobilization of impressive proportion.
Out of a total population of approximately
seven million Cubans at the end of 1961, one
and a quarter million had been drawn actively
into the campaign as either students or teachers.
Subtracting approximately two million Cubans
from the total population as having been too
young to be eligible for the campaign in any
role whatsoever, we are left with five million,
of whom one out of four participated directly
in literacy work. If we add to these direct
participants the tens of thousands of others
who contributed in some fashion through the
mass organizations, and the hundreds of thousands
who were linked emotionally to the effort because
of family and friends, it is probably safe to
say that the campaign affected in some real
way the lives of most Cubans who by 1961 were
old enough to have even minimal political
awareness....As the campaign progressed, it
assumed a scope at any time or place except
under conditions of war. It is not surprising
then, that the revolutionaries adopted a military
metaphor to characterize both the organization
of the movement (the literacy army) and the
desired national psychology (crush the enemy).[174]

The literacy campaign was basically political in aim rather than technical or even economic. The leaders believed that "only when techniques and pedagogy are subordinated to the revolutionary power of the people and the organization of the masses can they really be of service in a political project like this."

The Committee for Defense of the Revolution was launched also as a political mass movement. Castro declared,

> In answer to the imperialist campaigns of aggression, we're going to set up a system of revolutionary collective vigilance so that everybody will know everybody else on his block, what they do, what relationship they had with the tyranny (the Batista government), what they believe in, what people they meet, what activities they participate in. Because if they (the counter-revolutionaries) think they can stand up to the people, they are going to be tremendously disappointed. Because we'll confront them with a committee of revolutionary vigilance on every block.... When the masses are organized there isn't a single imperialist, or a lackey of the imperialists, or anybody who has sold out to the imperialists who can operate.[175]

By 1963 the CDR grew into an impressive national mass organization purged and reorganized after the Bay of Pigs experience. The following statistics was the way the CDR was organized in 1963.

Number of Committees:	102,500
Total Number of Members:	1,500,000
Number of Women Members:	660,000
Number of Youth:	500,000

Since the total population of Cuba is approximately seven million, the regime claims that better than one out of every five Cubans is a member of the CDR. In terms of adult population, the claim is that 34 percent of the urban residents and 30 percent of the rural residents belong to the CDR. When these membership figures are added to the figures from other mass organizations and the militia, the total exceeds four million.[176]

Although the CDR did perform productive functions, its symbolic and ceremonial capacity among others contribute also to the sense of Cuban solidarity and egalitarianism.

Mobilization of this sort is most interesting when it is predominantly symbolic and ceremonial, when it has no instrumental or productive function. The occasion on which this happens most dramatically and extensively is the annual anniversary celebration of the CDR. On each of the eight anniversaries to date (1968), there has been a gigantic mass meeting in Havana, a major address by Castro, and innumerable lesser speeches and celebrations throughout the island. The anniversary of the CDR is one of the three or four most important revolutionary birthday parties; it is a solidarity rite, a time for organizational stocktaking, and a public fiesta all rolled into one.[177]

Finally, the Schools of Revolutionary Instruction were inaugurated as part of the mass mobilization project, whose function was to be "the ideological formation of revolutionaries, and then, by means of the revolutionaries, the ideological formation of the rest of the people."

After Castro took power in January 1959, ideological formation became an established part of the programs of public education given in almost all sectors of revolutionary organizational life, although the most developed programs continued to be those offered through the Department of Instruction of the Ministry of the Armed Forces. Throughout this period, however, these programs continued to be public and nonselective. Classes were on a part-time or after-hours basis, and the very broadest mass attendance was sought, if not required. Moreover, the subject matter, though it may have been nationalistic, anti-imperialist, and anti-American, was not overtly Marxist. After the founding of the EIR (the Schools of Revolutionary Instruction), mass programs of this sort continued, with Marxist-Leninist doctrine forming more and more of their content. But the EIR should not be understood as merely a continuation or extension of this tradition. Rather, they were an organizational response to a need created by the revolution in power. The need was not just for an expanded program of ideological-training, but for the educating

of Marxist-Leninists in a revolution going
Marxist with neither a party to supply
the cadres nor a rich indigenous Marxist
tradition to draw on.[178]

Further, the EIR was gradually transformed into a system for technological instruction, especially beginning in 1965. The heavy emphasis on ideological indoctrination was replaced by emphases on technology and scientific research, which the leaders recognized as significant in the development of a Cuban revolutionary era. Increasingly, the EIR was viewed as having completed its mission as an ideological instrument in the revolutionary process. By the end of 1967, the leadership decided that the EIR was becoming more obstructive than helpful to the revolution:

> Therefore, with little hesitation and no ceremony, the schools were closed. It was an action quite in keeping with their earlier history, for the schools had always developed and changed in response to the top leadership's idea of the revolution's needs. When the masses needed an introduction to Marxism-Leninism, the basic EIR were founded. When the technical revolution became the focus of attention, the EIR were given responsibilities in the field of technical education. When social research was needed, the EIR formed special commissions for research. Thus the system of revolutionary instruction was used as a flexible instrument to attach a series of problems cast up both by the revolution itself and by the changing views of Castro and his lieutenants.

Such practices in mass mobilization in Castro's Cuba directly follows an established manual on modern revolution. As the French Revolution represents the theoretical and rhetorical pattern after which all later Enlightenment-Liberal transformations have been modelled, the technical and practical aspects of contemporary Radicalization-mass mobilization being one-have been learned mainly from the Soviet experience. Hence, the modern techniques and ideological justification for mass mobilization have invariably derived from the legacy of the Bolshevik Revolution, especially from the Stalin era of regimentation and industrialization. By the time of Stalin's death, Russia was already brought into one national unit, created and maintained by the decades of mass mobilization and collectivization.

The opening up of the Russian heartland
suddenly brought the local inhabitants,
their traditional way of life still hardly
touched by 150 years of Russian domination,
face to face with the modern world and the
rapidly increasing influx of Russians.
Though the official policy continued to
emphasize the full equality of all languages,
creeds and cultures, the arrival of large
numbers of Russian workers and technicians
with their families inevitably made inroads
on the local culture. A career, whether
political or technical, in the Soviet
Union had by now become unthinkable without
complete command of the Russian language.
With few exceptions, only Russian-language
schools provided the new technical and
scientific education which was fast becoming
the exclusive avenue for managerial and
technical careers--as it had been before
1917. Official policy with regard to
minority cultures had begun to take on
something of a romantic quality which tended
simply to ignore the hard facts imposed
by an increasingly Russian-speaking era of
modernity. There were, of course, genuine
concessions to the national feeling; for
instance, in the staffing of top Party
and government posts Russians often alternated
with leaders of local origin. But during
the twenty-five years of Stalin's rule
such locally born leaders had in practice
become entirely 'russified' through common
Party experience. Genuinely local leaders
had been eliminated almost entirely in
the early 1930s.[180]

Efforts by the revolutionary regime to expand communication,
thereby bringing the masses into the collective orbit of
national life and awareness, have been made by all contemporary
Radical societies as both ideological and practical instruments.
The organized labor in the revolutionary China has become
legendary; Egypt created the Liberation Rally through which the
Revolution Command Council controlled various social and
professional organizations; Israel's kibbutzim and later
Moshavim (semi-cooperative settlements) have become the
unifying force in rural areas; Korea, after the military coup
of 1961, drastically expanded the social services system, the
workers from which covering every inch of rural ground to

to instruct on various matters ranging from birth control to cooperative management. In many of these societies in the Radical stage, women have been both encouraged by and drafted into active life with men both to ease labor shortage and to uphold egalitarian spirits in many instances.

9. OPPRESSION AND TERROR

One of the most intriguing turns of the events in Radicalization can be seen in the conflict between the desire to express and practice the Marxist and/or Enlightenment spirits of equality, justice and freedom for all citizens, on the one hand, and the oppression and prejudice against minorities (be it national, cultural, or religious), suddenly surfaced with the tides of nationalist feelings and sentiments on the other. It is ordinarily the case in a Radical state that the new regime attempts to rally the entire citizenry behind its cause. Yet, ironically enough the new regime may find itself in need of creating and/or dramatizing the presence of an enemy, both in the physical and the psychological sense. It is in this situation that some minorities are chosen to be the target of political expediency to unite the more homogeneous population; the minorities in this case are almost entirely dispensable, the repeated and guaranteed pronouncements of egalitarianism notwithstanding. Oppression and prejudice against these minorities are often more symbolic and strategic than inspired by absolute necessity.

A good case in point is the conflict facing Israel and Egypt and other Arab nations in the Middle East. The charges of oppression and prejudice inside Israel against the Arab miniority, and the mass exodus of Jews, Copts and other non-Muslim minorities from Egypt, especially after the 1956 conflict with Israel which expelled all but a handful of Jews from Egypt, are too contemporary to need any further elaboration.[181] Such oppression and prejudice prevalent in times of revolutionary changes are of course not confined to nationality minorities alone, but include other socially and politically "undesirables". Consequently at no other times in the history of mankind are there such strong feelings of animosity toward what the regime considers evil and obstructive to its collective endeavors than in a transformed Radical society as part of its new social character.

Similarly, political revolution and terror are often taken as synonomous, and for good reason. The legacy of revolutionary terror may be said to have begun with the execution of Charles I in the English Revolution, which, being unprecedented, properly shocked the pious and loyal subjects of England. Since then practically every revolution has been accompanied by varying measures of terror, purge and bloodbath. As the expressed ideology of the revolutionary forces gathers more logic and inevitability in the minds of those involved, the methods and justification for terror become more thorough and methodical. It is true both in Enlightenment revolutions and in Marxian socialist revolutions. In the second half of the twentieth century, however, the practice and/or threat of terror in Radicalization tends to wither away, for often the ideological demarcation itself becomes blurred in the hybrid of Marxism and Enlightment. Similarly the prime revolutionary preoccupation tends to be a national reconstruction with the united citizenry solidly behind the regime rather than the annihilation of a specific class of individuals for ideological reasons alone.

The French Revolution stands as the classic example of terror which began under the "Terror" Convention and establishment of the "Revolutionary Tribunal," which, between March of 1793 and the summer of 1794, tried and sentenced to death some 2,600 persons. King Louis was charged with treason soon after the monarchy as an institution had been demolished. Convicted, he was executed in January 1793. The indictment began, "Louis, the French people accuses you of having committed a multitude of crimes in order to establish your tyranny by destroying its liberty," and continued with numerous "crimes" against the sovereign people. The ensuing internal disorders and counter-revolutionary movements, especially that of Vendee, spurred tightening of security measures, of which the establishment of the Revolutionary Tribunal was one. Note the familiar ring of the phraseology in Article 1, which has its facsimiles undoubtedly in many of the later-revolutionary legislations in other nations, in which a similar practice of revolutionary courts has been carried out to purge and terrorize the counter-revolutionary movements:

> A special Criminal Court shall be established at Paris to take cognizance of all counter-revolutionary activities, all attacks upon liberty, equality, unity, the indivisibility of the Republic, the internal and external security of the State, and all plots on behalf of the re-establishment of monarchy or of any other authority hostile to liberty, equality, and the sovereignty of the people, whether the accused be civil or military functionaries or ordinary citizens.[182]

The Reign of Terror, conventionally designated as the period between June 1793 and July 1794, took on three seperate spheres in its exercise: political, economic and ideological. The

Terror Government, like its counterparts in other revolutions in later times, was an institutional response to the internal as well as external crises that the Revolution faced. Although numerous individuals, many of them innocent, lost their lives during the Terror, from the viewpoint of the Revolution it was a matter of expediency. The Government declared that "Terror is the order of the day." In September 1793 the famous Law of Suspects, a sweeping legislation giving the Revolutionary Tribunal a total judicial power, was declared, which begins,

> Immediately after the publication of the present decree, all suspected persons within the territory of the Republic and still at liberty shall be placed in custody. The following are deemed suspected persons: 1st, those who, by their conduct, associations, talk, or writings have shown themselves partisans of tyranny or feudalism,[183] and enemies of liberty; 2nd, those who are unable to justify, in the manner prescribed by the decree of 21 March last,[184] their means of existence and the performance of their civic duties; 3rd, those to whom certificates of patriotism have been refused; 4th, public functionaries suspended or dismissed from their positions by the National convention or by its commissioners, and not reinstated, especially those who have been or are to be dismissed by virtue of the decree of 14 August last;[185] 5th, those former nobles, husbands, wives, fathers, mothers, sons or daughters, brothers or sisters, and agents of the emigres,[186] who have not steadily manifested their devotion to the Revolution....[187]

The economic crises were met by enacting legislation for compulsory loans, establishing price control, the "absolute maximum" law, and further centralizing economic activities. As we have seen in a previous section, the ideological form was manifest in their attempt at dechristianization and the establishment of a "revolutionary gospel." The crises gradually passed and with the fall of Robespierre the Thermidorian Reaction finally brought some measure of stability to the Republic, and the era of Bonaparte began.

The legacy of terror of the French Revolution largely remains as one legendary aspect of the revolutionary period. But that of the Russian Revolution still is a living memory to those who have lived it. The terror of the Bolshevik revolution has come to represent something of a proto-type nightmare of ideological revolution in the twentieth century, although the Bolsheviks' "Red Terror" of 1918 was, like that of the French counterpart, primarily a defensive and politically motivated retaliation against the counter-revolutionaries and other rival opponents. "The machinery of counter-terror (mainly against the Left Socialist-Revolutionaries) and repression grew piecemeal but rapidly from each challenge to Bolshevik authority." By mid-1918 the Bolshvik Party was the only governing body, and the Soviet organs merely discussed the Party's policies and officially ratified them.

The Cheka, the secret police, declared that it "must defend the revolution and conquer the enemy even if its sword falls occasionally on the heads of the innocent." Among the suspects of the counter-revolutionary tendency were those linked with their former positions against the Bolsheviks, and especially the heavy burden of persecution fell upon the Left Socialist-Revolutionaries. "The necessity of the Cheka for the Young Soviet State was, of course, clear, because from the days of the revolution the opposing forces were so great that without using the most drastic measures against them, the Bolshevik government would have been overthrown quite easily." The officers of the Russian Army, who pledged loyalty to the new regime, had been tactfully integrated into the Red Army under Bolshevik supervision. But there remained those demobilized yet still organized officers who presented a real threat of counter-revolution. Consequently, the first of the Cheka's punitive measures was directed against these officers who openly opposed the new regime. Mass arrests and executions followed, eliminating a good number of commanding personnel who became less useful since the war with Germany had already been declared ended. The old bureaucracy, landlords, clergy, and capitalists were also exterminated.

In August 1918 on the night following the attempted assassination of Lenin and the murder of Urizky--which occured simultaneously--there were executed in Leningrad 500 prisoners, in Kronstadt 400, in Moscow over 1000 and, during the following week, over 15,000 throughout the country. The executed, of course, had no connections with the murders, but were just taken in alphabetically order. In 1919, after the explosion in the Moscow HQ of the CP, there were shot over 20,000 hostages hitherto detained in prisons for various reasons.[188]

Peasants' revolts soon followed suit in which one instance alone cost at least 4000 lives, all executed by the Cheka in

March 1919. Over several tens of thousands of officers from the "White Army" who failed to escape abroad were executed in Crimea alone in 1920. Consequently during this period of national crisis the concept of justice was administered solely by the revolutionary necessities and arbitrary decisions made by the courts of law:

> Among other authorities the Courts of Law of the Soviet Union had "extraordinarily wide powers" in the early days of the revolution and were expected to be guided by a "Socialist sense of law" and a "revolutionary conscience." It was assumed, in fact, that all those entrusted with legal powers would be in touch with <u>the sources of inspiration of the revolution and would guide their decisions accordingly</u>. In the early days of the Civil War the dominating conception was that of the "Class Struggle" and the declaratory decrees of the Government were assumed to be sufficient guides in the conduct of that struggle.[189]

With the start of New Economic Policy terror in Russia declined, during which about 3,000,000 persons were taken prisoners under various political reasons, and the Cheka became the GPU, the State Political Administration, which would become the dreaded state secret police during the Stalin era. The confusion and diffused concepts of legal administration even during the Civil War and military communism, however, demanded a further clarification of the legal codes. Hence in 1922 the Criminal Codes, among others, came into being, which defined the counter-revolutionary activities and their penalties in the broadest terms, strongly reminiscent of the French experience. "Aiding or abetting the Counter-Revolution," and "offenses against the Public Administration" were declared criminal offenses against the Government of the Soviet Union. Further,

> Any action calculated to destroy, injure, or weaken the existence of the USSR, or to assist that part of the "International Bourgeoisie" which does not recognize de jure, is described as Counter-Revolutionary. Any act or intention which may even indirectly threaten the "basic political and economic conquests of the Proletarian Revolution" is included. Clauses 58-67 inclusive decree the death penalty, with total confiscation of property, for

the following offences, whether actual
or intended: armed insurrection, or the
invasion of the territory of the RSFSR,
or any attempt to usurp local or central
authority; breach of treaties concluded
by the RSFSR; incitement to foreign Powers
or their representatives to make war on
the RSFSR, or assistance to such Powers
when war has been declared; incitement to
civil commotion, to non-payment of taxes
or to non-performance of duties; any act
which may cause obvious injury to the
Dictatorship of the Proletariat, even though
such injury is not the prime motive of
such act; any action tending to prevent
or check any normal function of the Government
and any attempt to use Government
institutions to the detriment of Government
activities in industry, trade and transport,
aqueducts, public works of every kind;
espionage of all kinds, including the giving
out or transmitting of confidential information;
activities directed against the working
class by ex-Tzarist officials, terroristic
activities against the representatives of
the RSFSR.[190]

The terror of the Bolshevik revolution during this period is real and terrifying enough, but the terroristic measures taken by the new regime must be understood in terms of the organization problems and the policy oppositions the new regime faced, whose threats were enough to endanger the very revolution itself. Lenin, often accused of intolerance for opposition, was essentially a futurist, looking ahead and attempting at solutions for the present problems rather than holding grudge against the past events and ideological differences.

It was Stalin who "invoked the past in order to justify and arrange the present." The concept of legal authority, accordingly, changed gradually from Marxist-Leninist to Stalinist. However, as late as 1930 optimism still prevailed.

We have a system of proletarian politics
and upon it law should be oriented (wrote
Pashukanis). Once we even wished to arrange
the curriculum so that, for example, the
course in land policy and law, because
among us law can play no independent and
final part: this was the design when War
Communism was going out. During the years

> of the New Economic Policy and of the
> rehabilitation period, the system of the
> codes was introduced and began again to
> develop, and at the same time attempts to
> pack and to tie all law into a system were
> renewed. Now, when we have passed to
> the reconstruction period, the utmost dynamic
> force is essential....Revolutionary legality
> is for us a problem which is ninety-nine
> percent political.[191]

By the end of the Stalin era, Soviet laws became thoroughly instrumental whereby "enemies of the state" were broadly defined and arbitrarily punished. Ironically, the Great Purge of 1936 coincided with the establishment of the new Soviet Constitution, which was expressively egalitarian and Enlightenment in many respects. During the Great Purge, something like 9 million persons were arrested, including (1) all the surviving Old Bolsheviks; (2) the high and middle levels of the Communist Party, including the district level leaders and two members of the Politburo itself; (3) political suspects of various kinds; (4) members of the Soviet Transport Organization; (5) the top leaders of the Soviet Army (which Harrison Salisbury estimated to be about one-third of all high ranking officers); (6) technicians and specialists in industry; (7) foreigners within the Soviet Union and those citizens connected in any way with them; (8) national minorities within the Soviet Union; and (9) personnel of NKVD, etc.[192]

> What appears to have happened is that
> Stalin indicated to his chief of the secret
> police in the general categories he wished
> eliminated or decimated. In turn, it appears
> that the secret police were instructed to
> operate in some kind of bureaucratic order
> on the basis of "confessions" of guilt which
> would implicate individuals in alleged
> conspiracies to assassinate Stalin or otherwise
> overthrow Stalin's regime with foreign
> assistance. The method of gaining "confessions"
> was to exert extreme and especially sustained
> psychological and physical pressure to induce
> some form of admission of guilt from the
> prisoners and, in addition, to induce them
> to list as many other persons as possible
> allegedly implicated in the alleged plots.
> Most prisoners, under the techniques of
> terror available to the secret police,
> agreed to a form of confession and named
> other persons. The secret police then

proceeded to arrest those named; and a kind
of wild geometric progression of arrests
resulted, ramifying out far beyond any
narrow group of categories. Thus, despite
the public attention given to the major
trials of higher echelons of Soviet official
life, it developed a direct momentum and
memorable knowledge of the regime's capabilities
for terror.[193]

"By the end of 1936 a wave with and without subsequent trial was swamping the Soviet Union. The most distinguished old Bolsheviks were arraigned and executed in batches. Perhaps a formal trial was the only concession to their rank; for every one of these, hundreds and thousands of people simply disappeared into the prisons and labor camps of the secret police and thence all too often to the grave. No one really knew how it had all started, and certainly no one knew how it was going to end. Safety of a very uncertain kind lay in denouncing others, and so the gruesome immolation went on for two years."[194]

World War II came almost as a relief upon which the citizens of the Soviet Union caught their breath and felt a sense of intellectual liberation from the choking regimentation of terror and industrialization effort. One observed toward the end of Stalin's regime, however, that

> Where the stability of the regime
> is threatened, law goes out the window.
> No fundamental legal opposition is tolerated.
> Where real opposition is even suspected,
> it is dealt with by "suppression and the
> use of force." The Soviets have the
> delicacy at least not to call this law.
> Yet the line is not always easy to draw
> and the inherent conflict between law and
> force results in some strange paradoxes.
> The law punishes discrimination on the
> basis of nationality, yet the Ministry
> of the Interior removes and disperses
> whole national groups which have been considered
> insufficiently loyal--the Volga Germans,
> the Crimean Tartars, the Chechen and
> Ingush in the North Caucasus. Anti-
> Semitism is a crime in law, but Zionists
> are sent to labor camps as counter-revolutionaries.
> Legal guilt is purely personal, but political
> guilt may be avenged against relatives and
> friends.[195]

Today the legacy of legal abuse and a terrorist form of law enforcement persists: "The man who is brought to trial is as good as convicted.[196]

In the subsequent revolutions, except for the Chinese Revolution, this "Jacobian" Radicalism in the form of mass purges has become rather mild by comparison. Although in the Egyptian Revolution all parties were ordered to "purge themselves" to remove "corrupt elements" and general Naguib warned that "the most evil elements, extending to the very top, still remained untouched," Nasser disavowed any intention of vengeance.[197] Purge commissions were set up to investigate and supervise the corrupted officials, as a result of which about 800 civilians and about 100 military and police officers were removed, nothing compared with the scale or scope of the predecessors.

The element of terror and purge did also exist to some measure in the Cuban Revolution; yet neither the intention nor the scope resembled in any sense the ruthless and cruel purges of the past. However,

> On 12 January 1959, the shooting began. Seventy-one supporters of the Batista Government, mostly police officers, soldiers and spies, were executed by firing squads for crimes against humanity, after summary courts martial. United States Senator Wayne Morse appealed to Castro's men to postpone judgement until passions had cooled. The new Cuban authorities replied in effect that such summary justice was necessary if those who had suffered under Batista were not to take the law into their own hands and possibly lynch innocent people.[198]

There were more "Kangaroo Courts" to follow in which the defendants were charged and the assembled crowd usually gave its thunderous approval of their guilt.[199]

"Setting an example" is often used to justify summary judgements and executions, which may be viewed as the most effective way of maintaining the revolutionary momentum and minimize bloodshed. This is the purpose of the following statement expressed by Korea's Park soon after the military coup in 1961; the tone of the revolutionary terror in this is a long way from the great purges of the past.

> There are still persons found to be reverting to the past, being too deeply engrained in habits of injustice

> and corruption. Such persons must be
> punished severely for their malfeasance
> in the name of our people and for the
> future of the nation. Furthermore,
> those involved in injustice and
> corruption under the old regimes must be
> held responsible for the sake of our
> national spirit, though we may pity them
> personally. The surgical operation excising
> the injustice and corruption of the past
> must be carried out under the principle
> of "punishing one to set an example for
> the multitude" and on a priority basis.
> In the revolutionary period, this will
> have to be completed within the shortest
> time possible. It must be noted, however,
> that such measures are not intended to stir
> the emotions of the people or to oppress
> the general public. The basic aim of
> this surgical operation is to establish
> a basis for building a cooperative society
> which is bright, healthy, and democratic.[200]

Barrington Moore's observation on the use of coercion and terror reflects this singularly utilitarian" purpose in these Radical societies:

> Economic and social change that is
> not the spontaneous product of attitudes
> and social relationships widely prevalent
> throughout the society require terror and
> enthusiasms as their motive force. Whether
> spontaneous or forced, a rapid pace of
> change is likely to produce widespread
> human suffering. Hence the situation in
> which a socialist regime comes to power
> is crucial in determining the probabilities
> of terror, as is widely recognized in
> socialist writings. If the socialists
> are content to take over the situation left
> by their predecessors without making fundamental
> changes, relatively little terror may be
> needed.[201]

10. CONCLUSION

Two pertinent observations may be made at this point as concluding remarks:

(1) The key to the transition of a Radical society to a

Liberal society (the path of which is not entirely clear historically) is its reasonable mastery over technology. However, technology in itself does not guarantee the transition, for technology can be utilized in two separate ways: the "sovereign" way and the "utilitarian" way. The use of technology in the Soviet Union--at least a considerable portion of it--is strictly for the "sovereign" purposes, that is, in military hardware and armament rather than in the promotion of individual wellbeing, or in the "utilitarian" purposes. In the Liberal West, on the other hand, technology has been intimately tied to the corporate commercial structure which oversees its manufactury and distribution, thus directly linking technology to the "utilitarian" ends in each individual. Hence, while the level of overall technological mastery may be considered even in the Soviet Union and in the Liberal West, the former is still considered to be in the Radical stage of its social character development. How and when technological benefits (at least a majority of them) can be shifted to reducing human toil and increasing creature comfort in these Radical societies will determine their entry into the ideology and social character of the Liberal stage, or its socialist variations. The development of technological mastery for utilitarian purposes--although universally desired and attempted--is a tenuous and arduous premise for contemporary Radical societies, while such mastery and utility of technology are largely confined to the Liberal states of the West (and Japan) which underwent their respective Radicalization processes in the nineteenth century. It is for this reason that the future of the Soviet Union, when and if its technological emphasis shifts from "sovereign" to "utilitarian", is an intellectually and historically tantalizing topic of speculation. And,

(2) at the close of our discussion on the Radical type as an historic stage of human development between Traditional and Liberal stages, a mention must be made regarding the more or less "mutational" experiences of Fascism and Nazism as <u>special cases</u> of Radical type. Their expressed ideology is based neither on the Enlightenment nor on Marxism; yet their nationalism which forms the core of their supposed racial and cultural superiority is distinctively modernistic. The reason that the two phenomena represent special variations of the Radical theme is based upon the fact that (1) they performed the transitional role between Traditionalism and Liberalism by "reforming" the respective quasi-republics established after World War I. Their highly constitutional ideals notwithstanding, these republics were burdened with ineffectiveness and corruption, in common with many of our contemporary ex-colonies under a quasi-constitutional guise; (2) both Fascism and Nazism were characterized in their manifest ideology by many of the characteristics that we have just attributed to the Radicalization process, except possibly the absence of the egalitarian

spirit. In many respects, however, the two closely resemble other Radical regimes in their aims and methods, enough to classify them among the latter. What is suggested here regarding Fascism and Nazism is intended to incorporate them into our conceptual model of history, rather than to reinterprete them.

FOOTNOES

1. W. W. Rostow, The Dynamics of Soviet Society, op. cit., p. 130.

2. J. P. Nettl, The Soviet Achievement, Thames & Hudson, London, 1967, pp. 158-9.

3. P. C. Kuo, China: New Age and New Outlook, Alfred A. Knopf, New York, 1956, p. 18.

4. Ibid., pp. 24-5.

5. Ibid., PP. 36-7. (emphasis added)

6. Ibid., p. 118.

7. Ibid., p. 121.

8. Ibid., p. 119.

9. Ibid., pp. 31-2. (emphasis added) Mao's speech written to commemorate the 28th Anniversary of the Communist Party of China on July 1, 1949 titled On People's Democratic Dictatorship contains a passage that reads:

> On the basis of the experience of these twenty-eight years, we have reached the same conclusions that Sun Yat-sen, in his will, said he had drawn from "the experience of forty years." That is, "We must awaken the masses of the people and unite ourselves in a common struggle with those peoples of the world who treat us on a basis of equality." Sun Yat-sen had world outlook different from ours and he set off from a different class standpoint in observing and dealing with problems. Nevertheless, on the problem of how to struggle against imperialism in the 1920's, he reached this conclusion which was basically the same as ours.

On People's Democratic Dictatorship, Foreign Language Press, Peking, 1950, p. 10.

Tracing Mao's ideological origin, therefore, cannot be accomplished without taking the nationalist psychology of a long-oppressed nation by imperialism, although this point may be as futile and academic an exercise as tracing the Hegelian influence on Marx. For the latter, see Joachim Israel, Alienation From Marx to Modern Sociology, Allyn and Bacon, Boston, 1971, pp. 36-41.

10. P. C. Kuo, op. cit., pp. 123-4. This observation was made in

1956. However, the turn of the events since then only validates the nationalism-preoccupation of Communist China. In a broad historical perspective, this nationalism strongly coincides with Russia's "Communism-in-one-country" turnabout to give assurance that socialist (or Marxist) ideology was used well and served its function of abolishing the feudal order, which is at any rate the basic purpose of the Radical revolution. This point is treated here as a footnote, not because it is insignificant but because it is so obvious.

11. Leo Huberman and Paul Sweezy, *Cuba: Anatomy of a Revolution*, Monthly Review Press, New York, 1961, p. 145.

12. Quoted by Huberman/Sweezy, *Ibid.*; this is also the main thesis of C. Wright Mills's *Listen Yankee*, Ballantine Books, New York, 1960. Also consider Rene Dumont's remark in this connection that "socialism cannot put an end to underdevelopment by a purely political transformation," in *Cuba: Socialism and Development*, Grove Press, Inc., New York, 1970, p. 87.

13. Consider, for instance, Boris Goldenberg's observation that the Cuban version of "collectivization" patterned after the Russian "State Farm-Style" was not communistic at all, in Boris Goldenberg, *The Cuban Revolution and Latin America*, Frederick A. Praeger, New York, 1965, p. 221. Similar complaints are also found in other quasi-socialist states, e.a., Egypt, made by the orthodox Marxist quarters.

14. Ramon E. Ruiz, *Cuba: Making of a Revolution*, The MIT Press, Cambridge, Mass., p. 4. (emphasis added) However, we shall see more of the ephemeral role of ideological pronouncement as opposed to nationalist interest in the following pages.

15. Don Peretz, *The Middle East Today*, Holt, Reinhart & Winston, New York, 1963, p. 231.

16. *Ibid.*, p. 138. See also H. I. Katibah, *The New Spirit in Arab Lands*, published privately by the author, New York, 1940, for Arab nationalism prior to World War II.

17. Don Peretz, op. cit., p. 200-201.

18. A. G. Nasser, *Egypt's Liberation*, Public Affairs Press, Washington, D. C., p. 30. "Other forces" did not exist to the extent that the military did; the Wafd Party was inept in governance, the Muslim Brotherhood more religious than political, and the Communist and socialist faction virtually inactive.

19. Don Peretz, *The Middle East Today*, p. 225.

20. Compare Park's Administrative Democracy" with Nasser's "Guided Democracy."

> "The aim of our revolution was not to ignore the value of democracy but to lay a solid foundation for rebuilding true democracy. The characteristics of our actions and policies, in fact, are "democratic" even in this revolutionary stage because there is not tomorrow without today, and the future cannot exist without the present. In this sense, democratic factors must be implanted and developed among the general public as far as possible, now that the nation has entered the second and third stages of the revolution. For these reasons, the author believes that the democracy we aim to build in this revolutionary period should be the one that meets social and political reality, and not the unworkable West European democracy. This type of democracy can be termed 'Administrative Democracy.'" Chunghee Park, <u>Ideology of Social Reconstruction</u>, Dong-A Publishing Co., Seoul, p. 208.

21. Leonard Binder, <u>The Ideological Revolution in the Middle East</u>, John Wiley & Sons, New York, 1964, pp. 191-192. (emphasis added). The essential identity of democracy, nationalism, constitutionalism, and socialism as the general character of a twentieth century Radical government is of extreme importance to our thesis to merit a lengthy quotation:

> It is, perhaps, superflous to point out that there are important differences among democracy, nationalism, constitutionalism, and socialism. There is no reason why all four of these elements cannot coexist in a single political system, even as the Ba'th argue that all four will characterize the future of Arab state. There is, furthermore, something to the argument that <u>all four will be but facets of one and the same social reality</u>. While distinction among these four in a real state can be analytical only, they may be more reasonably separated from one another in discussing a theory and a

constitution.

Democracy is a system of government in which the people are the supreme authority for all official acts. While the people are taken as a whole, pure democratic theory postulates that ideally the will of all is the same as the will of each, given universal freedom, rationality and goodness. Theoretically individualism and social responsibility are reconciled in pure democratic theory. Nationalism insists upon the sameness of a certain group of persons and their difference from all others, whose distinctive character entitles them to a separate statehood. Nationalism also reconciles individualism and social responsibility by insisting that nationality determines interest, preference of political institutions, and modes of cultural expression. Nationalism does not, however, insist upon some manifest expression of the popular will as does democracy. Constitutionalism may be alternatively the principle of government under law or the limitation of governmental power. In relation to democracy, constitutionalism limits not only government but the operation of democracy itself. Insofar as the constitutional rules may provide for only periodic expressions of popular will, they also limit democracy, but in the interest of making it workable. Socialism involves not only public control of all economic activity, but also public ownership of the means of production, i.e., land and capital. Socialism postulates the identity of individual and collective interests once private property and private economic decision-making are eliminated. When the political is viewed as an aspect of the economic, socialism may become a necessary adjunct of democracy or nationalism.

If this brief explanation of these four exceedingly controversial concepts is accepted, it appears that the crucial assumption is that <u>the will of each individual is the same as that of the collectivity</u>. Insofar as the nation is comprised only of those who subjectively feel themselves to be its members, no theoretical problem arises. Ibid., pp. 187-188. (emphasis added).

Some concluding remarks may be necessary. If the above thesis is generally representative of modern political forms of governance, it may be positively asserted that the <u>social character types that are essentially post-feudalistic take up one or another of the above political forms, which means that anti-feudalism (in whatever variety) is the only underlying forces of modern revolutions</u>. The a priori presence of anti-feudal ideology (Enlightenment or Marxian) and industrial technology makes a deviation of all future revolutions from this formula almost entirely impossible. It is almost self-evident that to argue for human equality and dignity (either "individually" or "collectively") stands better to reason than to argue for feudalistic absolutism in which human equality and dignity are subsumed under tradition and/or the Divine Providence. Hence, the inevitability of Radicalization in our historical model.

22. This is certainly unfair considering the reform measures taken, massive economic plans launched, e.g., the Aswan Dam, and the absolute vote of popular confidence accorded Nasser in the election of 1958 which continued even after the 1967 defeat by Israel.

23. The regime also liquidated the Rightist Muslim Brotherhood which plotted against the new regime.

24. Anouar Abdel-Malek, <u>Egypt: Military Society</u>, Random House, New York, 1968, p. xxxiii. For his criticism in detail that the single-party policy is purely tactical rather than ideological, that "planning and statism are absolutely not synonymous with socialism," and that there is no deep rooted socialist ideology among the leaders and their policies, see <u>Ibid</u>., pp. 363-9.

25. Maxime Rodinson, "The Political System," in P. J. Vatikiotis (ed.), <u>Egypt Since the Revolution</u>, Frederick A. Praeger, New York, 1968, p. 111. Rodinson's observation must be considered in contrast with that of Malek quoted above:

> It may seem strange to those who, like the Americans, are convinced that democracy and Marxism are irreconcilable to see Egyptian Marxists defending with ardor during this period (this played an important historical role) both parlia-

mentarianism and the restoration of constitutional life. But this defense was free of Machiavellianism. It did not even necessarily reveal competition with other political groups. I am confident about these conclusions, having been myself in Cairo during this period in close touch and communion of mind with Marxist groups. The evolution of the regime, as far as problems of rule and authority are concerned, <u>would have been probably the same and along the same main lines had the Marxists been able to seize power.</u> But outside the Government, the Egyptian Marxists, as all Marxists in non-Communist States during this period, were advocating democracy and the free expression of the public will through the parties. They were evading the problems that would arise if they seized power in a country where the majority would refuse the Marxists solution. In that case it seemed conceivable to the Marxists that minority group expressing the unconscious or, if one prefers, the virtual or potential aspirations of the majority should be allowed to rule. But to them only the Marxist-Leninist ideology could express these potential aspirations. But the junta lacked this ideology and imposed on the people its own views: it followed thus a dictatorial and reactionary line. Ibid., p. 97. (emphasis added)

26. Hans Kohn, <u>Nationalism in the Soviet Union</u>, AMS Press, New York, 1966, pp. 11-2.

27. J. P. Nettl, <u>The Soviet Achievement</u>, op. cit., p. 176.

28. <u>Ibid.</u>, p. 167. See also Harrison Salisbury's popular <u>900 Days: The Seize of Leningrad</u>, for the patriotism, military purge, and especially the sacrifice made under the name of Russian nationalism, Avon Books, New York, 1970.

29. J. P. Nettl, op. cit., p. 188.

30. One salient point: American society began as a Radical type whose rhetoric came to be used in later Radical revolutions, even including the socialist ones. Hence the identity "Americanism" and socialist theme makes another socialist revolution not only theoretically superfluous but also practically unnecessary. This point was observed by Leon Samson in <u>Towards a United Front</u>, quoted in Seymour Martin Lipset, <u>Political Man</u>, Doubleday & Co., Garden City, New York,

1963, p. 346.

31. For the intellectual influence on the English Revolution, see Christopher Hill, The Intellectual Origins of the English Revolution, Oxford at the Clarendon Press, London, 1965, esp. pp. 266-75.

32. Brian Manning, "The Levellers," in E. W. Ives (ed.), The English Revolution, Edward Arnold (Publishers), London, p. 145.

33. Samuel R. Gardiner, The Constitutional Documents of the Puritan Revolution, op. cit., p. xiv.

34. Ibid., p. 2. Significantly, after a long struggle with the Parliament Charles I agreed to abide by this Petition, which was the first statutory limitation on his exercise of authority. See Ibid., p. xxiii.

35. Christopher Hill, The English Revolution, Lawrence & Wishhart, London, 1949, p. 8. The impact of this first historical change from pre-modern to modern periods, dramatized by the execution of Charles I, is reflected in the fact that hearing the news: "Women miscarried, men fell into melancholy, some with consternations expired" throughout England. Christopher Hill, The Intellectual Origins of the English Revolution, op. cit., p. 5.

36. This Bill of Rights was the basic text that bore the Universal Declaration of the Rights of Man adopted by the United Nations in 1948; the six members of the Soviet Bloc, Saudi Arabia, and the Union of South Africa abstained from signing the Declaration. Quoted in Hans Kohn (ed.), The Modern World, MacMillan Book Company, New York, 1963, pp. 306-11.

37. John Hall Stewart, A Documentary Survey of the French Revolution, MacMillan, New York, 1963, 106-9.

38. Ibid., pp. 142-3.

39. This Declaration may be thought in part derived from the American Declaration of Independence. However, the American revolutionary slogans cannot be compared with those of the French Revolution. See Martin Gohring, "Historical Significance of the Declaration," in Herbert H. Rowen (ed.), From Absolutism to Revolution, MacMillan, New York, 1967, pp. 190-3, for a stirring recapitulation of the Enlightenment via the Declaration.

40. Referring to the August 1789 Declaration considered above.

41. John Hall Stewart, A Documentary Survey, op. cit., p. 231. Cf., the Constitutional Bill of the first Parliament of the Protectorate written after the revolution in England.

42. The First Propagandist Decree, November 1792, Ibid., p. 381.

43. The Second Propagandist Decree, December 1792, Ibid., p. 384.

44. Karl Marx, "The Critique of the Gotha Program," Lewis S. Feuer (ed.), Marx & Engels, Doubleday & Co., Garden City, New York, 1959, esp., 118-20, for the socialist conception of establishing equality by practicing inequality: "From each according to his ability, to each according to his needs!"

45. Walter Russell Batsell, Soviet Rule in Russia, MacMillan Co., New York, 1929, p. 40. In 1977, the Soviet Union revised the Constitution without altering much of the basic content.

46. Ibid., pp. 43-44. It must pointed out that Batsell's thesis is that "any similarity is one of words and not of ideas." p. 40. See the following comparisons by Batsell, p. 45:

Rights of Man (Theory)	Practice in Russia
"Law is the expression of the general will."	Only the "laboring masses" have legal rights.
"All citizens...are equally eligible to all public dignities, places, and employments."	Communists are shown preference over all others. No fairly important official is a non-Communist.
"No man can be accused, arrested, or detained except in the cases determined by law and according to the form that it has prescribed."	Any person may be put to death on simple report of the political police (OGPU).
"The free communication of ideas and opinions is one of the most precious of the rights of man; every citizen then freely speak, write, and print, subject to responsibility for the abuse of this freedom in the cases determined by law."	The right of assembly is given only to the working class with consent of the Communist Party. The government controls all printing and thus precludes any non-Communist criticisms of its actions.
All the taxes shall be "equally apportioned among	The government levies high taxes on all private industry

all the citizens according in order to drive it out of
to their means." business.

47. Ibid., pp. 84-5. These articles are from No. 10, 13, 14, 15, 17, 20, 21, and 22, Chapter V: Of General Principles of the Constitution of the RSFSR. Also the Civil Code, November 11, 1922, Clause 4 declares that "....Sex, race, nationality, religion and birth shall have no bearing whatever in relation to legal status." Quoted in L. Haden Quest, The New Russia, Thornton Butterworth, Ltd., London, 1925, p. 93. The Communist Chinese Constitution also states that all citizens are equal before the law, and all their freedoms are guaranteed by the State.

48. Batsell, op. cit., p. 44.

49. V. I. Lenin, The State and Revolution, in Emile Burns (ed.), A Handbook of Marxism, Victor Gollancz, Ltd., London, 1935, p. 756. (emphasis original)

50. Richard Fagen, The Transformation of Political Culture in Cuba, Stanford University Press, Stanford, Calif., 1969, p. vi.

51. Leonard Binder, The Ideological Revolution in the Middle East, op. cit., p. 11.

52. Quoted in Rinehard Bendix, Nation-Building and Citizenship, op. cit., p. 91.

53. John Hall Stewart, A Documentary Survey, op. cit., pp. 506-13.

54. Christopher Hill, The Intellectual Origins, op. cit.; some, like William Harvey, however, still sided with the king.

55. Samuel R. Gardiner, The Constitutional Documents, op. cit., p. liii.

56. Ibid., p. 302.

57. John Hall Stewart, A Documentary Survey, op. cit., p. 168.

58. Crane Brinton, French Revolutionary Legislation on Illegitimacy, Harvard University Press, Cambridge, Mass., 1936, p. 19.

59. Ibid., p. 72.

60. John Hall Stewart, op. cit., p. 333. The Revolutionary regime in China enacted a similar divorce law in 1950 that made

women equal to men in all aspects; see S. Chandrasekhar, Communist China Today, Asia Publishing House, New York, 1961, pp. 78-82. In Russia a divorce law was passed in 1926 which made divorce much easier than its 1917 enactment; see J. P. Nettl, The Soviet Achievement, op. cit., pp. 109-10. Cf., the ERA movement in the United States in the 70's.

61. John Hall Stewart, op. cit., p. 514.

62. J. P. Nettl, The Soviet Achievement, op. cit., p. 110.

63. Maurice Hindus, Humanity Uprooted, Jonathan Cape and Harrison Smith, New York, 1929, p. 35.

64. W. W. Rostow, The Dynamics of Soviet Society, The New American Library, New York, 1954, pp. 107-8.

65. J. P. Nettl, The Soviet Achievement, op. cit., pp. 111-2.

66. Quoted in W. W. Rostow, The Dynamics of Soviet Society, op. cit., p. 108; see also Rene Fullop-Miller, The Mind and Face of Bolshevism, Alfred A. Knopf, New York, 1929, pp. 223-43.

67. J. P. Nettl, op. cit., pp. 109-10.

68. Maurice Hindus, Humanity Uprooted, op. cit., pp. 140-1.

69. Christina Harris, Nationalism and Revolution in Egypt, The Hoover Institution Publications, Stanford, Calif., 1964, p. 195.

70. Ibid.

71. Don Peretz, The Middle East Today, op. cit., p. 235; see also Leonard Binder, The Ideological Revolution in the Middle East, op. cit., p. 87, for the decline of religious influence in Egyptian life.

72. Naguib recalled in 1955 that "Although we (the revolutionary government) were preparing the ground for the establishement of a secular republic, we had no intention of dispensing with religion. Islam would continue to be the offcial religion of Egypt." Quoted in C. P. Harris, Nationalism and Revolution in Egypt, op. cit., p. 195.

73. Article 43; The Constitution of January 16, 1956.

74. Christina P. Harris, op. cit., pp. 206-7.

75. See Footnote #71 above.

76. Christina P. Harris, op. cit., pp. 210-1. The parenthical remarks are not original but taken from another paragraph in the same reference.

77. Ibid., p. 224.

78. Alice and Roy Eckardt, Encounter with Israel, Association Press, New York, 1970, p. 78.

79. Don Peretz, The Middle East Today, op. cit., p. 238. The introduction of a new currency, executed under complete secrecy until the moment of announcement by the Korean military regime in 1961, aimed at the same effect of freeing capital for industrial circulation. See Rashad El-Barawy, The Military Coup in Egypt, The Renaissance Bookshop, Cairo, 1952, pp. 227-34 for the Agrarian Reform Law.

80. Ibid., pp. 238-9.

81. Anouar Abdel-Malek, Egypt: Military Society, op. cit., p. 83. Cf., Stalin on liquidating the "kulaks": "We must smash the Kulaks, eliminate them as a class....We must strike at the Kulaks hard that they will never rise to their feet again." For the reasons for liquidating the Kulaks, see J. P. Nettl, The Soviet Achievement, op. cit., pp. 115-123. With this liquidation of a middle class peasantry the characteristic industrialization and rigidification of Russian life began under Stalin's iron dictatorship, which marked the end of one era and the beginning of another in Russian revolutionary history.

82. Rene Dumont, Cuba: Socialism and Development, Grove Press, New York, 1970, pp. 165-6, has the following observation:

> Along with this debatable suitability to local conditions of a socialist ideology that was not always perfectly understood, there is also the historic, ethnic, South American heritage that can often be described as underdevelopment. For Cuba, the terms misdirected, distorted, unbalanced, or disjointed development would seem to be more exact, for the sugar industry was not really behind the times. As for the capital with its deluxe tourist attractions, which once pumped dollars into the economy, its catering to the luxury tourist trade was overdeveloped; this stood in the way of austerity becoming a general practice even though it is indispensable for socialist development.
>
> The lack of precision and exactitude, both

in the way Cubans think and in the way they keep appointments, the absence of any predilection for true facts set down in exact figures, the lack of prestige of technical jobs, the expressions "momento" ("in a while") and "mañana" ("tomorrow") which crop up all too often in conversation are to be classed among the essential characteristics of this underdevelopment.

83. The propaganda illustration of collective farm, pointing to the benefits of pooling small individual holdings together, in J. P. Nettl, op. cit., p. 72, is a good explanation.

84. L. Huberman and P. Sweezy, Cuba: Anatomy of a Revolution, op. cit., p. 122.

85. Boris Goldenberg, The Cuban Revolution and Latin America, Frederick A. Praeger, New York, 1965, pp. 221-2.

86. L. Huberman and P. Sweezy, op. cit., pp. 123-4. Cf., Egypt's "guided democracy" and Korea's "administrative democracy." Huberman and Sweezy envision a Cuban version of democracy possible via "guidance" and "administration" by the State through cooperatives.

87. Ibid., p. 123. See Goldenberg, op cit., pp. 223-4 for a description of dramatic changes that took place in a cooperative within a year of its state control.

88. Joseph North, Cuba: Hope of a Hemisphere, International Publishers, New York, 1961, pp. 64-5.

89. Loree Wilkerson, Fidel Castro's Political Programs From Reformism to "Marxism-Leninism", University of Florida Press, Gainsville, Florida, 1965, p. 84. Land reform and other measures in China are essentially similar in method and character For the reform measures in China, see P. C. Kuo, China: New Age and New Outlook, op. cit., p. 167, pp. 173-88; for the changes in the first decade of agricultural and industrial development in the revolutionary China, see S. Chandrasekhar, Communist China Today, op. cit., pp. 34-75; for the Russian-styled First Five Year Plan, see New China Advances to Socialism, Foreign Language Press, Peking, 1956, pp. 79-101.

90. For example, Nasser's address at the opening meeting of the second session of the National Assembly, Cairo, November 12, 1964, pp. 22-3.

91. "Profits on the Kibbutz," Time, July 3, 1972, p. 40.

92. *Israel's 20th Year*, Government Press Office, Israel, 1968, p. 2, 54.

93. Chunghee Park, *Ideology of Social Reconstruction*, op. cit., p. 200.

94. For this shift of emphasis in both industry and agriculture, see Richard Fagen, *The Transformation of Political Culture in Cuba*, op. cit., pp. 122-7; Lee Lockwood, *Castro's Cuba, Cuba's Fidel*, MacMillan Co., New York, 1967, p. 87; Loree Wilkerson, *Fidel Castro's Political Program*, op. cit., pp. 47-8.

95. For caricatures of the "scientific management" fervor in Russia during this period, see Rene Follop-Miller, *The Mind and Face of Bolshevism* op. cit., p. 23; Lenin's complaining about "bad working habits" of Russian workers is described in V. I. Lenin, *Selected Works*, vol. II, International Publishers, New York, pp. 332-3; for poor management, see Anton Karlgren, *Bolshevist Russia*, George Allen & Unwin, London, 1927, pp. 104-5.

96. J. P. Nettl, *The Soviet Achievement*, op. cit., pp. 126-8. This legacy still lingers on today as revealed by the Jewish immigrants from Russian. "In some cases the cultural shock can be enormous," one Israeli official said: "We had one Russian tailor who set up shop near Haifa. After a week he ran to us in tears: 'You didn't send me my work quota!'" in "Exodus from the USSR," *Life*, August 11, 1972, p. 60.

97. J. P. Nettl, op. cit., p. 129.

98. *Ibid.*, p. 141.

99. Peter Schmid, *The New Face of China*, George E. Harrap & Co., London, 1958, pp. 164-5.

100. Dunkwart Rustow, *A World of Nations*, op. cit., pp. 108-9.

101. S. R. Gardiner, "Introduction" to *The Constitutional Documents of the Puritan Revolution*, op. cit., p. xiv.

102. Harold J. Laski, *Reflections on the Revolutions of Our Time*, The Viking Press, New York, 1943, p. 42.

103. John Hall Stewart, *A Documentary Survey*, op. cit., p. 789. Edward H. Carr mulls over the wisdom that all the social ills of our times may have been "caused" by the French Revolution as a historical epoch-making event, in *The New Society*, Beacon Press, Boston, 1951, p. 1.

104. John Hall Stewart, op. cit., pp. 785-6.

105. See Alexis de Tocqueville, *The Old Regime and the French Revolution*, op. cit., pp. 32-60.

106. John Hall Stewart, *A Documentary Survey*, op. cit., pp. 786-7.

107. *Ibid.*, p. 787.

108. *Ibid.*, pp. 787-8.

109. *Ibid.*, p. 788.

110. *Ibid.*

111. *Ibid.*, p. 789.

112. *Ibid.*

113. J. P. Nettl, *The Soviet Achievement*, op. cit., p. 23, 32, 44, 48-9, 57. See Michael Karpovich, "The Historical Background of Soviet Thought Control," in Waldemar Gurion (ed.), *The Soviet Union: Background, Ideology, Reality*, University of Notre Dame Press, Notre Dame, Indiana, 1951, pp. 22-3, for the opinion that Lenin's preference for revolutionary Marxism, while the libertarian and democratic tendencies could have been chosen considering the native impulse for popular revolution, was due to "an unusually strong authoritarian and dictatorial strain."

114. Rene Fullop-Miller, *The Mind and Face of Bolshevism*, op. cit., p. 223.

115. *Ibid.*, p. 185.

116. W. W. Rostow, *The Dynamics of Soviet Society*, op. cit., p. 109.

117. A. A. Smirnov, quoted in Raymond Bauer, *The New Man in Soviet Psychology*, Harvard University Press, Cambridge, Mass., 1952, p. 132; see also A. N. Leotiev, "The Present Tasks of Soviet Psychology," in Ralph B. Winn (ed.), *Soviet Psychology*, Philosophical Library, New York, 1961, p. 36.

118. Rene Fullop-Miller, op. cit., pp. 54-5.

119. Okeg Anisimov, *The Ultimate Weapon*, Henry Regnery Co., Chicago, 1953, p. 47.

120. *Ibid.*, p. 45. Although this episode shows how thoroughly the thought-molding process in Soviet Russia had been in the prewar years, it may be indicative of something very significant in an entirely different way: that is, the basic principles

and theory of the proclamation in the Soviet Constitution are not too different from the "libertarian" forms of constitutional documents, as discussed in Section 2 of this Chapter.

121. R. A. Bauer, A. Inkeles, and C. Kluckhohn, How the Soviet System Works, Harvard University Press, Cambridge, Mass., 1959, p. 31.

122. Ibid., p. 35.

123. W. W. Rostow, op. cit., p. 167.

124. J. P. Nettl, op. cit., pp. 240-2.

125. Quoted in P. C. Kuo, China: New Age and New Outlook, op. cit., p. 31. Cf., Stalin on the destruction of the Kulaks, Footnote #81 of this Chapter.

126. The thesis that the Great Proletarian Cultural Revolution was basically an anti-feudalistic movement rather than anti-bourgeoise one is obvious in that (1) the Chinese Revolution did not topple a bourgeois class in the first place; and (2) by the time the Cultural Revolution took place, the duality of feudalism (Traditional) and revolutionary ideology (Radical) was the socio-political characteristic of new China, not the duality between socialists and bourgeosie.

127. Ibid., pp. 85-6.

128. Ibid., p. 91.

129. This was observed a decade before the Cultural Revolution.

130. Ibid., pp. 115-6.

131. Theodore H. E. Chen, Thought Reform of the Chinese Intellectuals, The Oxford University Press, London, 1960, p. 159; see also Colin Mackerras and Neale Hunter, China Observed 1964-1967, Thomas Nelson, Melbourne, Australia, 1967, pp. 118-21, 57.

132. Theodore H. E. Chen, op. cit., p. 66.

133. Ibid., p. 79.

134. C. Mackerras and Hunter, op. cit., p. 119.

135. Hugo Partisch, Red China Today, Quadrangle Books, Chicago, 1966, pp. 184-5.

136. Theodore Chen, op. cit., pp. 60-1.

137. Ibid., p. 70. For some examples of the "confessions," see pp. 185-8 and the list on pp. 209-11.

138. Hugo Partisch, op. cit., pp. 305-8.

139. Peter Schmid, The New Face of China, op. cit., p. 157.

140. Ibid., p. 159.

141. Hugo Partisch, op. cit., p. 307.

142. Ibid., p. 306. For the use of psychological research concerning "labor psychology" and "political thought work," see Robert Chin and Ai-li Chin, Psychological Research in Communist China: 1949-1966, The MIT Press, Cambridge, Mass., 1969, pp. 110-2.

143. Richard Fagen, The Transformation of Political Culture in Cuba, op. cit., p. 1.

144. Ibid., pp. 1-2. (emphasis added)

145. Ibid., p. 3. (emphasis added)

146. Ramon E. Ruiz, Cuba: The Making of a Revolution, The University of Massachusetts Press, Cambridge, Mass., 1968, p. 141.

147. Richard Fagen, The Transformation, op. cit., p. 3.

148. Ibid., p. 10.

149. Quoted in Elizabeth Sutherland, The Youngest Revolution, Dial Books, New York, 1969, p. 93.

150. Ibid., p. 102.

151. Ibid., pp. 139-40.

152. Ibid., pp. 140-1. (emphasis added)

153. Chunghee Park, Ideology of Social Reconstruction, op. cit., p. 212. (emphasis added)

154. Ibid., p. 6.

155. Ibid., p. 229. (emphasis added)

156. Richard Fagen, "Mass Mobilization in Cuba: The Symbolism of

Struggle," in *Journal of International Affairs*, vol. XX, (November 2, 1966), p. 257.

157. Quoted in Erick R. Wolf, *Peasant Wars of the Twentieth Century*, Harper & Row, Publishers, New York, 1969, p. 157.

158. V. I. Lenin, "Call To Action," in Hans Kohn (ed.), *The Modern World*, op. cit., pp. 202-3.

159. Quoted in P. C. Kuo, op. cit., p. 53.

160. Theodore Chen, *Thought Reform*, op. cit., pp. 51-2.

161. *Ibid.*, pp. 52-3.

162. Quoted in J. Halcro Ferguson, *The Revolutions in Latin America*, pp. 145-6.

163. Quoted in Loree Wilkerson, *Fidel Castro's Political Programs*, op. cit., p. 53.

164. Huberman and Sweezy, op. cit., pp. 93-4. (emphasis original)

165. W. W. Rostwo, *The Dynamics of Soviet Society*, op. cit., p.97.

166. David Wilson, "Nation-Building and Revolutionary War," op. cit., pp. 93-4.

167. *Ibid.*, p. 92.

168. Note again that no two Radical revolutions occur in the same country.

169. P. C. Kuo, op. cit., pp. 26-9.

170. Gamal Abdul Nasser, *Egypt's Liberation*, Public Affairs Press, Washington, D. C., 1955, pp. 32-4.

171. Joseph Schumpeter, *Capitalism, Socialism and Democracy*, Harper & Row, New York, 1962, pp. 216-7.

172. Reinhard Bendix, *Nation-Building and Citizenship*, op. cit., p. 215.

173. Richard Fagen, *The Transformation of Political Culture*, op. cit., p. 4.

174. *Ibid.*, p. 55.

175. *Ibid.*, p. 69.

176. Richard Fagen, "Mass Mobilization," op. cit., pp. 260-1.

177. Richard Fagen, The Transformation of Political Culture, op. cit., p. 89.

178. Ibid., pp. 106-7.

179. Ibid., p. 137. "Schools for the training of Party and other cadres did not, however, disappear with the closing of the EIR." Ibid.

180. J. P. Nettl, The Soviet Achievement, op. cit., p. 198.

181. See Sami Hadawi, Israel and the Arab Minority, Arab Information Center, New York, 1967, pp. 3-12, 17-20, 36-40; Sami Hadawi, Bitter Harvest, The New World Press, New York, 1967, pp. 238-40, 244-6; Israel's 20th Year, op. cit., p. 56; Alice and Roy Eckardt, Encounter with Israel, op. cit., pp. 10-2, 20, 114-9, 123-4, 236-237; Joseph Dunner, The Republic of Israel, McGraw-Hill, New York, 1950, pp. 159-70; Don Peretz, The Middle East Today, op. cit., p. 151, 191, 231-3; Maurice Samuel, Light on Israel, Alfred A. Knopf, New York, 1968, pp. 108-9, 111; Norman Bentwich, Israel Resurgent, Ernest Benn, Ltd., London, 1960, pp. 177-80, for charges and countercharges as well as pertinent facts about the conflict.

182. John Hall Stewart, A Documentary Survey, op. cit., pp. 409-10.

183. Referring to the "federalist" counter-revolutionary movements especially prevalent in the provinces.

184. Referring to the Order for the Establishment of Watch Committees, March 1793.

185. Referring to the law on the organization of registry offices.

186. A 1792 provision concerning the "common lands" to which the lands of the emigrés belonged.

187. John Hall Stewart, op. cit., pp. 477-8.

188. Vladimir Petrov, "Aims and Methods of Soviet Terrorism," in Waldemar Gurion (ed.), The Soviet Union, op. cit., p. 138. Much of this section is based on Petrov's good accounts of Soviet terror.

189. L. Haden Quest, The New Russia, op. cit., p. 87. (emphasis added)

190. *Ibid.*, pp. 132-3.

191. Quoted in W. W. Rostow, op. cit., p. 105. However, by the mid-30's Pashukani's theory was repudiated.

192. *Ibid.*, p. 106.

193. *Ibid.*, pp. 56-7.

194. J. P. Nettl, *The Soviet Achievement*, op. cit., p. 148.

195. Quoted in W. W. Rostow, *The Dynamics of Soviet Society*, op. cit., p. 106.

196. "Criminal Procedure: The Comrades & Their Courts," in *Time*, October 2, 1964, p. 118.

197. Gamal Abdul Nasser, *Egypt's Liberation*, op. cit., pp. 34-5, 59. Nasser abode by his pledge; when his relationship with Naguib ended in a bitter power struggle the resulting punishment for Naguib was merely "house detention."

198. J. Halcro Ferguson, *The Revolutions of Latin America*, op. cit., p. 129.

199. See Joseph North, *Cuba: Hope of a Hemisphere*, op. cit., especially the chapter titled: "You Had Your Nurenberg," pp. 36-42.

200. Chunghee Park, *Ideology of Social Reconstruction*, op. cit., p. 211.

201. Barrington Moore, Jr., *Terror and Progress USSR*, Harvard University Press, Cambridge, Mass., 1954, p. 173.

CHAPTER FIVE: LIBERALISM AS IDEOLOGY AND SOCIAL CHARACTER

1. LIBERALISM AS IDEOLOGY

The central thrust of the post-feudal mentality of man in the West may be simply and clearly characterized as liberalism, whose period of maturation as a theory ranges from Thomas Hobbes's appalling description of human nature to the apocalyptic-optimistic prediction of human future by Karl Marx (to be discussed later). The basic political thesis of liberalism from Hobbes to Locke and to Mill can be seen in what C.B. MacPherson called "possessive individualism," in which the competitive and "appetitive" human nature come to an anarchic (as Marx later described it) conflict and ensuing social control. One result of this "competitive" individualism, which was certainly antithetical to whatever the Middle Ages aspired to, as we have seen, was the legal and social justification of property as the main expression of that very individualism. This classic notion of liberalism can be summarily stated as follows:

(1) Human freedom consists of one's independence from the "will of others."

(2) Such independence means "freedom from any relations with others except those relations which the individual enters voluntarily with a view to his own interest."

(3) The individual is "essentially the proprietor of his own person and capacities, for which he owes nothing to society."

(4) "Although the individual cannot alienate the whole of his property in his own person, he may alienate his capacity to labor."

(5) Human relations can be summed up as a series of market relations.

(6) Independence from the will of others as the condition for freedom entails that "each individual's freedom can rightfully be limited only by such obligations and rules as are necessary to secure the same freedom for others." And

(7) Political society is a human contrivance for the protection of individual property and the maintenance of orderly market relations between individuals.[1]

Hobbes has presented the starkest nature of the market relations among individuals in terms of their value and the honor of that value, via strength, intelligence and knowledge: Essentially,

> The value, or WORTH of a man, is as of all other things, his price; that is to say, so much as would be given for the use of his power: and therefore is not absolute; but a thing dependent on the need and judgment of another. An able conductor of soldiers, is of great price in time of war present, or imminent; but in peace not so. A learned and uncorrupt judge, is much worth in time of peace; but not so much in war. And as in other things, so in men, not the seller, but the buyer determines the price. For let a man, as most men do, rate themselves at the highest value they can; yet their true value is no more than it is esteemed by others.[2]

The basic assumption of possessive individualism coincides with the structure of a market society, in which a man's freedom from the will of others reduces him to a series of market relations with fellow men whose strength and urge to gratify their desires are about equal to his own. For Hobbes,

> The model of the self-moving, appetitive, possessive individual, and the model of society as a series of market relations between these individuals, were a sufficient source of political obligation. No traditional concepts of justice, natural law, or divine purpose were needed. Obligation of the individual to the state was deduced from the supposed facts, as set out in the materialist model of man and the market model of society. The model contained the two suppositions of fact which Hobbes thought sufficient for the deduction of right and obligation: equality of need for continued motion, and equal insecurity because of equal liability to invasion by others through the market. The system, both mechanical and moral, was self-moving and self-contained. It needed no outside mover or outside standard of right.[3]

The right and obligation based on the presumably fair relations among equal individuals inevitably led to the rhetoric of individual property, a manifest fact of that very equality, and of libertarian political toleration. This was true among the radical Levellers during the Civil War and in the liberal political philosophy of Locke. Freedom in this case was contingent upon individual possession, which ultimately became the cornerstone of Western liberalism, and its other political and social implications went far beyond the western sphere of influence. Although theoretically the assumption of possessive individualism was independent of industrial development, its basic tenets became the desired, if not the intended, ideology of industrial technological states in the following centuries. The Levellers "saw that freedom in their society was a function of possession. They could therefore make a strong moral case for individual freedom by defining freedom as ownership of one's person."[4] This conception of equal rights and freedom presupposed the existence of a naturally balanced distribution of rights and individual rationality, which, by this very postulate, resulted in class differentiations between "natural" haves and have-nots. The triad of individualism, property and political liberty in Western societies, in the meanwhile, has functioned to serve the process of modernization, extending citizenship to lower classes and granting generally more expressive political, social and cultural exercises by them.[5]

Individualism as formulated by the thinkers of the Enlightenment and social contract theorists as well as by the proponents of modern technology has undergone a metamorphosis in two stages, that is, Radical individualism and Liberal individualism. For a Radical society, individualism is essentially an ideological device to demolish feudal (and quasi-feudal) political order of social relations, while in a Liberal state it is a resulting material condition of industrial technology. The former indicates liberation from ideological shackles whereas the latter indicates that from material wants. A Liberal state, as defined here, is one in which both the ideological and material conception of individualism is re-arranged and re-ordered in one stable and continuous social pattern of relations and a characterology appropriate to that setting. The changes in individualism are thus a function of industrial technology that transforms rhetoric into material reality. Liberalism is basically a materialist ideology in its world outlook and behavioral manifestations, science, technology and industrial rationality of managerial variety serving the model of Liberal epistemology.

Our model of historical development so far has been based upon two basic factors: namely, (1) the egalitarian, anti-feudal ideology in both Enlightenment and Marxian forms, and (2) the presence of industrial technology, universally accepted as the next logical step toward a "better" society.

Modern historical development in any given society has evolved, or will evolve, around these two central themes. Our main task has been that of constructing a model based upon this empirico-logical observation and inference. We have also seen that the process of the Radical break consists largely of struggle, rhetoric and planning--around the theme of equality and economic development through industrial technology. Liberalism is essentially the only historico-logical sequence to that development, given the premises that (1) all men are created equal; and (2) industrial technology transforms man's innate equality into reality.

The Liberal state is thus defined by a reasonable measure of political stability and technological distribution on a permanent scale. The process of the emergence of Liberalism thus follows a successful political transformation by various means and ways as we have seen, and full use of industrial technology as the dominant mode of national production. Obviously, a relatively stable political system, either Western Parliamentarian or monolithic one-party control, and a reasonably well distributed income per capita will have to enter our definition of a Liberal state. This simplified definition of Liberalism leaves, of course, much to be desired, e.g., the role of GNP in this connection.[6] Political stability refers not only to the form of uninterrupted continuity and consistency, but also to those qualities that are fundamentally post-feudal regardless of the specific forms and the variety of methods employed. An increase in individual wealth and in general social well-being brought about by industrial technology, thus, necessarily presupposes a political reconstruction of the ideology and corresponding social character of the given society as the essential preceding factor for Liberalism. It is only with this historical development that we may speak of the Traditional-Radical-Liberal sequence as the logical outgrowth in our inquiry.

That Liberalism is a logical outgrowth of, and sequential to, Radicalism is not difficult to see. For the ideological and characterological expressions of Liberalism are already embodied in the rhetoric of Radicalism and given the physical utility and development of available industrial technology, the rhetoric in time is translated into reality to form a distinctive thought and action pattern--that is, Liberalism. We have insisted that history may be viewed in terms of the modal epochs, modern and pre-modern, and the "Radical break" from Traditionalism (or that which embodies whatever pre-modern ideology and social character) makes for the historical distinction. After the break, the only task that remains to be done is a logical follow-up, given the empirical grounds for collective welfare. Liberalism is, hence, the <u>lived</u> reality of the Radical rhetoric. This turn of event entails its particular ideological and characterological ramifications that are distinctive enough from those of Radicalism to warrant a separate classification as Liberalism.

2. LIBERALISM AS SOCIAL CHARACTER

In considering the prevailing social character traits in Liberal personality, certain general (and generalizable) characteristics emerge, which is true in the modal behavior of most societies that we can identify as Liberal states. One of the most characteristic features of Western liberalism is that its Radical phase is exceedingly short in duration. Liberalism as an insurgent ideology--that in the American, English, and French Revolutions, and now possibly in Northern Ireland--promptly turns into a conservative liberalism as soon as the action objective has been achieved. Once the absolutist feudal social order is dismantled, liberalism is unable to remain an insurgent ideology very long simply because there is no more objective to be accomplished, which would justify further organization of individuals. As will be discussed later, liberalism has been replaced in general by socialism as the insurgent creed. In its historical composition, contemporary welfare liberalism stands somewhere between the Radical liberalism of the eighteenth-and nineteenth-century, and the utopian liberalism of contemporary American society. At the heart of the transformation from Radical liberalism to welfare liberalism lie the utilitarian functions of technology and the subsequent rise in living standards, which also increase the size of middle class and the range of its civil liberty. The interaction, and balance, between libertarian politics and utilitarian technology is the most telling summation of contemporary welfare liberalism.

Political liberalism is thus a balanced state of affairs between the rhetoric and the realization of classic liberalism, steadily butressed by technological utility that characterizes its life style. The individualist notion of freedom and equality is advanced against the rationally and collectively determined needs of sovereign reality. This definition of sovereign reality in Liberal state is heavily colored by its traditional elements in daily perception and class interests in economic relations. These two factors serve as the brake in the utopian interpretation of the Liberal creed, although the traditional and class factors may be gradually undermined by the essentially egalitarian basis of technological mobility and bureaucratic rationality. Western European nations including Canada and Australia, and Japan find it impossible to advance their liberalism beyond this point of balance, checked by the historical residues of tradition and class interests. Free from these two factors, for example, the United States has been able to forge a utopian interpretation of liberalism in its social commitment and behavioral ramification. These Liberal nations define the liberal creed as the object of human aspiration, but not necessarily as the object of daily practice in reality; they confront the liberal process of social relations and politics necessarily within the limitations of collective reality. In doing so, the sovereign state occupies a legitimate place in the management of collective affairs.

In theory, the liberal individual possesses no biographical history; each person is considered complete in and of himself without the restrictions placed upon him in his relations with others. His association with others is solely determined by the survival necessity of his person and the exchange value that his person brings into the market system of human relations. The economic premise of individual freedom is insured by the simple fact that their survival capacity, therefore their worth, is evenly distributed among them. There is no ascriptive social history, no artificial bondage, and no predetermined recognition in the liberal person that he is obliged to uphold in the determination of his person. The Liberal state is, for the reasons of tradition and class interests, however, quite incapable of assuming and practicing this pure notion of liberal man. The residual historical past is such that no liberal state is completely free from its impact on present modes of social structure and human relations. Economic as well as intellectual disparity among members within a liberal state is taken as a given, though not desirable, part of its reality.

The extent to which the egalitarian notion is balanced in a political liberal state, partly hampered by tradition and class interests, is determined primarily by the extent of industrial technology in use; this technological utility is one singular factor that also differentiates the Liberal state from the Radical state, although the extent of its utility is not as extensive as in the post-Liberal state--the United States. The rather wide use of technology facilitates a certain degree of personal freedom from undesired relations with one another and from excessive physical toil; yet the desire for social freedom is greatly counterbalanced by traditional ties and class interests, while the commercial limitations on technological utility tend to impede the formation of extensive physical inertia. Social norms are considerably relaxed and deviation from public norms much tolerated, to the extent that such relaxation or deviation does not jeopardize the sovereign state itself. The soap-box tradition in Great Britain may be an appropriate illustration of this delicate balance in its political relations. This balance between the libertarian creed and the legitimacy of collective imperative generally characterizes the political behavior in Liberal society.

The classic formulation of liberalism assumes that man is a perfectable being, given the appropriate social structure and human relations. Under this assumption, a purist interpretation of liberalism requires that the social structure and human relations must be reflective of this perfectability. Perfection is considered an immediate reality rather than an ideal state of things that men may aspire to. Liberal states find themselves unable to adhere to this pure notion of human perfectability in their domestic organization as well as sovereign behavior. While professing considerable aversion to absolutism and rigid social control, they nevertheless admit defects in human reason and conduct. Their domestic as well as sovereign conduct reveals the conviction of human fallibility; rarely do they display a doubtful state of mind in moral decisions and in the choice of action open to them. Their way of goverenance and human relations reflects the simple principle that men are given to mistakes and mischiefs, viewed from the individual as well as sovereign perspective, including the moral and philosophical implications entailed by such mistakes and mischiefs. Neither the state nor the individual demands perfection from each other in their interaction. A reasonable degree of imperfection is taken into consideration in their governance and human relations. Internal as well as external affairs are managed on the basis of such imperfection, and to some extent they learn to live with it.

Implicit in the notion of human imperfection is also the way the individual and society interact with each other. The basically constitutional and libertarian mode of public administration is quite far removed from the rigid style of social control in Radical society, yet the notion of individuality is rarely allowed to obstruct public concerns. When confrontations occur between individual and social order in criminal justice, for example, the latter is rarely sacrificed to promote individual freedom. The protection of individual rights is considered only within the domain of public safety. Punitive measures are certainly not the predominant mode of criminal justice in Liberal society, unlike the Radical type. Nevertheless, criminal justice does not vacillate between the two polarities of public safety and individual liberty. Having learned to live with human imperfection, social justice is maintained on the basis of managerial practicality rather than ideal perfection. The process is predictably swift and certain, entailing the reality of human fallibility that they are prepared to accept. The sovereign state as the depository and dispenser of social justice exists neither as a totalitarian organ for social control nor as an extraneous public nuisance as in post-Liberal society. The Liberal state strives for a balance between totalitarianism and sovereign powerlessness. Public bureaucracy and commercial industry tend to come under the sovereign sphere of influence but half free and half determined; they are neither completely immune from the influence of sovereign politics nor completely dictated by it.

This state of balance characteristic of Liberal society, facilitated by industrial technology, is in considerable part contingent on the reduced conflict in global relations. Doctrinaire proclamations may be gradually replaced as the predominant national rhetoric by the pragmatic spirit of cooperation among nations. The sense of predictable life style brought about by political stability and industrialization makes the conflict theme of human relations rather inappropriate. Peace and tranquility, though limited, gradually replace the crisis-and-conflict mentality in global relations. Although never taken lightly, the military institution is reduced to the optimum level. Stable and at times thriving economic development makes armed adventures not only undesirable but also unnecessary. Since this variety of liberalism already contains provisions for human fallibility and imperfection, sovereign setbacks in diplomacy or even in limited armed conflict may even be accepted in stride; when and if armed conflict is inevitable, the liberal state views it from an exclusively practical perspective, relatively free from the utopian notion of human ideals for peace and harmony. Generally, Liberal men are neither war enthusiasts nor idealistic pacifists; they perceive war and peace as exclusively human affairs subject to the usual follies and moral righteousness. They are neither totally committed to a life of conflict like Radical men, nor absolutely oblivious to the nature of human conflict like the utopian liberals in post-Liberal America. There is an implicit understanding among Liberal societies that both a total commitment to conflict and a total negation of it are equally wrong in the interpretation of war and human conflict. War is to be considered strictly as a matter of global reality for self-defense and survival, nothing more or nothing less.

Barring international wars or economic disasters of catastrophic dimension, these Liberal nations are bound to move steadily but surely in the direction of greater political freedom in the liberal Enlightenment and greater physical freedom in industrial technology. Whether, however, the future for Liberalism is to become a replica of the ideological and behavioral form of contemporary American society is yet unknown, although the factors of tradition and class interests may play the balancing role in slowing (if not preventing) this historical development. In order to become a post-Liberal society, which is the logical alternative available to the Liberal stage, Liberal society must be history-less in its individual biographies; its tradition-and class-burdened social structure and human relations must be completely replaced by a fundamental variety of egalitarianism and technological mass production in order to envision the development of such a personality. A purist interpretation of classic liberalism and utilitarian technology is possible only in this historical milieu which has characterized the American setting. As long as the remnants of tradition and class interests continue to function as a potent determinant of human behavior in Liberal states, their ideology and social character will be suspended in this state of delicate, and at times uncertain, balance between ideal and reality, and between human follies and perfectability.

3. CHALLENGE FROM SOCIALISM: THE DECLINE OF LIBERALISM AS IDEOLOGY AND SOCIAL CHARACTER

To understand the "socialist" challenge to Liberalism as the new ideology for social change, it is essential that we recapitulate the very theoretical and practical foundations of the Liberal doctrine in the West. The following is that recapitulation, which should lead to the reasons for the emergence of socialism as the new ideology and social character especially in the Third World.

I. In what is known as the Modern Era, two major political theories have emerged to represent two varieties of human perception, international relations, and the future of man itself. They are the Enlightenment-originated liberalism and Marx-originated socialism. As C. Wright Mills observed,

> Since the Russian Revolution and the consolidation of the soviet bloc, the encounter of liberalism and marxism has become a world encounter of nation-states. In political fact, the communist variety of marxism, seated in the soviet bloc, is now the leading form of marxism. In political fact, the North American variety of liberalism, seated in the United States, is now the leading form of liberalism.[7]

To furthur simplify the ideological landscape, it can be stated that the political world is now divided into the two main camps of political and economic interest. In politics, liberalism insists on individual freedom; socialism insists on the collective management of human welfare. In economics, liberalism defends the virtues of 'free enterprise' in which each individual seeks his fortune by whatever talent he may possess; socialism advocates collective control of resource and distribution, and the elimination of individual competition. Against each other, they fight wars in battlefield; they debate at the United Nations; they compete for political and economic advantages and dominance; and they defend their respective ideologies with guns and rhetoric.

Viewed from a broad historical perspective, both liberalism and socialism have contributed to the coming of the Modern Era, from absolutism to democracy and from religious domination to secular rationality. In this making of the modern world, "Both liberalism and socialism have been insurgent creeds: in their several varieties they have been the rhetoric of movement, parties and classes on the road to power."[8] As insurgent creeds, both have been committed to the basic notions of freedom and equality, and to human reason. In both rhetoric and action, however, liberalism and socialism have been fundamentally opposed in the methods of achieving freedom, equality and reason: liberalism of the West has been committed to the natural way, and socialism of the Soviet bloc to the social way. Nature and society, as the pivotal theme in Western intellectual development, represent the fundamental tension in political theory, in economic relations, and in individual perception of reality.[9] Following a recapitulation on these origins of nature-liberalism and society-socialism, we shall also discuss how the very theoretical elements of the two ideologies bear upon the practical affairs of the Third World nation-states as systems of thought and action.

II. The origin of Western liberalism may be traced to the fall of the Middle Ages, and more concretely to the Copernican Discovery, the Reformation and the Renaissance, among other events.

It was articulated in the eighteenth century theories of society by men of the Enlightenment, which in the following century gradually acquired the broad framework of liberalism. Despite its national and theoretical varieties, liberalism continues to be the rhetorical as well as the practical backbone of Western civilization.

It was with the Enlightenment, however, that liberalism first became the spokesman of 'nature,' 'natural man,' and 'natural society.' As a political movement in revolution and as a theory of free economic relations, liberalism sought to expose the unnatural and irrational forces of the feudal system. Human nature was thought good, and any artificial control of it evil. Rousseau's oft-quoted passage precisely reflected this sentiment: "Man is born free, and yet everywhere he is in chains"[10] At the heart of the Enlightenment rhetoric--'Back to Nature', 'Natural Rights', 'Laws of Nature', 'Equality', 'Freedom'--stood the idea that social control with all of its oppressive implications was evil and nature good. Alexander Pope's praise of nature is typical of this notion:

> Thus then to man the voice of Nature Spake--
> "Go, from the Creatures thy instructions take:
>
> "Thy arts of building from the bee receive;
> "Learn of the mole to plough, the worm to weave;
>
> "Mark what unvary'd laws preserve each state;
> "Laws wise as Nature, and as fix'd as Fate."[11]

The notion of Nature became a 'benign' concept in the age of the Enlightenment, and human relations and social institutions as organized in society were viewed as unnatural and evil.. As Crane Brinton pointed out, "Class distinctions, the etiquette of society, the privileges of clergy and nobles, the contrast of slum and palace...were unnatural."[12] Further, the concept of natural order and natural law "was made the acid test of the legitimacy of the existing order of government and society. If an institution worked badly because of privileges, prejudice and tyranny, it was regarded as artificial. Hence, it was to be abolished, and a new, enlightened one established based on natural law."[13] In essence, the lineage of nature-Enlightenment-liberalism derived from the twin notions of freedom and equality, in which the individual was to define his course of action and pursue his happiness with (or without) other individuals in the process.[14]

Liberalism as the ideology of natural man, and more specifically as the standard theoretical justification (though somewhat modified) for the political and economic relations that now prevail in the West in liberal-capitalism, entails the following assumptions and ramifications. As indicated earlier, this paper argues that the very emergence of ideology of social man--that is, socialism--owes itself to such liberal assumptions and ramifications.

LIBERAL ASSUMPTIONS: Implicit in liberalism is the assumption that the work of nature in all things, including man, is 'fair' and 'random'. The notion of fairness and randomness implies its denial of any 'artificial-unnatural' rules of human relations which make some persons superior or inferior to others. Subject only to the fair and random work of nature, man is responsible only to his own person and his possessions entailed in the person. The total value of the person is entirely endowed by nature, and determined by its fair and random system of endowment, not by arbitrary rules imposed on men by society. As such, the person's nature-endowed value must be the sole criterion of his relations (or no relations) with others. It is the individual talent, and the worth derived from such talent, that determines his bargaining position in society in an open, competitive market. In this process, the social rules should not artificially and arbitrarily interfere with the work of nature on men, which should be determined freely and openly. There is to be a perfect balance in human relations, the liberal doctrine holds, because nature knows no prejudice or bias in endowing each person his share of talent which is to be equal to that of other person. Within this system of natural relations, each person defines the sphere of his freedom and individuality, unhampered by the arbitrariness of tradition, a dogma or faith contrary to reason and freedom, and nature.[15]

LIBERAL RAMIFICATIONS: Liberalism as a doctrine of nature and natural man entails within it a built-in contradiction--although not necessarily the Marxian notion of contradiction--while effective as a theory of governance and social relations in the making of a post-feudal world. The contradiction in liberalism is revealed when the supposedly free and equally endowed persons begin to form a new superior-inferior relationship in their social and political transactions which the liberal doctrine seeks to destroy in the first place.[16] If the work of nature is indeed fair and random, the new system of superiority-inferiority between _haves_ and _have-nots_ should not take place at all considering the assumptions of the even-handedness of nature, the universal endowment of human reason, and the open market, the new division between those who are _favored_ and those _disfavored_ by nature--which is actually a replica of the feudal system--proves to be the fatal weakness of the nature theory of social relations. In theory, each person's capacity and his worth should be more or less equal to that of any other person, and their ensuing social relations should reflect this equality of personal values, both in the person and in his property. In practice, however, the liberal doctrine of fair and random nature does not take into account the existing social structure for governance and human relations which is quite contrary to the assumed evenenss of men's affairs with fellow men; it turns out that in a liberal society of free competition it is _not_ the

177

work of nature (sometimes called the work of God), but the work of _men_, that determines the relative freedom and equality of each person in society. This process normally takes place in the following manner.

At birth, each individual confronts a set of pre-determined qualities and identities which exists prior to his coming into this world: family fortunes or misfortunes, relative positions in class/status allocation, abundant or scarce opportunities for success in life. Such qualities and identities the infant confronts are not the fair and random work of nature as liberalism defines, but a deliberate work of men against other men. An infant born a Rockefeller already entails a set of future possibilities entirely different from an infant born into a welfare family, although no one planned their respective births deliberately so that one goes to wealth and the other to welfare. While the process of conception is entirely the fair and random work of nature, what follows the conception is already beyond nature's hand. The Rockefeller baby may receive abundant attention and care during the pregnancy and at birth, while the welfare baby may never enjoy such amenities. What emerges after birth is even more unfair and unequal as the two respective infants face different fortunes and opportunities for success in life. Although fairly and equally conceived by nature, the Rockefeller and welfare infants have already been socially predetermined for their mutual relations so that the former is infinitely superior to the latter without the benefit of the free market competition to determine their respective capacities and worths. In short, some persons are born with a 'silver spoon, and others with a welfare identification number. Within this predetermined social structure which defines their social relations, they must stand with each exactly in that relationship.

III. Presented with this dilemma, many liberal theorists either avoided or defended the man-made differentiations specifically associated with property relations. Among the inconsistencies of John Locke, a classic liberal defender, for example, was that he recognized "the differentiation in his own society, and read it back into _natural_ society. At the same time he maintained the postulate of equal natural rights and rationality"[17] Although the early liberals were critical of the feudal system and the social inequalities it maintained, they defended by omission as well as commission the nature-created inequalities in social relations. And as an intrinsic component of natural inequality, private property represented the individual differentiations. As the Schwendingers have observed, "In the development of a classical liberal concept of man, social inequalities predicated upon the private ownership of property were perceived as being natural."[18] While assuming the free flow of social contract among men, liberalism "never understood, was never able to fully admit, that freedom of contract is never genuinely free until the parties thereto have equal bargaining power. This, of necessity, is a function of equal material condition....The idea of liberalism, in short, was historically connected in an inescapable way, with the ownership of property."[19]

The logical limitations inherent in the naturalist conception of equalitarianism which characterized the liberal doctrines from Hobbes to J. S. Mill contained the dilemma of having to exclude non-property owners from the category of rational, capable individuals who could participate in the political processes and social discourses as equals. The major tenets of this naturalist conception of human equality, i.e., individualism, property ownership and political toleration, thus invariably applied only to those naturally-endowed with personal fortunes. While assuming the emergence of a completely equal and free society, and its corresponding individual relations within it as modeled after the work of nature, liberalism failed to achieve both the nature-modeled equal and free social relations and a theory of mutual obligation in order to compensate for the loss of social cohesion resulting from the liberal practice.[20] In the eyes of the critics of nature-liberalism, formulating an ideology that could eradicate the logical defects of liberal tenets became necessary. Out of this liberal discrepancy between its natural theory and its unnatural practice emerged the theoretical foundations of socialism as the theory and practice of **society** and **social man**. Historically, the rise of the theory of socialism coincided with the theoretical defects of liberalism in the nineteenth century; the rise of the practice of socialism coincided with the practical decline of liberalism in the twentieth century.

Marxian socialism, in a nutshell and in contrast to liberalism, negates that the work of nature is fair and random, simply because its practical results contradict its theoretical designs. Where a system of governance and social relations totally free of inequality is expected in theory, it only results in a system bitterly divided between those well endowed by nature and those deprived by it. What is wronged by **nature** must therefore by righted by **man himself**. Those who are naturally deprived, constituting the have-nots, must be socially compensated for. Whereas **natural means** for equality results in inequality in a class-divided society, **social means** must provide complete equality among men regardless of their nature-endowed individual talent or its deprivation. Individuals must not be left to the whims of nature and their fateful meaning in social relations.

This transition of political theory from nature-originated liberal competition which results in inequality to the society-originated Marxian scheme of managed equality, is clearly stated in Marx's "Critique of the Gotha Program".[21] On the occasion of the 1875 Gotha Congress, uniting the two German socialist parties, Marx defined the notion of equality in socialism by way of critically examining the wordings of the occasion. Of particular interest in this context is Marx's analysis of the phrase "equal

Right" which appears in"...the proceeds of labor belong undiminished, with equal right, to all members of society," which refers to the method of distributing collective proceeds in a supposed socialist state. Marx examined the notion of 'equal right' in the sense that the "individual producer receives back from society-- after the deductions have been made--exactly what he gives to it." In this, "a given amount of labor in one form is exchanged for an equal amount of labor in another form." If equal right implies that each individual recives <u>his share</u> of the total social production, as his own labor contribution has created the total proceeds, according to Marx, it is still <u>bourgeois right</u> in that "The right of the producers is proportional to the labor they supply." What appears to be a fair way of distribution turns out to be an unfair practice, if one person is capable of supplying greater labor than another and is thus subject to a greater reward in return. This discrepancy results from the differences in men's individual physical attributes, some better endowed than others. As Marx describes it:

>This equal right is an unequal right for unequal labor. It recognizes no class differences because everyone is only a worker like everyone else, but it tacitly recognizes unequal individual endowment and thus productive capacity as natural privileges. <u>It is, therefore, a right of inequality, in its content, like every right</u>. Right by its very nature can consist only in the application of equal standard; but unequal individuals are measurable only by an equal standard in so far as they are brought under an equal point of view, are taken from one <u>definite</u> side only, for instance, in the present case, are regarded <u>only as workers</u>, and nothing more is seen in them, everything else being ignored. Further, one worker is married, another not; one has more children than another, and so on and so forth. Thus, with an equal performance of labor, and hence an equal share in the social consumption fund, one will receive more than another, one will be richer than another, and so on. To avoid all these defects, right instead of being equal would have to be unequal.

Although Marx views this unequal distribution as 'inevitable' in the early stages of socialism with the maturity of its development the method of distribution is also to be transformed. It is in this transformation of the method of equal distribution--from the naturalist-liberalist method to the managed one of socialism-- that the most fundamental differences between the ideology of nature and that of society crystallizes. In the liberal theory of equal distribution--and the entire notion of just social relations-- rests on the assumption that the nature-endowed (or nature-deprived) individual capacity in a series of open market transactions. The individual capacity which can be transformed into a valuable commodity thus acquires a corresponding value in the possessor's social relations. Social justice in a liberal society is insured by the fact (1) that such open market transactions in determining the form of social relations are entirely free of artificial and arbitrary rules; and (2) that the work of nature is endowing each man his share of talent is totally fair and random, which must result in a universally even distribution of such talent in every man.

The Marxian socialist theory of equal distribution, countering the liberal doctrine, recognizes that this nature-determined equality in economic distribution in liberalism is both theoretically and practically unworkable in insuring social justice for every member of society, as the "Critique" above illustrates. The socialist strategy which emerges from this recognition is that the unevenness of liberal-naturalist distribution of talent can be made even by establishing a notion of equal distribution from the society's end, rather than from the individual's end. That is, instead of determining social justice according to each person's talent or lack of it which is supposedly the work of nature, which results in inequality, his society or whatever acting in the capacity of his collective representation determines social justice by insuring that every member's economic needs are justly met regardless of his ability for the initial contribution to total production. Hence the Marxian formula: "From each according to his ability (nature-given or -deprived), to each according to his needs (socially determined)." The transformation of social justice from ability to needs is at once the core of socialist theory and the strategy for its economic justice, as an alternative to liberal theory.

IV. Many nations in the category commonly known as the Third World--nations nominally outside the West and the Soviet bloc--have acquired their independent statehood after World War II and made at least a formal transition to the modern era. The popular usage of the term 'Third World' connotes the peculiar ideological structure of these new nation-states, which implies that they are neither liberal-capitalist nor socialist in their definitions of politics and economics.

One of the most pivotal events in shaping the socialist tendencies is the success of the Soviet experience, which seems to point to the possibility of rapid development within a relatively short period of time by applying massive centralization. According to Horowitz:

> The development of Russia more nearly approximates the obstacles faced by developing areas in the modern world. Here, too, was a backward nation with uneducated, illiterate peasantry. Here, too, there was an imbalance between the agricultural and the industrial

sector. And here, too, there was a heavy investment of foreign capital in those areas which, prior to the revolutionary buildup, had already been subject to some degree of industrialization. Hence, it should occasion little wonder that the developing areas of the Third World would be magnetized--perhaps even hypnotized--by the Soviet model.[22]

Among the Third World nations, Goulet similarly observed, "Widespread admiration exists for the development achieved by the Soviet Union within forty years: a huge feudal society has become a world economic, industrial, scientific, military, and political power. The Soviet performance has made them think that rapid success is possible."[23] Along with the Soviet demonstration lies the perceived ineffectiveness of the liberal-capitalist doctrine for development as the adequate ideology for development. They reject "the capitalist method as slow, inefficient, and unsuited to their conditions. It is their view that rapid economic growth can only be attained by 'socialist' methods, although the precise meaning of this socialism is rarely defined in detail"[24] What are, then, some of the heuristic advantages of adopting socialism in these new nations, as opposed to adopting liberalism, advantages that are extraneous to their respective ideological doctrines on politics and economics?

The heuristic advantages of socialism, therefore its attractiveness to the Third World, can be identified in the following four categories:

(1) <u>Socialism is relatively clear of the 'colonial sins' (being essentially a newcomer in international mercantile history) while liberalism is not</u>. Most of the newly-independent nations have a history of colonial rule under Western powers which are now the predominant liberal-capitalist states. What was once a perfunctory or courteous relationship between new nations and their former rulers have increasingly turned into bitter accusations for the latter's past exploitations and what seems to be their continuing economic dominance. It is only an expected outcome that in this anti-liberal-capitalist conflict, the Soviet Union should preserve the image of a viable alternative. As the criticisms mount, the Western liberals find themselves increasingly defensive and apologetic about their colonial past.[25] In the world balance of power, the colonial experience has had, and will continue to have, a profound impact on the shift of ideological alliance. With old colonies now becoming independent states in all continents, it is highly unlikely as a historical trend that these new nations will take up the political theory of their colonial rulers. In denouncing liberal theory, socialism stands as the only established alternative.

(2) <u>For sheer logic of explanation for the state of the world, socialism contains greater clarity than liberalism</u>. It is no accident that the type of liberal democracy that prevails in the

West today is generally accepted and practiced only in relatively advanced and industrialized nations with sizable middle classes. In liberal theory, one has to be economically independent to insist on his freedom to dictate the needs or non-needs for his relations with other persons. One can remain completely isolated from others only when he is economically independent, if the liberal doctrine is to be literally practiced. The Third World nations find the liberal doctrine--which assumes an equal presence of economic independence through a fair and random work of nature--utterly incongruent with their political and economic reality. In the minds of the new leaders the liberal theory of naturally-determined distribution of equality seems to bear no relevance. From their perspective, the masses must be fed, clothed and educated, and in this, the liberal rhetoric of nature, private property and political toleration provides little, if any, explication for the current state of things. Although socialism itself provides only a marginal guide to such social action, its emphasis on collective method can lay the basic foundation from which rationale for social action can be derived.

(3) <u>Socialism is far more effective as rhetoric than liberalism for justifying centralized administration and economic planning</u>. One of the more compelling and practical reasons for the appeal of socialism lies in the necessity of state control for most of the political and economic institutions. The political and economic theory of liberalism negates state control, while socialism provides justification for centralization. Although the issue of centralized economy remains controversial, the underdeveloped nations attempt to solve their organizational needs by centralization of resources and institutions. The growth of different industrial sectors must be controlled, trade deficits minimized, and long-term economic plans established.[26] Often, the regime finds it profitable to nationalize foreign-owned corporations and capital. While such radical actions may not lead to actual national development, they can certainly more easily be justified in the name of the 'masses,' and 'proletariat,' or 'national liberation' than of the liberal doctrine. Finally,

(4) <u>Socialism has greater persuasive power than liberalism to compel men to action and sacrifice</u>. Socialist theory is also a theory of action. The rhetoric of socialism can extract extremely fundamental loyalties from its followers, of which little can be observed in today's liberal counterpart. Socialism provides a theory of history with its own logic, thus assigning each person his pre-determined role in the world drama. As such, the average socialist can perform tasks many times more arduous than what can be expected of a liberal believer. Even under the most difficult of circumstances, the socialist partisan can concentrate on who the enemy is, how to struggle to destroy him, and why socialist triumph is inevitable. For a faltering new nation, the liberal theory of natural social relations is capable of none of such vital functions necessary to the nation's organization and survival. Liberalism succeeds as a theory of social action only where there

is a sizable middle class and a good deal of potential upward mobility among those less fortunate to the ranks of middle class. Prolonged organization requiring single-minded dedication and sacrifice for years, decades, and centuries, if necessary, is simply impossible within the premises of liberal theory. Hence the advantages of the socialist doctrine to these nations in the Third World.

V. The ascendance of socialism in the new nations coincides with the decline of liberalism. The gradual decline of liberalism in its classic mold since the beginning of this century can be attributed to several mutually enforcing currents of social change. First, the expanding and free-roaming political and economic relations, especially true in the United States, which contributed to the validity of liberal theory in practice, ceased to be so with World War I. The United States closed its frontiers and its immigration flows; nations rushed to protective tariffs and nationalist restrictions on free trade; and world markets lost their openness by unwarranted competition. In this, the liberal theory of society which "requires and assumes a friendly universe of equal and open opportunities" declined with such illiberal changes.[27]

Second, the ascendancy of technological instrumentality and the "cult of efficiency" obliterated much of the emotive and rhetorical force inherent in ideology, courting what Daniel Bell termed "the end of ideology." World realities are translated into non-ideological technical problems which can be solved by technical means, without the inflammatory (and essentially functionless) ideological rhetoric. In this, according to Bell's contention, both liberal and socialist theories have lost their values.[28]

Third, there is the rise of corporate capitalism, and with it the individualist character of classic liberal economic theory has declined. Instead of the independent and free farmers and small businessmen, a mass of white collar workers grace the contemporary, economic landscape. In economic and political centralization, and in the consolidation of resources into corporations and bureaucracies, individualism which is the essence of liberalism has lost its meaning. Corporate capitalism has made the application of old classic theories of politics and economics confusing and somewhat obsolete; it is neither liberal-capitalist nor state-capitalist. In this confusion and obsolescence of the conventional frameworks, liberal theory functions no longer as the explanatory reference point of modern political and economic behavior.[29]

Finally, and most significantly, the decline of liberalism as the dominant rhetoric of the West, which began half a millenium ago, may signal the end of the natural era in human history. This liberal exercise in political and economic relations may turn out to be a brief interlude between the society era of the Middle Ages and the coming era of collective economy and centralized political life, the latter of which is being spearheaded by the Third World nations. It will indeed be an intellectual challenge to ponder the eventual changes that would confront the current liberal states when their liberal-naturalist experiment in social relations has finally ended. For the ideology of nature whose time has passed must be replaced by the only remaining alternative--that is, the ideology of society.

FOOTNOTES

1. C.B. MacPherson, *The Political Theory of Possessive Individualism* op. cit., pp. 263-264.

2. Thomas Hobbes, *Leviathan*, Collier Books, New York, 1971, p. 73.

3. C.B. MacPherson, op. cit., p. 265.

4. *Ibid.*, p. 266.

5. Reinhard Bendix, *Nation-Building and Citizenship*, op. cit., pp. 74-104.

6. See for example the ranking of national power by GNP in Herman Kahn, "Uncertain Road to the 21st Century" in Richard Kostelanetz (ed), *Beyond Left and Right*, op. cit., p. 342, in which Kahn places India and Canada (Traditional and Liberal states, respectively) on the same scale.

7. C. Wright Mills, *The Marxists*, Dell, New York, 1962, pp. 15-16. Mills rightly observed that "There is of course no one liberalism and no one marxism." p. 15.

8. *Ibid.*, p. 19.

9. The nature-society dichotomy is a more familiar concept in social psychological theories, e.g., Freud's *id* and *superego*, G. H. Mead's *I* and *me*, and Herbert Marcuse's characterization of human history simply as a conflict between "nature and society."

10. Jean-Jacques Rousseau, the first sentence of *The Social Contract*.

11. Alexander Pope, as quoted in Mulford Sibley, *Political Ideas and Ideologies*, Harper & Row, New York, 1970, p. 386.

12. Crane Brinton, *The Shaping of Modern Thought*, Prentice-Hall, Englewood Cliffs, New Jersey, 1963, pp. 109-110.

13. J. Salwyn Schapiro, *Liberalism: Its Meaning and History*, D. Van Nostrand, Princeton, New Jersey, 1958, p. 17.

14. For a comprehensive discussion on nature and man as an intrinsic component of Western intellectual theory, see Howard Becker and Harry Elmer Barnes, *Social Thought From Lore to Science v. II*, Dover Publications, New York, 1961, pp. 423-57.

15. A handy reference to the United States as the first genuine natural-liberal society is found in Arhur A. Ekirch, The Decline of American Liberalism, Atheneum, New York, 1973, pp. 22-23, and Hans Gerth and C. Wright Mills, Character and Social Structure, Harcourt, Brace & World, Inc., New York, 1953, pp. 464-67.

16. On the role of Natural Law as a revolutionary creed, Julia and Herman Schwendinger observed: "During the precapitalist period..., natural law relationships were also involved by revolutionary writers. Since it was assumed that natural law relationships were independent of human conventions, seventeenth and eighteenth century scholars relied on this basic assumption whenever they claimed that monarchies oppressed an individual's right to live naturally. Since, in their eyes, natural law was more valid than aristocratic (i.e., 'man made') law, natural law standards were used to justify the overthrow of monarchical regimes." Julia and Herman Schendinger, "Sociologists of the Chair and the Natural Law Tradition," The Insurgent Sociologist, v. III, Winter 1973, p. 5.

17. C. B. MacPherson, op. cit., p. 269.

18. Julia and Herman Schwendinger, op. cit., p. 6.

19. Harold Laski, The Rise of Liberalism: The Philosophy of a Business Civilization, Harper & Brothers, New York, 1936, p. 9.

20. C. B. MacPherson, op. cit., pp. 271-277.

21. Karl Marx, "Critique of the Gotha Program," as appears in Marx and Engels, Lewis S. Feuer (ed.), Doubleday, New York, 1959, originally translated by the Foreign Language Publishing House, Moscow. (Emphases are original.)

22. Irving Louis Horowitz, Three Worlds of Development, Oxford University Press, New York, 1966, p. 131.

23. Denis Goulet, The Cruel Choice, Atheneum, New York, 1975, pp. 28-9.

24. Paul Sigmund, "Introduction," to The Ideologies of the Developing Nations, Paul Sigmund (ed.), Frederick A. Praeger, New York, 1964, p. 12. Characterizing the kind of political process in modern Russia and other later emerging nations as 'socialist' is a matter of both practical and theoretical considerations based on the logic and experience of the nature-society dichotomy. If one is justified in identifying the competition and differentiation of 'natural man' as a theoretical concept, and further if a parallel could be at least

conceptually drawn between liberal-capitalism and this competitive and anarchic state of nature among differential power possessors, then it can be argued that the term socialism could be rightly applied to an orderly, positive system of human control by society for controlled distribution of social justice. Hence the theoretical justification for the Soviet model among the Third World nations. For the convergence of 'democracy,' 'nationalism,' 'constitutionalism,' and 'socialism' as one overriding ideology in the Third World nations, see Leonard Binder, The Ideological Revolution in the Middle East, op. cit., pp. 187-8.

25. For a short, comprehensive discussion on the United States and the Third World, see Ralph Stuart Smith, The United States and the Third World, U. S. Department of State, Washington, D. C., 1976.

26. See Barrington Moore, Social Origins of Dictatorship and Democracy, Beacon, Boston, 1966, p. 410, and Leonard Binder, op. cit., p. 9, for the needs of centralized authority in underdeveloped nations.

27. Hans Gerth and C. Wright Mills, op. cit., pp. 466-9.

28. Daniel Bell, The End of Ideology, 2nd ed., Collier Books, New York, 1962, pp. 393-407.

29. Andrew Hacker, The End of the American Era, Atheneum, New York, 1973, especially pp. 38-76; also see C. Wright Mills, White Collar, Oxford University Press, New York, 1956, pp. 3-59.

CHAPTER SIX: POST-LIBERAL SOCIETY AND ITS IDEOLOGY AND SOCIAL CHARACTER

1. UTOPIA AND POST-LIBERAL AMERICA

Now our basic contention that in contemporary American society we find of our world ideology and social character types is primarily based on the observation that the post-Liberal state is a logical extension, given the ideal formulas and technological means available, of historical development since the Radical transformation. The post-Liberal state, being contingent upon the two conditions, must be sought in the most advanced of all Liberal states. This post-Liberal stage may also be conceived of as the future frame of human affairs into which all current Liberal nations will be entering. It is in this sense of historico-logical supposition that contemporary American society is taken as the prototype of all future post-Liberal states. The oft-mentioned uniqueness of American characterology is simply that American society is the only human society that has attained the desired aims of the Enlightenment and industrial technology without much difficulty, unlike its European or Oriental counterpart. Thus, the uniqueness consists of the fact that the two universally desired human goals have been achieved in the United States with unprecedented speed and ease, owing to the physical circumstances which favored such a development.[1] It is empirically valid and logically sound to suppose that when the formulation of the Enlightenment ideals and the implementation of industrial technology reach their full and sustained maturity, which is no sheer fancy, our ultimate historical development will be toward this post-Liberal state via the Radical break, the Radical transformation and the Liberal state.

For America, the rhetorics of the Enlightenment began with the Revolution which has since become the unchanged policy for its governance and human relations. American political theory, then, has always been one or more variations on the same Radical rhetoric of the Enlightenment. Hence, the effort by some to radicalize America has therefore been futile and superfluous. America experienced the Radical transformation once and for all through the political break with England, which rendered the effort for America's re-Radicalization entirely redundant and unworkable.

In an increasing effort to account for the failure of socialism to take root in American society, Leon Samson has suggested that an important cause has been that Americanism is a political ideology with much the same value content as socialism. It endorses the progress of the society toward the more equal distribution of privileges that socialism demands. As a result,

> the rank and file members of American labor unions have
> not had to look for an ideology that justified the changes
> which they desired in the society.[2]

This Radical strain of American political and social thought is also seen in that

> When Americans celebrate their national heritage
> on Independence Day, Memorial Day, or other holidays
> of this sort they dedicate themselves anew to a nation
> conceived as the living fulfillment of a political doc-
> trine that enshrines a utopian conception of men's e-
> galitarian and fraternal relations with one another.
> In linking national celebrations with political events
> and political creed, the United States resembles such
> other post-revolutionary societies as France, the Soviet
> Union, or many of the new states. Nations whose author-
> ity stems from traditional legitimacy, on the other hand,
> tend to celebrate holidays linked with a religious tra-
> dition or a national military tradition, not with a
> political doctrine as such.[3]

The continuity of American thought basis resting upon Radical formulations and proclamations, and upon achieving a reasonable level of technological maturity, is essentially the central theme of understanding world history. American uniqueness (mainly consisting of its phenomenal success) must be seen in its fundamental similarity with the Radical and Liberal states which share the ideological and material basis of its social structure.[4] Many other "urbanized, industrialized, and capitalist" societies may vary in their "status systems, their political institution, parent-child relations, and so forth," which sets apart the pattern of American behavior as differentiated, having been exposed to no feudal past, and to the egalitarian strain of political thought from the beginning of its history. Yet,

> It may be argued that the entire Western world
> has been moving in the American direction in their
> pattern of class relationships, family structure, and
> "other-directedness," and that America, which was <u>de-
> mocratic and equalitarian before industrialization</u>,
> has merely led the way in these patterns. Thus, at any
> given time, the differences between America and much
> of Europe may have remained constant, but this difference
> might have represented little more than a time lag.[5]

According to Hans Kohn's observation, America has remained a "branch from the same tree" of English culture, like Canada and Australia.[6]

Among other heritages of English origin, the puritanical idealism and the infinite faith in human perfection, stemming from the

Enlightenment, have become the backbone of life and thought in American that is highly utopian in its conception and puristic in its aspiration.

> Blending with other ideologies, and modified by experience and environment, the puritan philosophy has formed an important part of that fundamental agreement of mind and purpose by which the United States has played its peculiar role in the modern world. The democratic creed of the Declaration of Independence formed a platform on which the insurrectionary colonies took their common stand. Interwoven as it was with economic and psychological motives...it has through American history been invoked whenever in times of crisis, such as the Civil War and the two World Wars, it has been necessary for Americans to mobilize their spiritual resources and find a common path amidst diverse and conflicting interests.[7]

The utopian character of contemporary American society was deeply molded by puritanism that coincided with egalitarian and industrial ideology. "It was expected of the puritan that he should clearly be distinguishable from other men by the perfection of his righteousness and piety, and by his uncompromising allegiance to the supreme good."[8] It was only one step away from this to conceive of the infinite perfectibility of man, so characteristic of the Enlightenment, and to a great extent, of Marxism, an offshoot of that rational-libertarian idea. This utopian preoccupation on human perfection in America was clearly, and not without optimism, observed by Tocqueville.

> In proportion as castes disappear and the classes of society approximate, --as manners, customs and laws vary, from the tumultuous intercourse of men, --as new facts arise, --as new truths are brought to light, --as ancient opinions are dissipated, and others take their place, --the image of an ideal but always fugitive perfection presents itself to the human mind. Continual changes are then every instant occurring under the observation of every man: the position of some is rendered worse; and he learns but too well that no people and no individual, how enlightened so ever they may be, can lay claim to infallibility: the condition of others is improved; thence he infers that man is endowed with an indefinite faculty of improvement. His reverses teach him that none have discovered absolute good, --his success stimulates him to the never-ending pursuit of it. Thus, forever seeking, forever falling to rise again, --often disappointed, but not discouraged, --he tends unceasingly towards that unmeasured greatness so indistinctly visible at the end of the long track

which humanity has yet to tread.[9]

One resulting consequence of utopian conception on human equality was the strange phenomenon of alienation among individuals, subsequent to failures of perfection and the competing mentality toward the fullest state of man's greatness. This loss of the sense of reality and an historical understanding of that reality reflected in daily life was made famous by David Riesman in the middle of the twentieth century; but as early as 1830s such a tendency in American characterology was observed by Harriet Martineau.

> (Americans) may travel over the world, and find no society but their own which will submit to the restraint of perpetual caution, and reference to the opinion of others. They may travel over the whole world, and find no country but their own where the very children beware of getting into scrapes, and talk of the effect of actions upon people's minds; where the youth of society determine in silence what opinions they shall bring forward, and what avow only in the family circle; where women write miserable letters, almost universally, because it is a settled matter that it is unsafe to commit oneself on paper; and there elderly people seem to lack almost universally that faith in principles which inspires a free expression of them at any time, and under all circumstances....[10]

One sardonic modern observer asked "why do Americans behave like Americans?" and offered the following account as the answer:

> As is well-known outside America, Americans lack souls. This makes them even simpler to understand. It makes them both simple and simple-minded. (Souls are notoriously correlated with complexity, and therefore with higher mental development.) It is therefore unnecessary to go below the surface to learn about Americans, because most of them only live on the surface. Being so simple and superficial, Americans thus create a uniform, superficial culture and civilization, based on standardization and mass production. They fear being different from their fellows. Consequently, few deviations from a standard pattern of family life ever occur.[11]

Against Riesman's thesis that proposed the character changes that have taken place since the colonial times, from tradition to other-directedness, Seymour Martin Lipset maintains that the distinctive "American" character traits, e.g., mistrust of authority, equalitarianism, "other-directedness," a value system unique in American society, etc., have always remained virtually the same, deeply embodied in the basic make-up of American psyche since the Independence.[12] The issue of the basic American character can be viewed from two different perspectives, that is; (1) American social character has remained fundamentally unchanged, for the ideal values and "social ethic" since the inauguration of the nation, or in short the Radical ideology of libertarian Enlightenment, have served the function of shaping the initial forms of political governance and of human relations. These values and ideals have only slightly been modified and altered by the technological ascendency; if equalitarianism was part of the basic American ideological system, technological abundance has only contributed to extending that ideology in reality, and (2) the change in American social character may be described and discerned validly <u>within</u> the frame of the basic ideological commitments, i.e. equality, human dignity, individualism, political toleration, etc. Obviously, Riesman's characterological typology is empirically sound and significant, insofar as it tells us the degree to which the basic character change in America has taken place within the pronouncement and proclamation of the Radical break. In this connection we already mentioned previously that it is the Radical break from Traditionalism that constitutes a fundamental change in history, and that the transition from Radical to Liberal, and to post-Liberal stages is merely a logical follow-up, given the existence of human ideals (Enlightenment and/or Marxian) and industrial technology. Viewing from this perspective, it is sociologically valid to assert that American character type has changed since the initial stage of the nation, but <u>not</u> from tradition-directedness as Riesman supposes, but from the Radical stage, and that within that Radical commitment America has moved from Radical to Liberal, and to post-Liberal stages in its character formation.

As the culminating point of this historical development, the post-Liberal ideology has created a powerful myth of human equality which entails numerous ramifications in political governance and in human relations, peculiar to this character type. David Potter observed that

> The myth of equality held that equality exists not merely as potentiality in the nature of man but as a working actuality in the operation of American society--that advantages or handicaps are not really decisive and that every man is the architect of his own destiny. It asserted the existence in the United States of a classless society, where no one is better than anyone else and merit is the only recognized ground of distinction. Despite their patent implausibility, these ideas received and still retain a most tenacious hold. Americans are notoriously unresponsive to the concept of class warfare, and American workers, while fully alert to the protection of their economic interests, have never accepted identity as members of a working class in the way in which workers in England and other countries have.[13]

Margaret Mead has made a similar observation on this post-Liberal conception of human equality: "the assumption that men were created equal, with an equal ability to make an effort and win an earthly reward, although denied by every day experience, is maintained every day by our folklore and our day dreams."[14]

We must now explore further some of the theoretical and actual ramifications of this egalitarian thesis in contemporary American society, one manifestation of post-Liberal ideology and social character.

2. THE FORMATION OF POST-LIBERAL IDEOLOGY

Ralf Dahrendorf observed that among the industrial societies America is the only country "in which there are many who believe that Utopia can come true."[15] With the utopian ideals already in formulation, this general persuasion comes about only as a result of technological maturity blended with the existing utopian ideals. The possible convergence of East and West is in important part the work of technological maturation.[16] The supra-ideological character of technology was succinctly observed by Jacques Ellul.

> Concerning the technique of human relations (it) is as true of a socialist as of a capitalist society. "Socialist rivalry" is only a psychological tool to force men to work harder. The effort to integrate man into large-scale enterprises is not restricted to capitalism; it stems from technical investigations which are universally valid. The most that can be said is that under capitalism psychological techniques are concentrated on the problem of integrating the individual into private enterprise. Under socialism they are more generalized.[17]

The utopian conception of post-Liberal ideals, including democracy and freedom, is exclusively tied to the maturity and sustenance of industrial technology, and this explains why the post-Liberal imparting of democracy, American style, almost always fails in nations with very little industrial technology.[18] One major concern of modern societies is thus integrating the democracy-conscious populace to its actual working. In Edward H. Carr's words:

> The problem of political organization in the new society is to adapt to the mass civilization of the twentieth century conception of democracy formed in earlier and highly individualistic periods of history. The proclamation by the French Revolution of popular sovereignty was a serious challenge to institutions which had grown up under quite different auspices and influences.

It is no accident that Athenian democracy, which has been commonly regarded as the source and exemplar of democratic institutions, was the creation and prerogative of a limited and privileged group of the population. It is no accident that Locke, the founder of the modern democratic tradition, was the chosen philosopher and prophet of the eighteenth-century English Whig oligarchy. It is no accident that the magnificent structure of British nineteenth-century liberal democracy was built up on a highly restrictive property franchise. History points unmistakably to the fact that political democracy, in the forms in which it has hiterto been known, flourishes best where some of the people, but not all the people, are free and equal; and, since this conclusion is incompatible with the conditions of the new society and repugnant to the contemporary conscience, the task of saving democracy in our time is the task of reconciling it with the postulate of popular sovereignty and mass civilization.[19]

Democracy and its other Enlightenment ideals, however, found their most prosperous footing in America, which Hans Kohn called "a gift of benevolent Nature." "The Anglo-Americans were the first to establish a nation on the basis of new civilization. Its characteristic features--a pluralistic and open society in place of an authoritarian uniformity of state and faith; reliance on the autonomy of the individual and voluntary association; a rationalistic and humanitarian regard for one's fellow man--gradually asserted themselves as the fruit of a long historical process."[20] John Adams, then 78 years old, wrote to Thomas Jefferson, "Many hundred years must roll away before we shall be corrupted. Our pure, virtuous, public spirited, federative republic will last forever, govern the globe and introduce the perfection of man."[21]

In its very origin as a nation the United States was the embodiment of an idea....The ideology was a supra-national ideology, the philosophy of the eighteenth century. But it was based upon, and limited by, the English tradition which continued to the single most important factor in the development of American life. Only by accepting and maintaining the English idea of constitutional liberty--and by thus remaining Anglo-American--could the English colonies in North America continue and solidify their political existence; only by transcending the English heritage and broadening it beyond the confines of historical-territorial limitation could they establish their distinctive political existence. In doing this, they lived up to the expectations of the age. A new chapter in the history of the West was inaugurated. The identification of the political rights founded upon the philosophy of the age, was self-evident to the Americans who grew to manhood in the 1760's and 1770's.[22]

It was only one step away, given this precondition for a utopian democracy in thought, to turn the founding ideals into practice. With increased material distribution through industrial technology, these ideals of post-Liberal state have thoroughly permeated every nook and cranny of American life.

> Abundance has influenced American life in many ways, but there is perhaps no respect in which this influence has been more profound than in the forming and strengthening of the American ideal and practice of the equality, with all that the ideal has implied for the individual in the way of opportunity to make his own place in society and of emancipation from a system of status.[23]

To a large extent, Lipset contends, stable Western democracies (including the United States) are in the "post-politics" stage, that is, "there is relatively little difference between democratic left and right, the socialists are moderates, and the conservatives accept the welfare state." In these societies the workers have won "their fight for full citizenship." Now the lower strata are represented in politics, and "the incorporation of the workers into the legitimate body politic has been settled."[24] Although democracy is neither conducive to creativity nor geared to reducing conformity, the American case represents, to Lipset, an optimistic view on the ramifications of abundance and democracy.

> There is considerable evidence to suggest that higher education, greater economic security, and higher standards of living strengthen the level of culture and democratic freedom. The market for good books, good paintings, and good music is at a high point in American history. There is evidence that tolerance for ethnic minorities too is greater than in the past. More people are receiving a good education in America today than ever before, and regardless of the many weaknesses of that education, it is still true that the more of it one has, the better one's values and consumption patterns from the point of view of the liberal and culturally concerned intellectual.[25]

The workability of democratic equalitarianism, especially in the United States, has apparently been fostered by the fact that enough opportunities have been present for those who strive to achieve them. The redistribution of wealth in the Old World, as a measure of effectuating equality, has always been conceived of in terms of taking it from one class, or stratum, of society and re-distributing it to those who are underprivileged. This conception of re-distribution has not been part of egalitarianization in America. In America, the distribution of wealth has been possible "without taking from others." "Hence, Europe cannot think of altering the relationship between the various levels of society without assuming a class struggle; but America has altered and can alter these relationships without necessarily treating one class as the victim or even, in an ultimate sense, the antagonist of another."[26]

Today in contemporary America, the ideal has seemed turned into reality.

> American social distinctions, however real they may be and however difficult to break down, are not based upon or supported by great disparities in wealth, in education, in dress, etc., as they are in the Old World. If the American class structure is in reality very unlike the classless society which we imagine, it is equally unlike the formalized class societies of former times, and thus it should be regarded as a new kind of social structure in which the strata may be fully demarked but where the bases of demarcation are relatively intangible. The factor of abundance has exercised a vital influence in producing this kind of structure, for it has constantly operated to equalize the overt differences between them, without however, destroying the barriers which separate them.[27]

Consider the following example,

> A man steps out of a sparkling white split-level house set on a green lawn bordered by flower paths. He wears well-tailored sports slacks and an Italian silk sports shirt. He waves to his children, who are splashing merrily in an inflatable pool near the patio. He shoulders his golf bag, carries it to his station wagon, and drives off for the golf course.
>
> Question: Is this the richest man in town, or one of modest means? Is he a social nonentity? Is he a political power or a machine voter? Is he a banker, a salesman, a plumber, a poet?
>
> Answer: You cannot tell.
>
> In a country as homogenized as a bottle of Grade A milk, almost anyone with sufficient desire and energy, underwritten by an average amount of good fortune, can own a pleasant home, wear good clothes, drive a late-model car, spoil his children, and play at pleasure that were once the sole province of the upper classes. If the average man does not have a staff of domestic servants,

he need not fear this will set him apart socially. The richest man in town probably does not have servants either, primarily because he cannot find any to hire.[28]

Armed with the utopian ideal of human equity and perfectibility of man on the one hand, and the reality of affluence brought about by the deployment of full industrial technology, on the other, a whole new generation of men and women has been brought up in a "germ-free, glasshouse." When they finally confront the ugly social reality contradictory to their ideal expectations and environment, they feel totally confused and often betrayed. Studying the youth movement, especially concerning the "Vietnam Summer" of 1967, Kenneth Keniston found this to be exactly the case. "The shock of confrontation" with reality was the factor that transformed them into radicalism against what they regarded as gross social injustice:

> For such young men and women, privileged and idealistic, the confrontation with social inequity--the first personal meeting with poverty, injustice, political manipulation, and institutional dishonesty--have a disproportionate impact. As relatively empathic and compassionate young men and women, when concretely confronted with the toll of American society, they quickly lost their "intellectual remoteness and felling of objectivity," and felt "personally responsible" for doing something to change things.[29]

"American idealism," wrote Gustavus Myers, "then, has been the mo potent, far-fetching tangibility. Yet to many Americans, affected by its suffusive influence but unmindful of it as an historic fact, the subject has seemed impalpable, blending into the unreal."[30] This surrealistic depiction of a utopian America by many optimists becomes strikingly hollow especially when one reads accounts like Utopia: 1976,[31] which casts American society in a stark framework of perfect utopia as a living reality. Contemporary American society is predominantly leisure-oriented and compared with past democracies, say that of Greece, it can truly be said that America is a society in which the majority can become leisurely gentlemen. Herman Kahn and Anthony Wiener predict that by the year 2000, about 70-80 percent of the population may truly become men (and women) of leisure, delving into "competitive 'partner' games (chess, bridge), (into) music, art, languages, or (into) serious travel, or (into) the study of science, philosophy, and so on."[32] Such a prediction appears rather out of place in view of the contemporary cultural landscape. First, we need not wait until the year 2000 to have the majority of the population in this utopian society to be leisure connoisseurs; male and female white-collarites combined already form the leisure mass, with enough time for art, science or philosophy. Second, those with leisure time are apparently inclined toward developing neither the "competitive" games nor the "speculative" contemplation on life; they merely form a frenzied mass seeking sensory pleasures and spectator sports to tame their most immediate and primitive nerve endings. A utopian society, i.e. contemporary America, displays the strange two-fold characteristics, that is, an extreme degree of mass conformity and self-centeredness. In the emphatic atmosphere of individuality and independence, the more subtle process of mass conformity gradually takes place. We shall now turn to the consideration of mass conformity and self-centeredness in utopian America.

3. UTOPIA AND MASS SOCIETY

Modern rationalism, as the state ideology in post-Liberal society, as the pattern of production, and as the constitution of higher learning, began with the classic materialists in the seventeenth century, then was elaborated as the empirical mode of inquiry in the hands of the British empirical School, which dominates the scientific rationalism (knowledge through controlled observation, experiment and sense perception, etc.) into technological rationality was made chiefly with the surge of industrialization in the nineteenth century and into our own era, which includes, among other more subtler elements, these characteristics: technological application in life in general, and more specifically, mass production, mass consumption, mass mind-molding, and mass organization that breeds conformity in thought and action through bureaucratic organizations, institutional ethos, etc.; in short, it is what constitutes the mass characteristics of a post-Liberal society.

The major theme of modern technological organization is, as Max Weber so thoroughly observed, rationality and efficiency, which tends to transcend all hiterto dissonant political ideologies as each nation races toward one variety or another of the Welfare State.[33] These characteristics of technological application, then, inevitably become cross-ideological. One safe prediction is that this characteristic of a utopian society will be a world phenomenon, regardless of the specific historical stages in which each society is currently passing through. The technocratic rationality means its most efficient, and most rational, means of achieving the Welfare State's goals and purposes. Added to this efficient and rational fascination with technology is the fact that much of the world has been in constant scarcity. Technology has come of full age at last in post-Liberal society.

We shall examine in this brief section the extent to which technology is a form of conformity-producing mechanism in contemporary America which is the front-runner in this repsect. More specifically, we shall call attention to the major areas in which this tendency is more pronounced: Mass Media, Mass Consumption and Mass Education.

Also briefly, we will look at the social-psychological implications brought about by the technological rationality in terms of their role in the post-Liberal state.

The first TV broadcasting in the United States began in 1941, although quite a few millions had seen the wonder at the New York Fair in 1939. Its rapid distribution since that time is phenomenal; by 1950 less than four percent of the U.S. households owned TV sets,[34] but by 1960 the percentage rose to 45 percent, and by 1970 nearly one hundred percent. Today, nearly every household in the United States owns a TV set; new distributions parallel the increase of natural population only. The utility of the TV medium by the general audience is more staggering. Nearly all Americans after the age of two spend an average of twenty-five hours a week, as reported by the Nielsen Company, before the TV screen. As a means of commercial advertisement, only TV increased in its utility by the sponsors while other media either declined or merely marked time.[35] When the entire nation spends its major portion of leisure time before the screen as an established way of life, it is difficult to estimate its more subtle, longer-range character implication. For one thing, the average American is a person molded by the TV medium in his daily action, conversation, thinking and reaction. His opinion is generally guided, either consciously or unconsciously, by the constant bombardment of TV viewing; neither capable of breaking away from it nor intellectually controlling such dominance, he is living a life in a pure vacuum, molded, shaped and controlled by TV. Just the sheer amount of time America as a nation spends watching TV is mind-boggling--two million times twenty-five hours a week, and the trend is sure to go upward. Blue collar workers and low level white collarites are the greatest TV-watchers, the ones whose leisure time is increasing faster than any other social strata.

The domination of TV in every nook and cranny of modern life is real and countable, but hardly accountable. Every little nuance of TV broadcasting affects human minds that absorb it in three dimensions, but there is very little concrete argument that one can make **against** TV. This popularity of the TV medium is not difficult to explain. Printed matters require and demand an active and critically concentrated mind on the part of the reader, but TV eliminates this active participation by relieving its tension through three dimensional images on the screen. The viewer is not required to be critical, for the images require no more than natural ability to distinguish the sensory experience in the most crude distinctions. The fleeting pictures demand no more than an average mind can muster. Intellect gives way to senses, reason to impulse, and imagination to visuality in post-Liberal society.

American politics is dominated by TV indirectly or directly; although there is a recent report that the candidate's appeal on the screen is not as crucial a factor in a campaign, we may humbly submit that it can be restored by innovating the appealing techniques in programming the image, the time and the location. If the 1960 election was a TV debacle for Nixon, then his 1968 one was a triumph in the utility of TV. The 1968 campaign for Richard Nixon was a TV campaign, once his foe but now his savior; he carefully selected image-managers and during the entire campaign these TV specialists ran the show with great care. They changed the length of TV speeches, affecting not only the tone and nuance but also the content itself, such as the candidate's direct ideas and ideals about the world affairs. In short, it was not what the candidate had to say about the course of human fate individually and collectively that mattered, but what the TV specialists judged to be appealing to the TV viewers. As expected the TV campaign expenditures steadily rose with each election in the last two decades as the potency of messages grew with the growing number of TV sets in American households. In the 1956 general election about six million dollars was spent on TV advertising; ten million dollars in 1960, twenty-three million in 1964 and in 1968 some thirty-eight million dollars was spent on TV campaign.[36] "Americans sit in the dark," writes David Potter, "for no one really knows how many hundreds of millions of hours per night in front of the screens on which the pictues are projected. Television has become a major element in American life, and many travellers, who eighteen years ago had never seen a television set, today will not stay in a motel room overnight unless they are provided with one."[37]

It has been already observed that America has been established on the utopian ideas of egalitarianism and consequently mass culture has flourished without the feudal or class tradition prevalent in Europe or in Asia. For better or worse, in societies where class or nobility was distinctly associated with the model of subtle quality and manners of behavior men of lower origins eagerly aspired to as a desirable, if not attainable, style of life. The absence of this tradition has made America much more prone to mass fetishism and conformity. From the very beginning of American history massism was the dominant mode of cultural model in literature, art and notably technological application. A mass society, in its taste, has historically demonstrated a preference for the inferior. There is only an upward trend in this aspect of massism in post-Liberal America. We may now turn to our second topic of mass culture, Mass Consumption.

Mass consumption is only one constituent aspect of utopian society in its most prodigious realms. Mass production which entails mass consumption derives its rationality from the rules of <u>scientific</u> and <u>technological</u> efficiency. Technology produces the goods en masse, and the masses consume them en masse, whose process is no longer a natural one, that is, producing and consuming for an essential human existence that is naturally (bio-socially) determined. Consumptive behavior at the mass level implies a special meaning in our times; it tells something about the singular effect on the physical as well as the psychic life of men and women of the post-Liberal type. Consumption hiterto concerned itself with meeting the natural demands of human existence, and man's activity almost solely consisted of meeting such demands. In post-Liberal society, technological rationality in production results in overproduction, and hence consumption takes up a strange character: many working men and women live to consume, few to produce. Conspicuous consumpti today is no longer an idea associated with the leisure class. If one avoids consumption on credit he is looked upon as an odd one indeed.[38]

Modern consumptive behavior is a credit phenomenon. One's life in post-Liberal society is a constant race to consume, and consume, and meet the credit deadlines. Mass consumption is an historical product of post-Liberal technological rationality, and credit consumption its way of complying with the historical trend.

Outstanding consumer credit grew from twenty-one billion dollars in 1950 (not including mortgage) for both installment and non-stallment items to one hundred and twenty billion dollars by early 1970, during which period credit consumption grew at an annual rate of 10.5 percent while personal income increased by only 5.5 percent.[3] In other words, in the period of 1950-1970 the American consumer learned to consume twice as fast as the increase in his income. Credit consumption is indeed a mass phenomenon, cutting through every stratum, race or age, in American society. The application of mass production and consumption is rationally derived from the rules of technological rationality and efficiency. It is only that such consumptive behavior reveals a frenzied desperation, socially and psychologically, to comply with the utopian ideals.

The rise of credit consumption largely coincides with the rise of white collarites, the new middle classes, the rise of mass media and the subsequent mass conformity in life and thought. The new middle classes no longer claim its status on property ownership, and consequently are pressed to maintain their status, not only by conspicuous consumption, but also by credit consumption aided by its somewhat standardized state of income. Social attitude toward credit consumption has changed; now it has become a legitimate, and highly normal, way of American life in its post-Liberal stage. It used to be a disgrace to be in debt, but today it is an oddity if one is not in debt of some kind. Theoretically, every family in the United States is only three months away from total financial bankruptcy owing to credit consumption. Being in debt means also that someone watches to make sure that the debt payment is regularly carried out. There are the Big Brothers closely watching every person in debt.

These Big Brothers are the invisible overseers of modern mass consumptive compulsion. There are offices charged with investigation and information file in every city and on nearly every citizen who can consume, from junior high schoolers to those on social security. "A man's credit record follows him like his shadow."[40] Every square inch of U.S. society is covered by the post-Liberal way of life, mass media, mass consumption, and by necessity the Credit Bureau can unearth in one push button one's past, present and future rate. However, Americans are relatively well adapted to the credit way of life so that even during the Depression failure to make installment payment did not exceed five percent. This good conditioning is also reflected in the lavishness of credit card usage, Visa, American Express, Carte Blanche, Diner's Club, Master Charge, etc. The now-increasing credit violations, however, do not seem to discourage their commercial appeal. This mass behavior in consumption is constantly promoted by the mass media, and no less by mass education in utopian America.

Mass Education in America has truly lived up to its liberal-utilitarian promise, especially in this century. Over ninety-five percent of those between the age of fourteen and seventeen years were enrolled in high school in 1950, but by 1970 nearly ninety-nine percent. Among those, some fourteen percent were in college, but by 1970 the percentage more than doubled.[41] Today, more than seven million youths are in the institutions of higher learning in the United States. Two expected ramifications have followed: First, the quality of education has appreciably declined; second, education has contributed to the molding of a mass-mind.

Characteristically, the education in the United States is neither directed toward acquiring the wisdom of life, nor geared to making the world more intelligible. The educated mass remains intellectually inactive and culturally unimaginative, but intelligent enough to function as consumers, as TV watchers, and as easily-swayed educated "idiots," using C. Wright Mill's term. The quality of education brings them up to the level of sufficient functionality in the established social order, but not enough to examine it critically, nor to act responsibly in the arena of politics and human relations. The liberal arts education in colleges and universities leaves students as intellectually illiterate as they enter. These colleges and universities produce mainly sales persons, school teachers, and other basic level functionaries in bureaucratic social organizations. Learning in the United States today does not lend one to discovery, nor to creativity; it merely turns the educated masses into what technological efficiency and rationality requires, i.e. TV viewers and credit consumers. The classic notion of education, in the tradition of "know thyself," as the pursuit of noble human knowledge has no place where education means only maintaining the status quo in a post-Liberal America.

The totalitarian character of utopian massism presupposes the uniformity of individuals in thought and action. And this is constantly insured by the mass education in American society. One of the most important premises of mass education is that one should never learn more than what is taught, and never more than the average level of society itself. The crisis of higher learning in American sums up in its concentration of learning on satisfying social demands--more technicians, salespersons, bureaucrats--toward rationality and efficiency. Aesthetic and moralistic teachings rarely draw serious attention. There is a fearful effort to "be more scientific" in all academic disciplines. In post-Liberal society, moral problems are transformed into technical ones, to be planned, managed and corrected, if necessary.

The current state in higher learning is, then, only one part of a larger matrix which confronts an historical era characterized by post-Liberal ideology. Technological rationality tends to be viewed as self-correcting and self-directing, and to some extent benign. In reality, it is self-perpetuating and belligerent, with its own purposes and aims over which one scarcely has control or knowledge. Its subtlety of dehumanization, the mechanization of the mind, toward a totalitarian massism is one of the most pertinent characteristics of a post-Liberal America.

4. THE SELF AND THE PURSUIT OF HAPPINESS IN POST-LIBERAL SOCIETY

The individual right and prerogative to equality and happiness were already contained in the Enlightenment formula, and the ensuing success in industrial technology has rendered a real or supposed possibility of practicing the highly utopian ideals in actuality. This being the observable historical trend, post-Liberal America has become a society of "sovereign individuals," or what Andrew Hacker calls "two hundred million Egos."[42] When these two conditions (egalitarianism and industrial technology) met finally in a post-Liberal society, the analytic unit of social analysis is eventually brought down to the individual. The whole community (or society) may be considered one unit for a Radical state and the family for a Liberal state. Now it is the individual himself that constitutes the whole of this new historical type. The logical extension of fulfilling the egalitarian promise, when made possible by industrial technology's mass production, is that the general range and scope of individual perception come to be limited only to the individual himself. We need not quote Thomas Hobbes's account of greedy human nature; it is an empirically generalized fact that when our ideology is shaped by the wish to fulfill individual happiness, as consolidated and solidified in national tradition, and our material condition is such that the ideology is transformed into daily reality, the utopian state of mind is a matter of opinion as to whether it is real or unreal. Our general observation on this historical trend bears out the contention that the primary concern of a "privatized" society is essentially the utopian degree of individual happiness and freedom. In the last analysis, post-Liberal America may be characterized as a society of utopian pleasure pursuit. The social system and its institutional arrangements are geared to creating and maintaining the sources of this vast pleasure game. This assertion is based as much on empirical observation as on logical analysis, bearing upon the relationship among ideology, social character and specific human behavior that we discussed earlier. Post-Liberal society thus embodies the last stage of our conceptual model of history, and the time and place is Contemporary America.

Tocqueville earlier observed that "in America, the passion for physical wellbeing is not always exclusive, but it is general; and if all do not feel it in the same manner, yet it is felt by all. Carefully to satisfy even the least wants of the body, and to provide the little conveniences of life, is uppermost in every mind."[43] This preoccupation with physical wellbeing and conveniences has reached a massive scale today, having been incorporated into the academic field under "recreation" or "physical education."

The recreationist today is all too eager to shoulder the responsibility of teaching Americans how to play. To begin with, he is seeking to dignify his work as a profession. More than sixty-five colleges[44] give full four-year courses leading to Bachelor's, Master's, and even Doctor of Philosophy degrees in recreation. The catch is that all save a handful of these courses are in departments of physical education, and are oriented almost entirely toward sports and games. Students take tests on such subjects as badminton rules: "When using the Eastern forehand grip, the top plate of the handle comes in the middle of the V made by thumb and forefinger--True or False?" "In announcing a badminton score, whose score is given first?" Ph.D. theses are written on such topics as "The Validity of the Miller Forehand-Backhand Test for Beginning Tennis Players," and "A Comparison of the Correlations with the First Centroid Factor and with the Composite Criterion in the Wall Bounce Test." This pseudo-scholarly attitude is carried over into "research studies." Recreationists made one elaborate survey that "proved," for example, that as men get older they tend to give up such pleasures as calisthenics, weight-lifting, and casual dating. They can also tell you to within a few decimal points what percentage of men and women between eighteen and thirty-five spend their free time hiking, collecting dolls, or playing in a fife and drum corps.[45]

What is so characteristic of pleasurist post-Liberal society, among other respects, is the blurred line "that separates luxuries from necessities," which has "become trappings without which we cannot go forth to enjoy ourselves." Those pleasure luxuries can become burdens rather than the instrument of pleasure. Lobsenz observes that "it is sad that we buy so much in the name of pleasure. But it is sadder still that so much of what we buy we do not really want." "Perhaps never before in history, except for absolute rulers and absolute ascetics, has there been such a person as 'the man who has everything.' Yet he is with us everyday."[46] The pleasure principle runs across every aspect of life in post-Liberal society, and provides an excellent basis for commercial fodders.

    None of life's little rituals is too insignificant to be <u>enjoyable</u>. The mildest <u>divertissement</u> is ballooned into a wild delight; the simplest pleasure becomes an ecstasy. Advertisers, never slow to sense a trend, have leaped on the burbling bandwagon, and there is now hardly an artifact or an activity that is not intimately connected with spine-tingling happiness. Brushing your teeth--with a certain toothpaste, of course-- is "fun." Cutting the grass--with a certain lawnmower-- is "exciting." Do you want to know "the real joy of good living?" Drink a certain beer. The newest jet plane is "relaxing"...Soapflakes give "glamorous" suds. It is "fun" to paint your house with so-and-so's paint. Eyeglasses are "bewitching." Light bulbs are "romantic." Yeast suddenly becomes "fun to knead and braid." Kitchen appliances are "smart."...Even paying the bills for all these items is "a pleasure" if you have an account at a certain bank.[47]

    This excessive pursuit of pleasure in America was earlier observed by Herbert Spencer, Matthew Arnold and Max Weber. Spencer remarked that "exclusive devotion to work has the result that amusements cease to please; when relaxation becomes imperative, life becomes dreary from lack of its sole interest--the interest in business." Arnold similarly observed that Americans were "extremely nervous because of excessive worry and overwork." In the 20's Weber noted a high degree of "submission to fashion in America, to a degree unknown in Germany."[48] In contemporary terms, "the current obligation of the American is to be eternally occupied. We are all mailmen, letting neither snow nor rain nor gloom of night deter us in the swift completion of our self-appointed rounds." Also, "free time is something that has to be filled up; a blight that must be excised." It was observed that many American families participated in as many as seventy-four different activities as a means of relaxation.[49] A sardonic European observes in a similar vein that "Americans produce so much that...their life is a frantic race to consume what they produce....Americans, in gaining their wealth, have become as culturally barren and impersonal as the machines they operate. The average American is drowning in a sea of standardized abundance. He must thrash and kick his life away, consuming and wasting, to keep his head above the suffocating flow of shining luxuries and gadgets that pour from the <u>laissez-faire</u> industrial system."[50] Contemporary America was characterized as "lost in the midst of the unprecedented material condition of our time...peculiarly (ignoring) the harsh lessons of historical reality."[51]

In this utopian society, the attitude towards work also changes, to the extent that work and play are increasingly intertwined in terms of pleasure-at-work ethic.

> American industry is becoming one vast playing field. Labor leaders who barely a generation ago were battling for the five-day week, or for minimally decent working conditions, now spend much of their time and energies negotiating such fringe benefits as paid holidays for employees and on their birthdays, free uniforms for members of the company bowling team, and daily rest periods. The "pause in the day's occupation" has been multiplied tenfold. In many instances it has been written in as an integral part of the union contract. A brewery recently yielded to demands for a "beer break"--a foamy interlude during which the workers may knock off and quaff a free seidel of suds.[52]

What epitomizes the tendency of work-as-pleasure is perhaps the "coffee breaks," which, according to the U.S. Labor Department, are guaranteed by one out of every four union contracts signed. "Plants have been struck for violation of the coffee break clause." All in all, each worker enjoys "three weeks of coffee drinking a year--with cream, sugar, and full pay."[53] Geared towards fulfilling individual pleasure and happiness, post-Liberal America is one gigantic playground engaged in pursuit of commercialized and privatized pleasure and happiness. This is easily reflected in the expenses the pleasure industry creates.

> The best and latest estimate of the amount of money spent each year in this country for various aspects of pleasure is forty billion dollars. This sum approximately equals the annual cost of the national defense.[54] It is greater than the total of all personal income tax receipts. It is a Gargantuan 8 percent of the gross national product. It includes such fascinating figures as one billion dollars spent on backyard pools; a quarter of a billion dollars on women's bathing suits; twelve billion dollars on tools and materials for "do-it-yourself" projects; twenty-three million dollars on baseball gloves; five million dollars

for children's sleds, and nearly a fifth of a billion dollars on fishing supplies. We pour one billion dollars into bowling and another billion into hunting; two billion into gardening, two and a half billion into boating. Over one-third of a billion dollars goes for photographic equipment. The outdoor barbecue craze costs one hundred million dollars for grills and twenty-five million dollars just for paper plates. We spend six million dollars for tennis balls, thirty million for golf balls, and another thirty million for sunglasses and goggles.[55]

Since this pleasure pursuit is more or less an individual activity, there is the fear of loneliness and isolation consequent to the pleasure pursuit. Hence there is so much concern for insurance protection, and guaranty regarding everything "from earthquakes to moth damage." To ease the sense of loneliness and powerlessness when confronting the world alone, the post-Liberal man furiously indulges in building model kits to display his power of creativity, whereas the model kits are labelled as "ingeniously, designed and require little or no skill to assemble."

Somewhat regularized as to the time and place for fun, the post-Liberal man feels guilty if he "lives it up" on Wednesday evening rather than on Saturday evening, caught between the traditional work habit and contemporary demand. As a result, "leisure has become a time of tension rather than relaxation." More accidents, more hostilities between married couples and more boredom and unhappiness are manifest on holidays and during summer vacations. "In trying so hard to fulfill this new duty to be happy, most Americans are taking the fun out of their play. Pleasure is no longer man's servant but his tyrant."[56] One result of this tyrannical pleasure, which is no longer pleasurable, is what Lobsenz calls "pleasure neurosis," a syndrome to "go to almost any lengths to avoid it."

The "pleasure neurotic" may be defined as a person who suffers from deep psychological fear of relaxation. He is equipped, often brilliantly, for all the workaday functions of life. But he is lost when work is over. So deep is his fear of leisure that he <u>must</u> remain in harness as long as possible. The pleasure neurotic is the man who brings home enough work from the office to carry him through the hiatus of the evening. He is the man who can't stand Sunday. He is the man who, at the behest of his subconscious, fritters away the hours of the day so that he will have a legitimate excuse to work overtime at night. He is the slave to lists and systems and routines--devices all nicely calculated to protect him from having time on his hands. He is the man for whom pleasure is equated with the defiance of authority; this creates feelings of anxiety and guilt;

> the only way he can appease these feelings and that authority--which is in fact the conscience of his childhood--is by hard work. He cannot give himself permission to let down.[57]

The pleasure neurotic, one of the proto-types of post-Liberal man, is unable to relax and enjoy his rare moments of leisure, driven by guilt and restlessness. His forced leisure activities are, then, rationalized into the realm of necessities, e.g., reading for business, golf for improving the waistline, a motion picture for an intelligent conversation piece, etc.

> The pleasure neurotic, as a result, takes part in enjoyable activities only furtively or defiantly. Either avenue leads inevitably to a deeper guilt. On occasion the pleasure neurotic secretly savors the delicious possibility of not only *not* enjoying himself, but of simultaneously being able to delude himself about his true motives and thereby to feel martyred for having to "give up" the pleasures he does not want in the first place. Deliberately, the pleasure neurotic sets himself impossible schedules calling for enormous stints of concentrated endeavors.[58]

With the enormous emphasis placed upon each individual to enjoy his life, pleasure neurosis is one of the many symptoms that characterize a post-Liberal society which is committed to the ideology of happiness and to technological means to fulfill the ideology. An extreme degree of self-centeredness, then, is the logical consequence of this post-Liberal mentality.

5. THE INSIGNIFICANT OTHERS

The breakdown of the family ties, among others, in contemporary America has been well noted by many. The underlying causes, however, have been a moot issue. Pleasure-seeking in this post-Liberal society implies, imperatively, a presupposition of individuality and freedom. When this supposition is analyzed in terms of its actual workings in pratice, we discover that individualism breeds self-centeredness and this self-centeredness, in turn, creates an intensive degree of intolerance, and to some extent, hatred for others as long as they are not part of one's pleasure-promoting process. This intolerance and/or hatred for others, which is rather historically rooted as we have seen, is the underlying cause of the general institutional decline in America including the family structure.[59] The so-called generation gap is neither caused by a failure to communicate nor by the monstrous rebellious spirts of the youth; it is simply a testimony that the individuals--old and young--have found each other intolerable, expensive and emotionally burdensome. Since the economic factor as the unifying basis of family cohesion has long been obsolete, they find no reason to tolerate each other's presence which may obstruct the road to pleasure-pursuit. Eric Larrabee remarked that the argument that it is for "the children's sake" whenever the parents find themselves in need for an excuse is often meant: "In order not to have to be bothered by the children."[60] Andrew Hacker also made a similar remark that the parents would rather go to Las Vegas for a vacation than save it for their children's education. The disintegration of the family structure, and of the general collective solidarity at large, are some of the most salient characteristics of post-Liberal society, increasingly shaped by the ideals of utopian variety and the increased confidence in the hands of industrial technology. As a society reaches its economic maturity, as in a post-Liberal state, heavily armed by the idea of individual happiness, the sacrifice demanded by the traditional institutional bondage becomes intellectually incongruent and socially unbearable. Joseph Schumpeter made this cogent observation on the changes within the family and the "utilitarian" causes underlying those changes.

> As soon as men and women learn the utilitarian lesson and refuse to take for granted the traditional arrangements that their social environment makes for them, as soon as they acquire the habit of weighing the individual advantages and disadvantages of any prospective course of action...they cannot fail to become aware of the heavy personal sacrifices that family ties and especially parenthood entail under modern conditions and of the fact that at the same time, excepting the cases of farmers and peasants, children cease to be economic assets. These sacrifices do not consist only of the items that come within the reach of the measuring rod of money but comprise in addition an indefinite amount of loss of comfort, of freedom from care, and opportunity to enjoy alternatives of increasing attractiveness and variety--alternatives to be compared with joys of parenthood that are being subjected to a critical analysis of increasing severity. The implication of this is not weakened but strengthened by the fact that the balance sheet is likely to be incomplete, perhaps even fundamentally wrong. For the greatest of the assets, the contribution made by parenthood to physical and moral health...particularly in the case of women, almost invariably escapes the rational searchlight of modern individuals who, in private as in public life, tend to focus attention on ascertainable details of immediate utilitarian relevance and to sneer at the idea of hidden necessities of human nature or of the social organism....It may be summed up in the question that is so clearly in many potential parents' minds: "Why should we stunt our ambitions and impoverish our lives in order to be insulted and looked down upon in our old age?"[61]

When this "utilitarian calculation," which is the behavioral basis of post-Liberal human relations, reaches its ultimate logical limit: the bare framework of human relations in post-Liberal society becomes that of sheer <u>antagonism</u> unless the relations are seen as contributory to the utilitarian aims and processes. The general structure of contemporary American society bears witness to its very "antagonistic" nature of that utilitarian mentality. For American social institutions through which the post-Liberal men and women carry out their happiness-pursuit are arranged in such a way that the social system tends to discourage primary relations between them, and renders the need for personal ties obsolete by deploying secondary social agencies in human relations.

Left to its own resource for maintaining the day-to-day relations within the family, a drastically new pattern of family structure must emerge. This new pattern of mutual tolerance is essentially based on a tolerable amount of personal asset in attractiveness and charm. This is true not only in the parent-child relationship but also in the husband-wife transaction as well. The very presence of the dispute over the generation gap and dissolved marriages manifests the sheer importance of this arrangement in human relations of American society. If human ties are generally seen less enduring and increasingly precarious, it must be noted that the new rule of mutual tolerance based upon attractiveness and charm itself is notoriously unenduring and precarious. In a post-Liberal society characterized by utopian ideals of individual happiness, materialized by technological affluence, no human ties, including the family bondage, are to be taken for granted; being a parent is no guarantee for his (or her) enduring authority or purpose for presence in the family. The parent must prove himself (or herself) worthy of the status through passing that tolerance test. In short, within and outside the family, a person must be "liked" in order to legitimize his continuing relations with others. A cogent point may be made by quoting an actual case.

> I have five children grown and married and nine grandchildren. For a time, after the two youngest married and left home, I was desperately lonely. I had been widowed seven years before. Suddenly life was completely empty and meaningless. Coming back to an empty house was unspeakably painful. I fell into the habit of making myself a good strong drink and turning on the TV.
>
> Soon I was spending hours before the "boob tube." After almost a year of this I examined myself. I hadn't heard from any of my children for weeks and weeks. I could have died and rotted before any one of them would have become aware of it. But I was too proud to call them so there was lack of communication.

I am now in my 60's, was never a shameful or nagging mother, I am five feet tall and weigh 100 pounds. I have always been neat and well-groomed. Suddenly, and for no apparent reason, I became aware I was still an individual, quite apart from my dependency on my children. It wouldn't be fair not to admit that twice I tried to commit suicide. But after I determined to remake my life, all this changed.

My hair was thining rapidly. I had it tinted and bought a wiglet. I joined a swimming class. Since I had been frugal, I had money with which to buy some new, modern clothes with exciting new fabrics and lines. I kept my mind open to reading, learning to like abstract paintings, listening to new music, going to good plays and movies. The whole point is this: I raised five children and I babysat with all nine grandchildren, but after all, I am still me, with probably 20 years ahead, since I come from a family who live into their 80's and 90's. So why not enjoy truly and whole-heartedly the remaining years? The strange reward is that I have regained in the process the affection and admiration of my kids! They are delighted with my wiglet and my new hair-do. They are pleased that I can speak their language when it comes to music and art. Grandma is suddenly and uproariously a lot of fun. I have a new respect for myself. I don't need them--they need me! I dance, I go out for dinner, I date, I read. I bought a new stereo. My sons and daughters bring their friends to my house.

Every widow who can, should make her life her own and her children will be eager to share it.[62]

Comment: she had been thoroughly ignored by her children until she had her hair tinted, bought a wiglet, went mod in dress and music, etc., to regain her children's attention from whom she had not heard for weeks and weeks. Her motherhood must depend on how long she can maintain these attraction devices to keep her children coming. It is, apparently, not her as mother that renewed the relationship; anyone with that much attractive desperation deserves to be liked by others.

The American family structure has changed clear-cut along the Radical-to-post-Liberal transformation, in which the generational relationship in the family has also changed from what might be called the "vertical" to the "horizontal" relationship. That during the Colonial and Revolutionary (Radical) period in America the parent-child relationship was stiffly vertical, superordination-subordination oriented, requires no further elaboration. However, it may be mentioned that the vertical parent-child relationship was not only socially and religiously sanctioned, but also legally defined.

> If any child or children above 16 years old of competent understanding, shall curse or smite their natural father or mother, he or they shall be put to death unless it can be sufficiently testified that the parents have been very unchristianly negligent of the educating of such child...if any man have such rebellious or stubborn son of sufficient years and understanding, viz., 16 years of age or upwards, which shall not obey the direct voice of his father or the voice of his mother, yet when they have chastened him will not harken unto them...such son shall be put to death, or otherwise severely punished.[63]

Contemporary America is a horizontal society, shrouded in the myth of equalitarianism and individualism, and a pursuit of happiness, where no traditionally defined authority is to be recognized as such. This historical trend from vertical to horizontal human relations has made the sustenance of parenthood well-nigh difficult, if not outright impossible, in post-Liberal society. The parents must win a vote of "attraction" from the child, and winning this is no small task. According to the post-Liberal conception of parenthood, made no less difficult by advocates of a post-Liberal parent-child relationship, e.g., Benjamin Spock, winning the vote of attraction, or qualifying as parents, must satisfy some of the most stringent demands. The following are some of the demands compiled which makes the relationship reflective of an horizontally-based utopian democracy and its equalitarian ideology.

Understanding (of the child)
Love
Discipline (not too much)
Patience (for mischievous children)
Helpfulness
Kindness
Availability (when needed)
Fairness (in treating children)
Humor (at all times)
Good disposition (well-controlled temper)
Easy to talk to
Sets good examples (of behavior)
Able to listen (to children)
Respect for children
Does not interfere with children's social life
Honesty (never tell a lie)
Can admit mistakes
Provides companionship
Firmness

Gives enough freedom (to children)
Provides guidance
Is fun to be with
Not too strict[64]

The mutually equal basis of the egalitarian theme is the outline of the vertical-to-horizontal transformation in human relations and ways of governance, in which "two hundred million feudal lords," using Hacker's term, claim the right to be heard. To some, this change reflects a depletion of morality in society.

There are those who claim that we live in a time when no moral system exists. The preconditions necessary for morality, they say, are missing. In a sense, they are right. The moral rights have gone out for millions. Those who still hold to the traditional codes are either the children of good fortune who live lives of isolation or the determined remnants of an age which passed out of existence with the birth of technologies and superstates. There is something almost quaint today about the man who defends the moral ideals of his forefathers. (Except for ministers, of course, for whom quaintness is often thought to be a virtue, and a hearty regard for the institutions of the past is considered a necessity.)[65]

In 1880 the United States' divorce rate was one out of every fourteen marriages; at the turn of the century the ratio climbed slightly to one to twelve; in the 70's the ratio is roughly one to three.[66] The divorce rate, among other empirical evidence of family breakdown, may be indicative, if anything, of the degree to which post-Liberal individuals have become increasingly intolerant of each other, or "horizontalized," which is peculiar only to the post-Liberal society with its corresponding ideology and social character. Tocqueville somewhere remarked that once the situation is deemed escapable, it becomes intolerable; once the ideological basis of human relations is perceived as based upon certain horizontal e-qualitarian premises, fundamental to the human ideals fostered in the Enlightenment, any slight irritation or provocation is deemed intolerable and, much more, <u>unreasonable.</u> Ensuing social isolation and the sense of loneliness and alienation must be explained in terms of these ideological premises and the characterological implications of those premises. Hence, in contemporary America, the rules of human relations represent the historical commitment with which men and women in the past have been preoccupied. If history is seen as the history of human progress toward freedom, post-Liberal society represents the ultimate destination, real or imagined, of that freedom. Committed to a society of horizontal milieu of equal rights and equal anonymity, the post-Liberal individual vacillates between the utopian ideals he beholds and the ease with which his life is transformed into meaninglessness. For the first time in history, the aspirations and hopes of the Radical rhetorics are seen as an actual possibility to be realized in post-Liberal society.

If the eighteenth century witnessed the end of the utopian homeward movement in the fictive sense, the twentieth century has seen the grounding of the idea itself: the appearance of the self-proclaimed ideal commonwealth on earth, not in the happy future but in the dismal present. Utopia...thus loses its etymological and philosophical denotation of "nowhere" and becomes a well-defined geographical reality for millions of totally controlled populations. The process of transformation is complete. However, an element of make-believe persists because descriptive and coercive utopianism all have presence--the assertion that the ideal can be or has been substituted for the real--as their common base.[67]

Virtues and merits as well as socio-psychological repercussions are associated with the post-Liberal ideology and social character. It is not an exaggerated assertion that all the struggles and conflicts of the recent past, since the dawn of the modern era, have been based on the moral strength of the egalitarian (both naturalist and socialist) promises of the human future. The agony of the modern age, epitomized in post-Liberal society, only reflects the degree to which the demarcation between an ideal and its reality has been blurred. As David Potter has observed:

> So long as these beliefs can be maintained intact--so long as they approximate reality closely enough to be convincing--they exercise an immense moral power. From them are derived many of the attitudes that make for decency in American life. The optimism with which Americans have confronted the future; the confidence with which they have grappled with difficult problems; their conviction that merit will be rewarded and that honest work is the only reliable means to attain success; their integrity in social relations; and their respect for the human dignity of any man or woman, regardless of that person's social credentials, are all by-products of the ideal of full equality in a classless society. But, with all its value, this ideal has never been maintained without a certain cost, for it breeds great expectations, and, in so far as these expectations fail of realization, social and personal tensions result. As we move past the mid-point of the twentieth century, it is becoming increasingly clear that the ideal confronts two serious and growing difficulties. One of these difficulties is that we really cannot attain a classless society, and the other is that we have sacrificed some very valuable qualities of the now repudiated status

system in an effort to attain it.[68]

The quality of life that has been sacrificed in an attempt to create an ideal classless society, of which Potter has spoken, may be located, in part, in the generally low level of cultural and intellectual taste that American society as a mass has consistently preferred. This chapter may come to a close with a brief consideration on that aspect of post-Liberal ideology and social character.

6. ON THE QUALITY OF SOCIAL LIFE

It would seem that excellence in taste and judgment is incompatible with the ideal basis of equalitarianism, and perhaps much more so with the ascendency of industrial technology in life. Almost by definition quality refers to a certain natural limitation by which only the select few are qualified. The mass phenomena in post-Liberal society, then, may be considered, though not necessarily, conducive to the decline of public taste in aesthetics, literature, and philosophy in preference for a more sensuous repertoire. Benjamin Disraeli once said that "increased means and increased leisure are the two civilizers of man,"[69] which turned out to be what Walter Buckingham calls a "Victorian mirage."[70] With a sustained enjoyment of economic abundance, cultural life has made a new turn in post-Liberal society.

> Abundance value comes from keeping consumption going. Advertising is its characteristic industry. And the entertainment business--which serves a similar purpose, surrounding high consumption with an atmosphere of cheerfulness--sets many of its styles. The great Abundance value is conferred on the evanescent, on that which is most quickly consumed--especially personality, or mere celebrity. Income for writer, as an illustration, tends to be inverse ratio to the permanence of their product. Writers for television comedians, whose work is fragile and quickly forgotten, live in the Abundance economy. Poets, whose work is likely to be more durable, are paid in Scarcity money, if at all.[71]

The academia, once the bastion of creative and serious thought, has become part of this mass culture, having accepted the bureaucratized standards and techniques of mass processes as its present and future academic goals. Lack of creative seriousness among academics has been noted and deplored by many a sensitive observer.

The transformation of the material world has been accompanied by revolutionary discoveries in the human as well as in the natural sciences. Recent anthropological, archeological, paleontological, sociological, psychological, historical, and economic discoveries

> are not alternatives to the search for wisdom. Nor is
> the search for wisdom a threat to advances in knowledge.
> It should help to reveal, to the advantage of truth,
> not only the limitations of scholarship in all the sciences,
> natural as well as human, but the most noble uses to
> which new scientific discoveries can be put....What is
> lacking today in the study of history, and in social,
> economic, and humanistic studies generally, is a hier-
> archy of aesthetic, moral, and intellectual values.
> Such a hierarchy is no less important in the realm of
> scholarship than in the realms of architecture, music,
> literature, and the other arts.[72]

Hence, this general state of intellectual affairs is reflected in the way in which the higher learning in post-Liberal society is organized toward the personal and social pre-requisites thus formulated and accepted. In this sense, the following observation makes the poignant point on the post-Liberal education.

> The multiplication of colleges, universities, and
> research centers during the past century has been accom-
> panied by an increasingly disharmony in (the) ancient
> philosophical sense. It is almost as if learning had
> come to regard it as proper for desire to govern both
> the spirit and the mind. It is almost as if what the
> wise men of the past regarded as the order necessary
> to human happiness had been stood on its head. Almost
> the only curbs on the appetite which learning now re-
> gards as important are those which contribute to man's
> physical well-being and material wealth, without reference
> to his mind and spirit. Thus the satisfaction of men's
> desires has come to be sanctioned as a contribution to
> the welfare ultimately not of the soul but of the body.
> The disharmony between the various attributes of the
> soul seems to be at the root of our distress.[73]

The moral, intellectual and aesthetic climate of a mass society, i.e. contemporary America has been largely shaped and conditioned by the social elite. The role of leadership in general culture and in the learned world by which an elite distinguishes itself from other social strata has largely been dispersed and diluted in the surge of mass technology that has rendered everyone his share of new egalitarian status. "Once upon a time in the United States," observed C. Wright Mills, "men of affairs were also men of sensibility; to a considerable extent the elite of power and the elite of culture coincided, and where they did not coincide they often overlapped as circles. Within the compass of a knowledgeable and effective public, knowledge and power were in effective touch; and more than that, this public decided much that was decided."[74]
But in contemporary America, the effective public has become diluted and stultified into an ineffective and incompetent, not to mention

vulgar, mass of morally confused and politically powerless individuals.

> The moral uneasiness of our time results from the fact that older values and codes of uprightness no longer grip the men and women of the corporate era, nor have they been replaced by new values and codes which would lend moral meaning and sanction to the corporate routines they must now follow. It is not that the mass public has explicitly rejected received codes; it is rather that to many of the members these codes have become hollow. No moral terms of acceptance are available, but neither are any moral terms of rejection. As individuals they are morally defenseless; as groups, they are politically indifferent. It is this generalized lack of commitment that is meant when it is said that 'the public' is morally confused.[75]

This moral confusion and political powerlessness does not necessarily represent the genuine sense of alienation, for, though powerless and confused as they are, they feel the sheer power of protected arrogance in the midst of commercial choices and mass-produced goods at their disposal. No sense of inferiority is experienced by the consumers of a vulgar culture where the culture is accepted as the standards of excellence and the established mode of authority. It is when the greatest common denominator is sought by the managers of the post-Liberal state that the mass vulgarity of an extremely inferior kind tends to stand out. J.K. Galbraith has made a similar observation when he remarked:

> Few would wish to argue that the popular taste is the best taste, that it reflects the highest aesthetic response. And it is quite clear that the ordinary industrial firm must produce for the popular market. There may be thus, by the artist's standards, a deliberate preference for common place or banal design. But the businessman, in the first instance, at least, is hardly to be blamed. When the Court and a few cultivated Parisians provided the principal market for French craftsmen, the standard of artistic excellence could be high. <u>The standard would certainly have fallen if France had suddenly become a prosperous, egalitarian democracy.</u>

> However, it seems probable that modern industrial design has managed to get the worst of a bad bargain. Taste is not static. And change begins with those who are in communication with the artist--who have a strong aesthetic response. Industry, alienated from the artist and with its eyes fixed by way of the market researchers on the popular taste, has regularly failed to perceive

those advances in taste which were rendering its designs
banal and otiose. Instead of being a little ahead,
it has been a little behind.[76]

The sexual obsession ranks prominently in a culture preoccupied
with physical fulfillments and sensuous pleasures, such as is observed in post-Liberal society. Since much of what could give men
and women the fleeting pleasure of sensory experience has been
well exhausted, now sex is seen as "the last frontier," using
Riesman's term, to conquer and exploit. One cynical European observer hits on this matter: "Americans of both sexes are poor lovers.
They bring to love-making, as to all other activities, two qualities
only: energy and speed. Admirable as such qualities are in turning
out unwanted consumer goods, they are not adequate substitutes
for the gloom which is so necessary for successful love-making."[77]
"The pleasures of sex," he continues, "are being diluted, if not
drowned, by its alleged intricacies."

> There is today, not only the question of whether
> a woman has had an orgasm (the technicians' sine quo
> non of female pleasure in sex), but of which particular
> section of her anatomy was responsible. There are questions of frequency, timing, style, position, and the
> quality of the preliminary skirmishing. The mass media
> are filled each month with such matters. The best seller lists are studded with marriage manuals that are to
> the pleasures of sex what the automotive mechanics'
> handbook is to the pleasures of motoring.[78]

This preoccupation with sex is a great part of one's early life in
which one is encouraged to be paired with the opposite sex for the
dancing classes and proms "as early as the fourth grade." Childdren become exposed to a most competitive aspect of social life
where popularity is an essential asset of their social career.
They are taught both openly and subtly how to be popular with the
opposite sex, without which there seems no life activity to speak
of.

> The arid artificialities of these early ventures
> into the world of male and female carry over into the
> age of puberty. The emotional lives of today's teenagers are built around a pattern resembling the sterile
> complexities of an involved but essentially meaningless
> ritual. The forms are there--dating, the petting,
> the pinning--but the emotional foundation is missing.
> The youngsters are social insects, going about their
> appointed sexual rounds and fulfilling their appointed
> sexual functions like termites, without any emotional
> or intellectual understanding of what they are doing,
> or why.[79]

This ritualization of daily life is true in all aspects of social existence in a society where a vote of attractiveness is the imperative factor in human relations and in the form they take. Because of the demanded conditions of equality and of happiness, coupled with the commercially provided personal power, the post-Liberal individuals are also the loneliest lot of all. The hygenic protection offered by routinized commerical affluence isolates each individual and confines him within the arrogant, but essentially programmed and conditioned, exercise of pleasure pursuit. The need for constant dramatics in life[80] maintains a kind of false crisis which contributes to the ever demanded public thrill and fun. As this need-satisfaction continues, via the mass media, the demarcation between what is real and what is imaginary rapidly disappears. Life in post-Liberal society approaches the essentially meaningless ritual of attraction-repulsion as the whims of the moment dictate. Caught in the dilemma between interpersonal intolerance and the terrifying fear of being alone, yet with all the consumerized pleasure and protection available to him, the post-Liberal man is entirely a new species different from the Traditional, Radical or Liberal type. Now he has finally come to himself as the sole possessor of his person. Half a century ago, Max Weber made this cogent observation on modern man--that is, the post-Liberal man of our time.

> No one knows who will live in this cage in the future, or whether at the end of this tremendous development entirely new prophets will arise, or there will be a great rebirth of old ideas and ideals, or, if neither, mechanized petrification, embellished with a sort of convulsive self-importance. For of the last stage of this cultural development, it might well be truly said: "Specialists without spirit, sensualists without heart; this nullity imagines that it has attained a level of civilization never before achieved."[81]

One can only guess at the course of human destiny, taking shape from this historical stage into the future.

FOOTNOTES

1. A clear development of American character with its ideological emphases in variation from Radical to Liberal and finally to Pure type can be discerned in the history of American ideas. See, for instance, Merle Curti, *The Growth of American Thought*, Harper & Brothers, Publishers, New York, 1943.

2. Seymour Martin Lipset, *The First New Nation*, Basic Books, Inc., New York, 1963, p. 178. Lipset here refers to Leon Samson's *Towards a United Front*, op. cit.

3. Ibid., p. 75.

4. Raymond Aron reluctantly postulates that industrial prosperity may make all industrialized nations resemble each other in the end. See Raymond Aron, *18 Lectures on Industrial Society*, Weidenfeld and Nicolson, London, 1967, p. 242.

5. Seymour Martin Lipset, *The First New Nation*, op.cit., p. 130. (emphasis added).

6. Hans Kohn, *American Nationalism*, The MacMillan Co., New York, 1957, p. 88.

7. Ralph Barton Perry, *Puritanism and Democracy*, The Vanguard Press, 1944, pp. 34-35.

8. Ibid., p. 247.

9. Alexis de Tocqueville, *Democracy in America*, (abridged by Richard D. Heffner,) The New American Library, New York, 1961, pp. 157-158. Tocqueville attributes the idea of perfectibility to democratic social structure: "Aristocratic nations are naturally too apt to narrow the scope of human perfectibility; democratic nations, to expend it *beyond reason*." Ibid., p. 158. (emphasis added).

10. Harriet Martineau, quoted in S. M. Lipset, *The First New Nation*, op. cit., p. 107. Tocqueville almost at the same time also remarked that he knew "of no country in which there is so little true independence of mind and freedom of discussion as in America." *Democracy in America*, V.I, Ch. XV.

11. Leslie James, *Americans in Glasshouses*, Henry Chuman, Inc., New York, 1950, pp. 57-58.

12. Seymour Martin Lipset, *The First New Nation*, op. cit., pp. 106-122. Also see Lipset's article "A Changing American Character?" in *Culture and Social Character*, (eds) Seymour Martin Lipset and Leo Lowenthal, The Free Press, New York,

1961, pp. 136-171.

13. David M. Potter, People of Plenty, op. cit., p. 97.

14. Margaret Mead, quoted by David Potter, Ibid.

15. Ralf Dahrendorf, quoted in Seymour Martin Lipset, The First New Nation, op. cit., p. 90.

16. Kenneth A. Megill, The New Democratic Theory, The Free Press, New York, 1970, p. 141, vii.

17. Jacques Ellul, The Technological Society, Random House, New York, 1964, p. 356. (emphasis added).

18. David M. Potter, People of Plenty, op. cit., p. 127.

19. Edward Hallett Carr, The New Society, op. cit., p. 61.

20. Hans Kohn, Is the Liberal West in Decline? Pall Mall Press, London, 1957, p. 20.

21. Quoted in Hans Kohn, American Nationalism, op. cit., p. 13.

22. Ibid.

23. David M. Potter, People of Plenty, op. cit., p. 91.

24. Seymour Martin Lipset, Political Man, op. cit., p. 82.

25. Ibid., pp. 451-452.

26. David M. Potter, People of Plenty, op. cit., p. 118.

27. Ibid., pp. 101-102.

28. Norman M. Lobsenz, Is Anybody Happy? Doubleday & Co., Inc., Garden City, New York, 1962, p. 36.

29. Kenneth Keniston, Young Radicals, Harcourt, Brace & World, Inc., New York, 1968, p. 126.

30. Gustavus Myers, The History of American Idealism, Boni Liveright, New York, 1925, p. 295. "The American people have provided the surprise of ages in writing an unprecedented species of history and they will more." Ibid., p. 349.

31. Morris L. Ernst, Utopia: 1976, Reinhart & Co., Inc., New York, 1955.

32. Herman Kahn and Anthony Wienes, The Year 2000, The Macmillan Co., New York, 1967, p. 217.

33. Daniel Bell, The End of Ideology, Collier Books, New York, 1962, pp. 355-404.

34. Compiled from Neilsen Media Research Division: Television, Chicago, 1970.

35. Compiled from Statistical Abstract of the United States, Department of Commerce, 1970.

36. Ibid.

37. David Potter, "The Historical Perspective," in Stanley Donner (ed), The Meaning of Commercial Television, University of Texas Press, Austin, 1967, p. 56.

38. Norman M. Lobsenz in Is Anybody Happy?, op. cit., p. 37, observes that "the leisure class has become the leisure mass."

39. Statistical Abstract of the United States, op. cit.

40. Quoted in Hillel Black, Buy Now and Pay Later, William Morrow and Co., New York, 1961, p. 7.

41. Compiled from Statistical Abstract of the United States, op. cit., and Standard Educational Almanac, (ed) A. Renetzky, Academia Media, Inc., Los Angeles, 1971.

42. Andrew Hacker, The End of the American Era, op. cit., See the chapter bearing the same title.

43. Alexis de Tocqueville, Democracy in America, (abridged) op. cit., p. 209.

44. This was written in 1962; the current listing is much longer.

45. Norman M. Lobsenz, Is Anybody Happy?, op. cit., p. 187.

46. Ibid., p. 108.

47. Ibid., pp. 15-16. (emphasis original).

48. Quoted in Seymour Martin Lipset, The First New Nation, op. cit., p. 115 and 115n.

49. Norman M Lobsenz, Is Anybody Happy?, op. cit., pp. 22-23.

50. Leslie James, Americans in Glasshouses, op. cit., p. 24.

51. J. H. Huer, Life, May 7, 1971, p. 25. Also see Jon Huer, The Dead End, Kendall/Junt Publishing Co., Dubuque, Iowa, 1977 for a psychological and historical analysis of the American Creed.

52. Norman M. Lobsenz, Is Anybody Happy?, op. cit., p. 84.

53. Ibid., pp. 84-85.

54. Again, written in 1962. The current ratio is more skewed in favor of pleasure expenses.

55. Ibid., p. 112.

56. Ibid., pp. 44-45.

57. Ibid., p. 166.

58. Ibid., p. 167.

59. See Arthur Calhoun's A Social History of the American Family: From Colonial Times to the Present, The Arthur H. Clark, Co., Cleveland, 3 volumes, 1919, for the clear changes that have taken place within the family in Radical and Liberal America.

60. Eric Larrabee, The Self-Conscious Society, Doubleday & Co., Garden City, New York, 1960, pp. 120-121.

61. Joseph Schumpeter, Capitalism, Socialism and Democracy, op. cit., pp. 157-158.

62. "Widow Readjusts," Pasadena Independent Star-News, July 13, 1968.

63. Arthur Calhoun, A Social History of the American Family, op. cit., V.I, p. 121.

64. Eric Johnson, How to Live through Junior High School, Lippinott, Co., Philadelphia, 1959, pp. 234-238.

65. Brooks R. Walker, The New Immorality, Doubleday & Co., Garden City, New York, 1968, p. 194.

66. Arthur Calhoun, A Social History of the American Family, op. cit., V.2, p. 263.

67. Leslie C. Tihany, "Utopia in Modern Western Thought: The Metamorphosis of an Idea," in Richard Herr and Harold T. Parker (eds) Ideas in History, Duke University Press, Durham, 1965, p.38

68. David M. Potter, People of Plenty, op. cit., pp. 98-99.

69. Quoted in Walter Buckingham, Automation, The New American Library, New York, 1964, p. 153.

70. Ibid., p. 152.

71. Eric Larrabee, The Self-Conscious Society, op. cit., p. 162.

72. John U. Nef, The United States and Civilization, The University of Chicago Press, Chicago, 1967, second edition, pp. 3-4.

73. Ibid., p. 70. See Pitirim A. Sorokin's The Crisis of Our Age, op. cit., the diagram that indicated a general decline of the West in creativity towards our time. p. 259.

74. C. Wright Mills, The Power Elite, The Oxford University Press, New York, 1956, p. 350.

75. Ibid., p. 344.

76. John Kenneth Galbraith, The Liberal Hour, The New American Library, New York, 1960, p. 55. (emphasis added). See also Pitirim A. Sorokin's The Crisis of Our Age, op. cit., pp. 254 ff, for contemporary taste that prefers quantity to quality.

77. Leslie James, Americans in Glasshouses, op. cit., p. 18.

78. Norman Lobsenz, Is Anybody Happy?, op. cit., p. 133.

79. Ibid., p. 136.

80. Eric Larrabee, The Self-Conscious Society, op. cit., p. 133.

81. Max Weber, The Protestant Ethic and the Spirit of Capitalism, op. cit., p. 182. Weber refers to the state of highest capitalist development in the United States where "the pursuit of wealth, stripped of its religious and ethical meaning, tends to become associated with purely mundane passions, which often actually give it the character of sport." Ibid.

CHAPTER SEVEN: SOME FURTHER SPECULATIONS

1.

It may be held generally true that one's ideological formation through socialization, in which his predisposed judgments are established, always precedes his rational and logical ability to choose what may be morally and intellectually correct. Since this is the case in general our most brilliant pronouncements and arguments may merely reflect the effort to defend our already existent, predisposed judgments, conceiving that the logic with which we make our points is essentially a product of pure reasoning without regard to the formation of ideological predispositions we have already acquired through socialization. The uncertainty of social studies consists mainly of this dilemma: Whereas we are led to believing that our judgment derives from an objective observation of the world, the frame of mind through which we observe the world has already been ideologically determined in our less logically scrupulous age. Not realizing this, we vainly try to give a logical basis to our pre-established propensities. If the process could be reversed, that is, if one could attain the capacity to utilize logic and experience to make the correct judgments <u>before</u> there could be any socialization, we might claim that unbiased knowledge is after all possible. But this is not the case in our reality unless we achieve a perfect utopia in which all is done, from an early age, according to some uniform correctness formulated by the constituted authority. Since this is not the case here, the best one can hope for is that he be aware of this fateful dilemma in his social analysis.

2.

We have observed that the Radical transformation (whether Liberal-Enlightenment or Marxian) represents the aspirations of human equality, which bases its rhetoric and theory, against the feudal ideology and social character, on the assumption that all men are equallly entitled to their persons and capacities. This Radical notion generally bears the strain of proletarian spirit. In the course of time after the transformation, the intervention of industrial technology makes this collective egalitarianism vulnerable to the rise and demand of individuation, encouraged by the visible material affluence that industrial technology has brought to the Liberal state. This individuation process increases sharply as Liberal society moves toward post-Liberal society, a state in which the individualist ideology and social character reach their peak. Such a state of historical change may be characterized as bourgeois ideology, except that the bourgeois individualism we now speak of is not the anarchist, "from below," "naturalist" competition as Marxism has it, but a "from above," "distributory" individualism controlled and sustained by state capitalism. Understanding that this process occurs sequentially in history, one cannot but ask the inevitable question resulting from such an observation: <u>Is it reasonable to state that the equality-oriented proletarian transformation almost always precedes the bourgeois constellation of its ideology</u>? This is exactly the reversal of the historical logic formulated in Marxism. The essence of this question may be further examined in the following: (1) the extent to which the "naturalist" conception of human equality, rampant in the nineteenth century, was true in terms of its individualism as both theory and practice; (2) the degree to which modern industrial technology has modified, and neutralized, the supposed class cleavage resulting from that naturalist conception; and (3) in what sense modern state-sponsored individualism, consumerized and commercialized, can be regarded as "individualistic." These are begging questions which require no more than mere suggestions at the moment, but future investigations may be fruitful in this area.

3.

The black-white relations in the United States, a post-Liberal society, will run along the predominant ideology and its corresponding social character. That is, blacks will eventually acquire an equal status, economically and politically, without a complete social integration, and <u>without</u> a further revolution. The increased material affluence accorded the black population takes the Radical steam out of their radical rhetoric and practice, which renders any political attempt at Radicalization in the United States both objectively and subjectively superfluous. One must not underestimate the human disposition to comforting surroundings created by industrial technology. This applies even to the most Radical of all individuals.

4.

To recapitulate the main theme of this model, we will postulate that most of those societies that fall under the Conservative type <u>will</u> have their Radicalization in one form or another, given the availability of Radical political formulas and visions that abound in the contemporary world. It is only a matter of time that these formulas and visions are put to a Radical practice by the Conservative populations, although a drastic reform from above, not necessarily from the elite, in some societies may be the chosen path for Radicalization. For the reason of available technological application in universal terms the Radical societies will race toward Liberalism through industrialization, as some have done already. There is no reason to believe that people prefer conventional ways of production when more productive and rational methods are made available to them. As the Liberal state achieves both political stability and industrialization, by which Liberalism is defined, its steady drift will be toward a greater practice of those ideological and characterological formulations, although in the post-Liberal state the specific form by which such utopian transformations occur may vary. In the long pull of historical time, however, the variation will be minimized by the conformity-creating technological universality.

5.

Accordingly, political conflicts involving a severe degree of violence, regional as well as national wars, will be <u>confined mainly to Radical societies</u>. It is the Radical type that generally initiates war and sustains that war effort, supported by the Radical rhetoric and aspirations which are generally absent in other social types. Traditional states tend to be the victims rather than the actors in this conflict. Liberal states attempt at reasonable settlements with dignity and honor on both sides. When involved in this situation the post-Liberal type responds according to the utopian ideals embodied in its social antecedents and political formulations; but as soon as the painful reality begins to make its impact the dilemma between ideal and reality becomes intensified, in which post-Liberal society is capable of neither extricating itself nor pushing the ideal, enduring the painful reality to its final agony. All in all, war games are generally the property of Radical societies, although the Liberal and post-Liberal states may become involved for one reason or another. War leverage is in the hands of the Radical state, and Liberal or post-Liberal states normally may counter it with extremely powerful brute force, mechanized and mobile, only to strengthen the determination of Radical men. This ideological and characterological involvement in modern conflict is what distinguishes it from pre-modern warfare in which purely military strategy and/or the magnitude of violence determined the outcome.

6.

Given the historical condition in which the move toward uniformity is more and more apparent and substantial, it may be stated rather wishfully that men and women today have achieved a state of existence in which they, for the first time in history, might truly become "full men and women," in both the Enlightenment and the Marxian sense. That every empirically observable fact defies this contention does not necessarily entail that it is both empirically and logically impossible. For the first time, a vast number of men and women today have access to information that was denied previously, and confined to few wealthy and limited individuals or select social strata. Whether this will turn out to be a modern revival of great human aspirations toward freedom and creativity only remains to be seen.

Jon H. Huer

APPENDIX:

There is one residual social type that fits none of the four types so far presented as the historical model of ideology and social character. It is the type in which the process of industrialization precedes the political transformation, which is to say that technology is imposed upon that society without prior political transformations. Hence modernity in the form of mechanization penetrates into what is essentially a Traditional structure, and this does not render the community a Liberal character ipso facto. The free medical care and education in Kuwait, for instance, may rival those of any well advanced Liberal state, but there is something quite inadequate about this comparison. What is absent in Kuwait is obviously the imperative process of political Radicalization, transforming the remnants of feudal society that still reign the desert society into a Radical social structure with its psychological as well as political re-arrangements in goveranance and social relations. Since the country's management depends solely and wholly on oil exports, a depletion of the natural resource, or its devaluation in world markets, may cause a return to the traditional order and pattern of social life. Micronesia's modernization process through American influence may be considered a similar case.[1] This type can only be defined in terms of reversed coming of what seemed to be an orderly historical sequence, that is, a political transformation preceding technological modernization.

We might do well by introducing a conceptual device by which we may be able to describe this residual social type in our model. World-history consists of constant exchanges of ideas and ideals and technological knowledge among nations. The ideals of the French Revolution or the Marxist formulation still inspire those in need of a revolutionary ideology, and Western science and technology are imported and emulated the world over. It is in terms of these "cultural exchanges" that the construction of a world-history becomes theoretically possible. It is also in terms of the world-wideness of these ideals and technology that a world-typology finds its empirical justification. However, in postulating that these ideals and technology are in constant exchange we must now conceptually separate two types of exchange: (1) the first type of exchange we may refer to as "voluntary cultural transmission" in whose process the borrowing community is in full possession of knowledge and control over what is borrowed, which including appropriate social policies regarding what must be borrowed and how it should be put to use. The world communication of ideals and technological knowledge among post-Radical societies is essentially of this kind. A new type of automobile engine may be invented in one society and other societies immediately adopt that invention with full control and knowledge over what is adopted. Concerning Kuwait or Micronesia we must speak of the second type of exchange process, (2) which we may term "involuntary cultural transmission" in which the borrower has neither control and knowledge over what is borrowed (or imposed upon it), nor a conscious awareness of the consequences and impacts of that cultural transmission. What distinguishes this type from other Traditional societies is the degree to which the process of "involuntary" modernization characterizes the given community.

Since we have very few of this residual type in existence today, a further speculation may not be of an imperative order. But as shown earlier concerning Egypt's abortive attempt at modernization prior to its political transformation, industrial modernization must presuppose a Radical social structure and human psyche geared to such modernization to be successful. The residual type, characterized by involuntary cultural transmission, then, is bound to be a failure in the long run. Modernization through industrial technology and its facilities must be accompanied by an appropriate social arrangement conducive to such a process, which is accomplished only through a Radical transformation. The residual type has entirely omitted that process, and in its consequence in world-history it is of no great significance that this type does exist today.

FOOTNOTES

1. "Micronesia: The Americanization of Eden, "National Geographic, V.131, No. 5, (May, 1967), pp. 702-744 for a pictorial account of modernization in Micronesia. See also "Out of the Stone Age, "Newsweek, August 28, 1972, pp. 35-36 for a similar infiltration of modernity in the Masai community in Africa.

INDEX:

America
    as post-liberal society, 5, 189-220
    as utopia, 189-194
Apter, David, 29
Arnold, Matthew, 206

Bendix, Reinhard, 1
Brinton, Crane, 41-42

Carr, Edward H., 194
Castro, Fidel, 1, 40, 43, 62-64, 120-121, 124-129, 131-133
Cuba, 43-44, 90-94, 120, 124-127, 129-135
    as Marxist, 75, 114-119
    as radical, 62-64
    and religion, 81
    transition to radical type, 40, 42
China, 6062, 108-114

Dahrendorf, Ralf, 194

Egypt, 43-44, 49-52, 66-67, 86-91, 94, 120, 127, 131
    as radical, 64-65
    as socialist, 65, 120
    transition to radical type, 40-42
Emerson, Rupert, 33

Galbraith, J. K., 218

Hacker, Andrew, 5, 204, 210

Ideology
    defined, 1
Industrial Revolution
    as historical event, 1
    in France, 101-102
    in Russia, 76-79, 95-97
Israel, 45-47

Kahn, Herman, 198

Liberal type
    as ideology and social character, 167-185
    classic liberalism, 167
    decline of liberalism, 174-175
    defined, 3-5
    functions of, 174-179
    individualism, 167-169
    liberal assumptions, 177
    liberal ramifications, 177

233

    transition to, 4
Lippmann, Walter, 1
Lipset, Seymour Martin, 192, 196

MacPherson, C. B., 167
Mannheim, Karl, 9
Mao tze-tung, 61, 81, 109-114, 122
Martineau, Harriet, 192
Marxist, 20, 43-44, 60, 70, 74-79, 99, 104-121, 130, 135-136, 167, 169, 179-181, 182, 184, 227-228
Mead, Margaret, 194
Mills, C. Wright, 1, 5, 11, 175, 203, 217
Moore, Barrington, 38, 144
Myers, Gustavus, 198

Nasser, Colonel A., 43, 49, 52, 64-65, 86-88, 94, 120-128
Nationalism, 30-34

Political revolution, 126
    as historical event, 2
    by coup, 47-51
    in China, 47
    in England, 70-71
    in France, 30-33, 41-42, 71-73, 98, 100-101
    in Russia, 67-69
    types of, 43
Post-liberal type
    defined, 3
    formation of ideology in, 194-199
    happiness in, 204-209
    insignificant others in, 209-216
    transition to, 5
    as utopia, 99-204, 189-194
Potter, David, 5, 193, 201, 215

Radical type
    as historical type, 145
    as ideology and social character, 59-146
    in Third World nations, 25-30, 34-36, 39, 44, 47
    defined, 3-4
    egalitarian spirit in, 69-80
        natural equality, 69-80
        socialist equality, 73, 75-80
    industrialization in, 94-97
    mass mobilization in, 127-135
    oppression and terror in, 135-144
    secularism in, 80-89
    revolution-by-coup, 47-51
    social reform in, 89-94
    theme of struggle, 121-127

    transition to, 3-4, 25-47, 145
Riesman, David, 5, 10, 192-193
Russia, 67-69, 76-79, 84-86, 95-99, 104-108
Rustow, Dankwart, 9, 33, 35-36, 41, 48-51, 98
Rostow, W. W., 18

Sartre, Jean-Paul, 62
Schumpeter, Joseph, 210
Slater, Philip, 5
Social character
    defined, 1
Spencer, Herbert, 19, 206
Spock, Benjamin, 213
Stalin, Joseph, 67-68, 81, 94-97, 104-108, 140-141

Tocqueville, Alexis de, 1, 41, 191, 205
Traditional type
    and conservatism differentiated, 9
    authority and legitimacy of, 11-17
    defined, 3, 9-11
    patriachalism, 13
    varieties of, 17-19

Weber, Max, 11, 15, 19, 199, 206, 220
Wilson, David, 41